AGRARIAN FEMINISM

In contrast to capitalist production, farming as household production is defined by the unity of property and labour. This unity means that production is organized through kinship and divided by gender and age. In *Agrarian Feminism* Louise Carbert demonstrates that farm women's opinions about feminism and politics are related to their role in agricultural production.

Farming   members. But the ten   ly pronounced in   DATE DUE   lity, and finances are closely   remunerated in wages driven by market forces, and their working conditions are not regulated through an employment contract subject to legislated labour codes. Instead, the terms of farm women's employment are established through marriage or cohabitation. The unity of work and family relations may account for the marked caution of farm women's feminist demands amid calls to save the family farm.

Farm women's proven track-record at mobilizing political participation can also instruct contemporary attempts to revitalize a sense of community. Their overriding enthusiasm for community-based service work emerges as both a collective strategy for fulfilling the larger needs of rural society and an individual strategy for personal happiness; it is simultaneouly agrarian and feminist.

In *Agrarian Feminism* a historical review of farm women's organizations in English Canada is combined with a recent survey asking Ontario farm women for their opinions on politics, feminism, and morality.

LOUISE I. CARBERT is an instructor in the Department of Political Studies, University of Saskatchewan.

Agrarian Feminism

The Politics of Ontario Farm Women

Louise I. Carbert

UNIVERSITY OF TORONTO PRESS
Toronto Buffalo London

© University of Toronto Press Incorporated 1995
Toronto Buffalo London
Printed in Canada

ISBN 0-8020-2931-0 (cloth)
ISBN 0-8020-7756-0 (paper)

Printed on acid-free paper

Canadian Cataloguing in Publication Data

Carbert, Louise I. (Louise Irene), 1960–
  Agrarian feminism : the politics of Ontario
  farm women

  Includes index.
  ISBN 0-8020-2931-0 (bound)   ISBN 0-8020-7756-0 (pbk.)

  1. Rural women – Ontario – Attitudes.   I. Title.

  HQ1459.06C3 1995   305.4'09713   C95-930795-8

University of Toronto Press acknowledges the financial assistance to its
publishing program of the Canada Council and the Ontario Arts Council.

This book has been published with the help of a grant from the Social
Science Federation of Canada, using funds provided by the Social Sciences
and Humanities Research Council of Canada.

Contents

Acknowledgments

This book owes a great deal to Len Sonmor; he is my editor, my statistics tutor, my systems manager, and my mainstay. I thank Naomi Black for suggesting this research and providing me with prompt and incisive criticism. Her intellectual curiosity has bolstered my enthusiasm throughout this project. The members of my thesis committee – Gail Cuthbert Brandt, Grace Skogstad, Robert Drummond, and Reg Whitaker – also provided helpful comments. Michael Hall, among others at the Institute for Social Research at York University, counselled me in statistics and provided access to previous survey data. This book has been published with the help of a grant from the Social Science Federation of Canada, using funds provided by the Social Sciences and Humanities Research Council of Canada. The University of Saskatchewan also provided a grant in aid of publication. At the University of Saskatchewan, members of the Political Studies Department and the Women's Studies Research Unit, especially Georgina Taylor, welcomed and advised me. The manuscript was improved greatly by the suggestions made by three anonymous referees for the University of Toronto Press. My friends Margaret Ogrodnick, Andrea Mozer, Barbara Crow, Katherine Fierlbeck, and Kalowatie Deonandan gave me their support. My parents, Ross and Maxine Carbert, helped with logistical support (camping equipment) while I conducted interviews. Robert, Mary, and Barbara Carbert, of Wingham, Ontario, extended their hospitality during my research. Jo-Ann Kidd at Visual Communications Services of the Ontario Ministry of Agriculture and Food helped the aforementioned Carberts search for photos. Anna Jackson and Janine Roelens-Grant, at the Guelph office of the Federated Women's Institutes of Ontario, were always helpful. Finally, I thank those who welcomed me into the world of Women's Institutes in rural Ontario: Peggy Knapp, Margaret Munro, Verna Maluske, Marion Dougall, Marg Krauter, Darlene Harding, and all the women who generously agreed to be interviewed.

Introduction

Germaine Greer credits farm women with inspiring her first clear view of feminism while she was an adolescent: 'If we lived in the country I reckoned Mother's energy would be absorbed, and not frittered away in flightiness. I didn't know women could be like that ... capable, proud, independent. Not vain, capricious, manipulative, affected, infantile' (1989, 209). In the same feminist spirit, Aritha Van Herk contrasts a farm woman's pride in her 'hard, clean, thin body' with that of her former self – a secretary's thickening body, victimized in hierarchical and coy sexual relations with her employer, a symbol of degenerate urban femininity (1978, 154–5). Sharon Butala, in contrast, exults in farm women's flower-print dresses and handicrafts as evidence of femininity defending itself against brutalizing landscapes and marriages (1988). Thus farm women[1] are often portrayed as epitomizing either feminism or femininity.

Why should images of such a demographically insignificant group (2 per cent of Canada's population) be so compelling to overwhelmingly urban audiences? And why should the images be seemingly at odds: strong and equal, on the one hand, and submissive and traditional, on the other? The answer to these questions lies in the universality of farming as a model for household-based production, which may be an increasingly important economic trend for the future. The associated integration of kinship, sexuality, and finances results in both higher status for women and opportunity for unchecked oppression.

The common-sense notion of 'farm' collapses when we consider the variety of products (agricultural and non-agricultural) sold by people universally recognized as 'farmers,' including, for example, the picturesque farm vacations that are a dominant commodity in certain rural regions of Europe. In order to encompass this variety, we must instead adopt a broad concept of household production that is not limited by the commodity sold (Friedmann 1980; 1986). In contrast to capitalist production, household production, which includes farming, is defined by the unity of property and labour. This unity means that production is organized through kinship and divided by gender and age. Most farm employees are family members waiting to inherit the enterprise; therefore, their 'wages' are more like dividends drawn against a capital investment. Although the husband/wife team is the mainstay of household production in both practical and emotional terms, that team relies on assistance from the larger extended family.

The future of family farming has generated a good deal of controversy.[2] Until recently, all production, whether the output of agriculture or of manual arts, was expected eventually to be incorporated into large-scale, industrial, corporate units that hire waged labour. Without access to the means of production (broadly conceived as land, tools, livestock, etc.) except through the sale of their labour, independent producers were expected to become wage workers. None the less, agriculture tends to resist corporate concentration of ownership and production (Buttel 1989, 69–70). Small-scale farming continues to be viable largely because, in Marx's terms, family members are 'self-exploiters.' There is, in general, very little profit to be had from the sale of raw, unprocessed agricultural commodities. Farm enterprises manage to extract profit by exploiting the virtually free labour of family members who work in return for mere subsistence. As one farm wife put it, she works for 'three-and-a-half per day ... not dollars – three meals and half the bed' (Taylor 1976, 151). When workers are not paid wages, almost all revenues can be turned back into the farm enterprise, thereby enabling it to persist under unfavourable economic conditions.

Family farming is further viable for reasons that are based in the very nature of plant and animal life. Capitalist investment prefers a continuous cycle of production and exchange, a cycle in which products are manufactured and marketed, and profits reinvested, all at the same time. But food characteristically requires a prolonged production cycle during which animals and crops take time to grow. Farmers are willing to tolerate exceedingly long production times; they wait all summer for crops to grow, harvest once a year in a single intense spurt of labour, and then live off the harvest's proceeds during the winter. Only when the production cycle is more concentrated in time, and more labour-intensive (as it is when fruit, vegetables, eggs, and poultry are the products), does the enterprise become more profitable, and hence more attractive to capitalist investment (Mann and Dickinson 1978). Another barrier to capitalist investment is the vast amount of land required relative to the volume and value of the commodity produced. Since the day-to-day work of farming is dispersed over a large area, supervising relatively unskilled and low-paid employees is difficult (Freshwater 1989). Finally, unprocessed food has very little potential for profit because scientific research keeps discovering cheaper and easier ways to produce more food faster than the rate at which world demand increases. In the end, those aspects of the food industry that are amenable to continuous cycles of factory production have already been taken up by capitalist investment, leaving farmers with whatever cannot be produced at a steady and secure rate of profit. Family farming thus continues to fill a necessary niche within capitalism.

This situation might not be unique to farming. There is emerging consensus, from left and right alike, that capitalism is at a turning-point which promises a greater role for household-based enterprises in the future.[3] Family farming is the most familiar, durable, and successful model of self-employed, flexible, skilled, and household-based production of commodities for capitalist markets. As such, it may be a useful reference point for anticipating the effects of larger economic trends. At a popular level, despite the benefits of permanent, unionized employment for wages, most people still hold out for the reputed independence of a small business that is capable of employing just themselves and their family members in return for a decent living. Seeing that a good many working people and a few intellectuals aspire to a self-employed or petty-bourgeois economy and society, it might be supposed, if only for argument's sake, that it is a viable alternative.[4]

Women's status will undoubtedly be affected by these trends. Early-modern Europe (roughly the fifteenth to the eighteenth centuries) presents a historical example in which household production for market exchange prevailed. Much feminist scholarship is devoted to this era on the premise that, when households were units of production, women's work in family enterprises ensured their near-equal status. Some feminists, and particularly those sympathetic to Marxist theory, argue that capitalism destroyed household production, deprived women of access to productive work, confined them to domesticity (in practice and ideology), and thereby subordinated women, denying them po-

litical and civic equality: 'The growing penetration of capital into
the economy undermined the basis of that [interdependent] family. As
a result, women could no longer combine in their general labour the
bearing, suckling and rearing of children ... Their dependence upon
their husbands increased. Wives became financial liabilities' (Hamilton
1978, 47).[5] The early-modern period holds considerable appeal for academic feminists because household-based production enabled women
to combine career and family, and thus avoid a chief cause of women's
contemporary economic disadvantage – namely, leaving paid employment with each pregnancy. Farming holds similar appeal for popular
culture and opinion at large. The idea of farming as an egalitarian
family enterprise may draw urban readers to a book like this.

Household production also has its perils for women. Unlike those
employed in capitalist enterprises, farm women are not remunerated
in wages driven by market forces, and their working conditions are
not regulated through an employment contract subject to legislated
labour codes. Instead, the terms of employment are established through
the sexual contract of marriage. When women's career in farming is
established through cohabitation, rather than through formal marriage
vows, the employment contract is even more starkly sexual. When reg-
istered either way with the state, the sexual contract regulates unin-
corporated farm assets and debt through divorce, credit and bankruptcy, and inheritance legislation (Meanwell and Glover 1985). When
farm women negotiate their work relations or claims to family assets,
they simultaneously negotiate the division of labour and authority
throughout the entire household. Because almost any occupational demand contains a latent threat to one's marriage, the unity of work
and family relations might account for the marked caution of farm
women's demands amid pleas to save the family farm. Farm women's
economic vitality and sexual subordination thus oppose each other
in determining their status. This tension may generate a distinctive
feminist analysis.[6]

The book's title, *Agrarian Feminism*, derives from *Agrarian Socialism*, S.M. Lipset's classic work on the rise of the Co-operative Commonwealth Federation (CCF) in Saskatchewan. Lipset set out to prove,
contrary to Karl Marx, that socialism could be initiated by farmers
rather than by industrial workers. His rebuttal was considerably weaker
than intended; he could not establish that the farmers' chosen party
was socialist or egalitarian in its leaders, program, or electoral support
(1971 [1950], xxi, 274-7). Lipset later regretted not having compared

the Saskatchewan case with the rise of Social Credit in Alberta (1971, xx). Social Credit also emerged from a rural population during the Depression of the 1930s but was closer to fascism than to socialism.

C.B. Macpherson's study of the Social Credit party (1953) addressed a perceived lack of theoretical analysis in Lipset's empiricism by employing Marxist class analysis. He argued that the Social Credit party was conservative because it defended a declining class of farmers against the advancing forces of capitalism. Later analysis decided that the CCF and the Social Credit party were unstable poles of North American populism, which swung back and forth between left and right because it represented a class of people – petty-bourgeois commodity producers – whose situation swung between entrepreneurship and waged labour (Richards and Pratt 1981).

These old approaches to agrarian politics were never designed to answer new feminist questions. Their principal goal was to judge whether or not agrarian protest movements had any potential to challenge industrial capitalism; any other political and social achievements were quite beside the point.[7] This goal had consequences for how research was done. In Canada, a political-economy approach relied on the influence of export staples (wheat and beef, in this case) to explain stages in national development. If protest movements make sense in terms of dominant commodities, it makes sense, accordingly, that very few empirical studies were conducted to discover farmers' individual opinions. We have no way of knowing how deeply leaders' critiques of finance capital penetrated or on what hopes farmers elected populist parties to power.[8] Individual voters' political opinions were subsumed in the ideology and careers of party theoreticians (for example, Henry Wise Wood and William Irvine) or in the platforms and policies of political parties, which were then taken, at face value, to represent the beliefs and interests of individual farmers.

A focus on partisanship is inappropriate for studying farm women in several regards. First, individual women are twice removed – via a farmer husband – from parties that were the typical focus of study. When women did belong to agrarian parties, they did so through a separate women's section.[9] Second, a partisan-centred focus neglected the bureaucratic arm of government, which was assumed to be subordinate to the parties in power.[10] Even allowing for much smaller state bureaucracies prior to the postwar period, the nuts and bolts of how various parties in power managed their relations with farmers, primarily through the ministries of agriculture, was neglected.[11] This neglect is important because rural women's most popular and active organization, the Women's Institutes, was, until the end of the 1980s, administered and funded by provincial ministries of agriculture. Third, the old approach marginalized community service. Although agrarian protest movements throughout North America were powerless to defend a declining class against the advancing forces of industrial capitalism and urbanization, they did sprout a variety of innovations in participatory democracy. Farmer's proven track record in mobilizing political participation in the face of considerable obstacles could instruct contemporary attempts to revitalize a sense of community among isolated individuals.[12] Any move in this direction also promises a renewed appreciation for farm women's community service.

I have attempted to address these issues by combining a historical review of farm women's organizations in English Canada with a contemporary survey of political opinions among Ontario farm women. Whereas Lipset's study described the socialist content in farm men's organizations, this book describes the feminist content in farm women's organizations. It goes farther than Lipset did in integrating the modifier 'agrarian,' by showing that women's opinions about feminism and politics are related to their role in agricultural production. Unlike Macpherson's approach, it does not emphasize the farm enterprise's external relations of commodity exchange in the market-place with creditors and merchants, but rather the internal relations of household production among family members and, in particular, between spouses.[13]

Chapter 1 relates the history of farm women's organizations in Canada, with particular attention to the 'old' Women's Institute movement. It situates the sampled population in historical and collective context within the broader Canadian rural scene, and in relation to the organized women's movement and government departments of agriculture. This chapter sets up a contrast between community-based and commodity-based political participation and at the same time observes the commonalities that unite farm women's collective activities.

Chapter 2 describes the survey. It begins with a geographical, historical, and cultural overview of Huron and Grey counties, where interviews were conducted. It then tells how the survey was designed and implemented, and discusses the methodological issues that arose in the course of conducting interviews. Finally, it compares demographic and farm characteristics of the sample to results from the 1986 Statistics Canada Agricultural Census.

The empirical bulk of the book is presented in chapters 3 to 6. Chapter 3 explains how agricultural tasks fall into four categories of agricultural work: animal husbandry, mechanical field-work, internal farm administration, and external farm administration. Chapters 4 through 6 address the contrast between conservatism and progressivism, the analogy in academic literature to the literary images of femininity and feminism. From the perspective of liberal progress and modernization, farm women are expected to lag behind almost everyone in relation to many social, economic, and political indicators. This issue is discussed in terms of standard politicization concepts and questions that have been developed over decades of survey research. Politicization comprises both political behaviour and opinions. Chapter 4 discusses three aspects of political behaviour: involvement, conceptualization, and participation. Political involvement comprises salience (how important are politics to a person's life as indicated by talk about politics or expression of interest in political issues); efficacy (how effective or influential a person feels about dealing with government); and partisanship (how committed a person is to party competition). Conceptualization refers to how well a person articulates abstract concepts of 'left-wing'/'right-wing,' 'politics,' and 'feminism.' The subjective, psychological indicators of involvement and conceptualization may be expected to culminate in concrete acts of direct political participation: voting, party involvement, lobbying, or volunteering. Chapter 5 addresses substantive conservative content as measured by voting preference, partisan ties, support for environmentalism, church attendance, sexual morality, and abortion. Feminism might be included among these, but it merits a separate chapter because of its special importance to this study. How farm women articulated in their own words, or conceptualized, the meaning of 'feminism' is at the core of chapter 6. In addition, chapter 6 discusses views on women in electoral politics and the changing roles of men and women.

Chapter 7 reports women's testimony in regard to farm marriages, families, and their personal happiness. It draws on a distinction between romantic or companionate marriage and a more traditional separate-spheres model of marriage.

Chapter 8 pulls together the empirical results of earlier chapters to summarize the impact of agricultural work on women's politicization. This synthesis reveals three patterns among farm women that differ on the basis of what type of farm work they did. The first pattern combines farm administration with a keen interest in politics among older women. The second pattern combines farm labour with a strong equality version of feminism among younger women, but not politics as conventionally defined in terms of partisanship and public affairs. The third pattern combines mechanical work with personal control. Notwithstanding these differences, the farm women interviewed showed striking similarity in several important regards that are then summarized. The book ends with an in-depth analysis of farm women's overriding enthusiasm for community-based service work as an individual strategy for personal happiness and a collective strategy for fulfilling the systemic needs of rural society at large.

Overall, 'agrarian feminism' should be approached with the same scepticism as 'agrarian socialism.' Indeed, Lipset beat his critics to the conclusion that the CCF in Saskatchewan was not socialist after all. The same goes for feminism. Instead of deciding who qualifies as an 'agrarian feminist' and who does not, this study observes women's politicization in relation to the agricultural economy and society that characterize rural Ontario.

AGRARIAN FEMINISM

1

A History of Farm Women's Movements in English Canada

A broad distinction between 'old' and 'new' farm women has come into use among academics, government bureaucrats, and some sectors of the farming population to describe the increasingly visible contribution of wives to agricultural production and management. In popular speech, traditional, or 'old,' farm wives are fundamentally housewives who happen to be married to farmers, whereas modern, or 'new,' wives are active partners in financial and agricultural decisions. One of the study's respondents, for example, explicitly identified herself as a 'new' farm woman: 'They [Women's Institutes members] seem pretty boring from the local newspaper articles. They seem like old-guard farm women, traditional women who aren't as involved in farming as modern women.' Similar themes of self-ascribed superiority and commitment to social change occurred during several interviews. For example, one woman credited her urban background for a marriage that she considered more egalitarian than those of her neighbours: 'A feminist will vocally stand up for women. Women around here are so ... husbands won't babysit and women can't get out to meetings. They defer to husbands' hard work. I go out to just as many meetings as my husband. [Because of my urban background] we don't defer to farm business, the house has high priority. Our marriage is more equal than others' around here. We discuss everything together.' On the subject of social change, another woman cited rapid implementation of employment equity legislation in local schools as a contrast to the social stasis of rural communities: 'But around here, farmers don't change. They still rule the roost and the women are passive. Who's getting through to them?' These three women implicitly relied on a model of modernization, operating through generational shifts and urbanization, to explain perceived social changes in rural communities.

The distinction between new and old farm women made one of its earliest official appearances in a report submitted to the Ontario Ministry of Agriculture and Food (OMAF) in 1984. The report's author, Molly McGhee, identified a 'new breed of farm women developing, anxious to discard the stereotype of farmer's wife and helper ... to be regarded as equal partners' (1984, 4). For Ontario farm women, this report was the equivalent of the report of the Royal Commission on the Status of Women (1970), which focused on Canadian women in general. After McGhee conducted hearings throughout the province, she reported that a perceived 'generation gap' corresponded to organizational affiliation in rural Ontario: 'Over half questioned whether the Women's Institute adequately represented rural women today. Because of the younger women's time pressures, their interest in single-purpose issues, they are reluctant to join the traditional organizations with their all-encompassing objectives and programs' (1984, 39). The Women's Institute (WI) movement is contrasted here with a series of organizations that have sprung up across North America, culminating in the new farm women's movement (Branden 1985). Ontario saw the emergence of Women for the Survival of Agriculture (WSA) in 1975 and Concerned Farm Women (CFW) in 1981. McGhee's recommendations to the OMAF included state services for farm women's activism through Rural Organizations and Services (ROS) and thereby spurred the establishment of the Ontario Farm Women's Network (OFWN) from the remnants of the WSA and CFW in 1989. The OFWN currently supervises the continued implementation of those recommendations.

Recent surges of activism in the new farm women's movement typically have been attributed to two causes. The first is the current economic crisis – caused by government fiscal policy leading to high interest rates, on the one hand, and agricultural policy leading to inadequate commodity prices, on the other – which threatens the continued viability of family farming and is often first on activists' agendas, ahead of feminism (Rankin 1989, 322–3). Women who actively contribute to farming operations are more likely to combine their gender-based concerns (discriminatory inheritance, tax, and divorce laws, and subsidy policies) with commodity-based concerns to protect farmers as a class (Haney 1983, 188; Miller and Neth 1988, 360–78). Second, urban-based feminism is presumed to diffuse from the centre to rural peripheries after a time-lag of a decade or more: 'The Women's

Liberation Movement has allowed Canadian farm women to see themselves in a new light. Following the example set by their urban counterparts, they are stepping out of their previous, stereotyped role' (Bruners 1985, 19). The new farm women's movement has thus implicitly relied on parallels with critical or progressive new social movements. These interpretations are not wholly inaccurate, but they lack historical perspective since both the farm crisis and the women's movement have been with us for over a century in Canada.

From the historical perspective established below, it appears that the prevailing distinction between old and new farm women's movements is inadequate, chiefly because it does not account for the central place of the WI movement in the history of rural Canada. The WI has its origins in state-directed programs of agricultural modernization that occurred alongside, and in response to, agrarian protest movements throughout North America from the end of the nineteenth century onwards. The history of the WI and agrarian protest movements has periodically intersected with that of the organized women's movement, but, as is discussed later in this chapter, their involvement is still better understood in relation to agricultural policy communities. A historical perspective shows that the WI movement still remains a viable option, in part, because it shares programmatic, organizational, and ideological continuities with the newer, often crisis-oriented, farm women's movement. The force of this apparently modest claim becomes intelligible only in terms of ongoing claims that farm women's organized activity in agrarian protest movements was historically, and continues to be, politically superior to activity in the WI movement.

THE AGRARIAN ORIGINS OF THE WOMEN'S INSTITUTES IN ONTARIO

Although the Canadian Women's Institutes did not promote farmers' interests as a producer class in parties of agrarian protest, their activities were no less agrarian, and their origins cannot be understood apart from those of agrarian populism in Canada. Agrarian populism arrived in Canada during the 1870s, when the Grange movement from New England expanded into Ontario (Wood 1975 [1924], 24, 30). The non-partisan Grange flourished briefly in the 1870s, and then was overtaken after 1892 by the Patrons of Industry, a more radical movement that originated in the American Midwest; the Patrons intended to run partisan candidates in a Labour–Farmer coalition (ibid, 109, 115). In the 1894 Ontario election, the Patrons had considerable success, electing fourteen candidates, but were less successful in the 1896 Canadian general election, which saw only three of their candidates elected, all in Ontario. After 1896, agrarian protest declined until the United Farmers of Ontario was formed in 1914 (ibid, 147). Meanwhile, in 1885, the Ontario government established educational, non-partisan Farmers' Institutes, after which the Women's Institute movement was modelled. L.A. Wood infers that the purpose of the Farmers' Institutes was to 'coddle [farmers] in order to neutralize the effect of independent thought among the farmers' (ibid, 275). If not-yet-enfranchised farm wives were to be likewise 'coddled,' astute partisan foresight on the part of Ontario politicians may have motivated the founding of the Women's Institutes in 1897, but the movement's origins are better located in the government's more non-partisan program of agricultural reform. For all that administrators in the Ontario government knew at the beginning of the twentieth century, agrarian populism as a partisan political strategy had been decisively defeated in recent elections, but the rural crisis remained and had to be dealt with.

At the turn of the century, Ontario agriculture was undergoing its own version of the extended and prolonged crisis that occurred as North America made the transition from a rural, unstable, and financially unreliable staple-exporting economy to an urban capitalist economy dominated by industry and the availability of local markets (Cohen 1988, 59–117; Graham 1988, 211–91). This transition was, even within Ontario, geographically uneven. In Huron County, the town of Goderich on the shores of Lake Huron became an important shipping port for grain early on, but the Grey–Bruce peninsula was characterized more by forestry than by farming. The areas inland from Lake Huron were settled later and were more isolated from major centres of commerce such as Hamilton and Guelph (Scott 1966).

During the nineteenth century, Upper Canada/Ontario exported wheat to Britain until the expansion of railways and a new wave of immigrants opened up wheat and grain cultivation on the western prairies. Just when Ontario's virgin soils, depleted by half a century of reckless farming practices, had given up producing high grain yields without fertilization or conservation, technological innovations arrived to encourage Ontario farmers to shift to dairy production and animal husbandry. The invention of the automatic separator allowed, first, creameries and, later, individual farmers to separate cream from milk quickly and hygienically. A network of creameries collected cream to produce butter, which was distributed not just to Ontario's growing urban population but also down the Saint Lawrence and overseas to Britain (Cohen 1988, 109-12; Graham 1988, 282-7). Dairy receipts had supplemented unreliable wheat crops throughout the nineteenth century, but the wholesale shift to dairy production could not take place until Ontario was sufficiently developed and populated to support a network of creameries. Grain products, being less perishable, could be cultivated in the back reaches of Upper Canada or on the prairie frontier, far from eventual consumers, but large-scale commercial dairy production had to wait for the advent of refrigerated transport and marketing networks. Agriculture in Canada, therefore, developed in tandem with the creation of an adequate financial and transportation infrastructure.

Although the shift to dairying marked an increase in farm income after the prolonged depression in grain prices that occurred after the American Civil War (which, incidentally, gave rise to populist revolt), people were still leaving rural Ontario, either to take up homesteads, first, on the American prairies and, after 1900, in Saskatchewan and Alberta, or to take waged labour in cities. Agricultural reform happened in the context of the overall transition from a rural, not entirely commodified agricultural economy to an urbanized, industrial capitalism in North America (Cohen 1988, 36-41).[1] A generation before Canadian farmers became fully aware of the transition's scope and organized coherent political opposition to the new order, the Ontario government prodded reluctant farmers to modernize. When a provincial commission on agriculture observed 'a very large amount of defective farming,' the Ontario Agricultural College was founded in 1874 to reach out to isolated and stubborn farmers through its Agricultural and Experimental Union, which later subsidized the educational Farmers' Institutes that had been established in 1885 (Cohen 1988, 112-5; Graham 1988, 263-4).

The Women's Institute movement's own account of its origins, which seems somewhat mythologized when read from a critical perspective, reveals how urbanization intersected with agricultural reform.[2] The organization's reputed founder is Adelaide Hoodless, wife of a wealthy Hamilton furniture manufacturer, who lost her eighteen-month-old son to a bacterial infection from contaminated milk. (Urban households bought unpasteurized milk from farmers who drove into town to sell it from open canisters.) Overcome with grief and guilt, Hoodless is said to have then made it her life mission to have housekeeping and child care conducted according to her, albeit limited, understanding of scientific principles. While promoting the new discipline of home economics or domestic science at the Ontario Agricultural College, she was invited to speak to women at a meeting of the Farmers' Institutes at Stoney Creek, just east of Hamilton. After suggesting that women form their own organization in affiliation with the Farmers' Institutes, Hoodless had very little to do with rural women.

In view of her minimal contribution, the Hoodless cult is entirely unwarranted and distinctly odd.[3] Reconsider the story of Hoodless's speech to Stoney Creek women critically: a wealthy urban woman warned farm wives about the danger of unhygienic dairy practices, women who almost certainly breast-fed their children and gave their older children freshly drawn milk. Adelaide Hoodless lectured to them as producers, not consumers, of milk. As cities became more densely populated and passed by-laws to prohibit the keeping of cows and chickens in backyards, the quality and delivery of fresh farm produce to urban populations had to be improved and regulated. Using the rhetoric of all women's common maternal responsibility, the WI's original program directed farm women to imitate urban, scientific standards of hygiene and sanitation, but as producers, not consumers or housewives. Whether farm women actually believed in and took precautions against bacteria is not known. Contrary to the belief that 'slovenly' farm wives lost control of dairy production to large-scale, government-inspected commercial creameries because they deserved to, blame is better shifted from farm wives to inadequate marketing networks (Cohen 1988, 111; Graham 1988, 261–3).

The WI's account of its origins clearly illustrates how the farm population was directed to reform agricultural practices in imitation of commercial manufacturing processes, but still in their capacity as producers of foodstuffs for a rapidly expanding urban population. And, while the WI's original program apparently imitated bourgeois urban housewifery, it made their members no less farm women; such was simply the rhetoric and content of agricultural reform at that time. Even the apparently trivial suggestion that WI members cultivate flower-beds makes sense in terms of the agriculture ministry's simultaneous campaign to plant trees along concession lines after fifty years of settlers' reckless deforestation (Graham 1988, 278, 287). Agricultural reform intersected with the logic of maternal feminism, epitomized by the tragic death of Hoodless's infant son, to persuade WI members of their particular agricultural responsibility, as mothers, to all other mothers. Although WI members were less politically sophisticated than populist radicals, their activities were perhaps no less agricultural. And finally, they were dedicated to preserving the agrarian and rural way of life despite the onslaught of urbanization and rural depopulation.

The three fledgling Women's Institutes at Stoney Creek, Whitby and Kemble, floundered until George Creelman was appointed superintendent of the thriving Farmers' Institutes. The WI movement did not really expand until 1900, when he extended to women the same subsidies and access to resources and speakers enjoyed by the men's organization. Three years later, there were fifty-two WI branches and a paid-up membership of 4,151. By 1905, the Ministry of Agriculture had hired seventeen instructors from the Ontario Agricultural College to travel the province, lecturing and giving demonstrations, primarily in dairying techniques, to Women's Institutes. To promote membership in the Women's Institutes, Creelman pointed out the contrast between improvements made to barns and stables by progressive farmers, and 'badly planned and poorly equipped' dwellings.[4] He still associated the dairy and poultry yard with the household, and thus suggested that women learn modern techniques in dairying, butter-making, bee-keeping, and market gardening. Creelman 'saw the [Women's] Institutes as the way to make the female sector of the rural economy more efficient, just as the male sector had become' (Crowley 1986b, 80).

But dairying was already slipping out of women's control as agriculture became increasingly commercialized. Whereas wives previously received dairy cows as wedding gifts to contribute to the household's subsistence and perhaps supplement its income, they lost financial control when dairy cattle became farm property controlled by its sold owner, that is, by husbands (Cohen 1988, 43–7). Marjorie Cohen is sceptical about the provincial government's efforts to promote women's dairying through the WI because, in her view, government clearly intended cheese and butter production to be shifted from farm households to factories (1988, 112–17). She faults the WI for focusing on production techniques rather than marketing, which might have kept dairy production in women's control. Although commercial creameries did not overtake domestic production of butter until the mid-1920s, it is difficult to see how women, even assisted by government subsidies, might have competed with better-financed commercial creameries. The uneven process of rural electrification surely gave commercial creameries an additional advantage. Regardless of the shift to factory production of butter, government policy during this period seems confused as to whether dairying was men's or women's work. In 1903, when Creelman designed the WI's program, husbands' access to dairy income was

not yet secured, or even in the process of becoming so uniformly secured across the diverse regions of Ontario.

Unlike the Cercles de fermières in Quebec, which maintained a
strong commitment to household production of commodities by its
members, the WI movement turned inward to consumption and home
economics, subjects that were part of the larger, urban-led 'domestic
science movement' (Prentice et al. 1988, 156-8, 183).[5] After acquiring
the franchise, the hitherto unified 'woman movement' dispersed into
three broad segments. Whereas one segment of the movement pressed
on to secure further citizenship rights (Cott 1987) and another segment
turned to labour militancy (Prentice et al. 1988, 226-32), yet another
segment, to which the WI movement belongs, retreated from electoral
politics to seek practical improvements to women's household work
(ibid, 242-52).

This apparent retreat on the part of the WI might be redeemed by
Veronica Strong-Boag's argument that, during the interwar period,
'home economics [had] some of the same consciousness raising and
research goals of the modern women's studies programmes' (1986, 44).
Moreover, the criticism that the WI was too domestic in orientation
does not quite account for the full range of responsibilities and heavy
manual labour involved before plumbing, electricity, professional
butchers, central heating, birth control, or spending money became
widely available to farm women. Home economics, at this time, entailed the growing and preservation of a substantial amount of food,
including canning adequate quantities of meat to feed entire families
during the winter months. In 1927-8, Violet McNaughton led a joint
campaign with the WI to install running water in farm homes: 'I suf-
fered so much from carrying those pails of water which are a part
of the burden of a country woman that it burned into my mind this
water question very deeply ... so that the idea of woman power for
handling the water will be abolished.'[6] A few years later, the prev-
alence of malnourished and ill-clothed children on the Canadian
prairies during the Depression lent further strength to the salience of
home economics and domesticity to women (Burnet 1951, 20). Even
as recently as the 1940s, wartime rationing of food and petroleum further increased the importance of household subsistence production for
rural households, and hence the relevance of domestic-science programs, which were rapidly becoming obsolete in urban Canada. The
WI's program is an example of a pragmatic feminist strategy focused
on household work that was appropriate for that stage in Canada's

development but which, present-day critics charge, has failed to move on to more pertinent issues.

THE WI AND AGRARIAN PROTEST ON THE PRAIRIES

The new farm women's movement also has antecedents in first-wave feminism. Because the new farm women's movement is oriented principally to agriculture, it is supposed to descend, in a conceptual sense, from such organizations as the Women Grain Growers' Association (WGGA), founded in 1913; the United Farm Women of Alberta (UFWA), founded in 1915; and the United Farm Women of Ontario (UFWO), founded in 1918.[7] These organizations were all affiliated with male-dominated agrarian protest organizations and parties. The farmers' protest movement was geographically based in prairie opposition to the National Policy promoted by central Canadian industrial interests, but it was able to encompass farmers' interests as a class when it spread to rural Ontario.

The history of farm protest movements intersects with that of the women's movement. According to one interpretation, farm women were an exception to first-wave feminist conservatism because they chafed against the dominance of bourgeois, urban suffragists.[8] Together with labour women, women involved in organized agrarian populism suspected that the suffragists' associations with provincial and central Liberal parties precluded more radical economic and social reforms. American farm women participating in populist politics in the 1880s are likewise credited with anticipating urban women's political mobilization and transcending their political analysis (Wagner 1988, 330–5). (In contemporary diction, populist feminists put class ahead of gender.) In contrast, members of the largest farm women's organization in Canada, the Women's Institutes, were conservative exceptions to the rule of generally progressive farm women because the WI was aligned with bourgeois urban housewives and Liberal governments. In addition to promoting gender to the exclusion of class, WI branches were further suspect because they were sponsored and subsidized by provincial ministries of agriculture. Although explicitly non-sectarian and non-partisan (Walker, Collins, and McIntyre Hood 1948, 30), the latter quality did not prevent the WI from being state-funded, and possibly state-directed, in order to thwart competition from the women's auxiliaries of populist parties. Provincial Liberal governments were suspected of funding the WIs in order to purchase women's partisan loyalty soon after women were enfranchised. In like manner, when farm organizations became partisan in the 1920s, their women's auxiliaries were expected to convince women to vote for agrarian parties and against the Liberals, who had given women the vote. According to this interpretation, the thousands of WI members were conservative aberrations among rural women, while populist leaders such as Violet McNaughton in Saskatchewan and Irene Parlby in Alberta spoke for the vast majority of unaffiliated farm women.

The actual evidence concerning rural women's affiliations is mixed. During feminism's first wave of collective political action, Canadian writer and activist Nellie McClung shifted back and forth among populists, suffragists, and Liberals; she did not distinguish between two opposing farm women's movements, both of which she considered superior to urban suffrage organizations: 'The Women's Institutes and the United Farm Women were not afraid to tackle social problems and their reading courses and discussions showed serious purpose. The women of the cities were more likely to be entangled in social affairs and in danger of wasting their time, but there was real stuff in the countrywomen' (1946, 182). Nellie McClung, moreover, was present among the members of the Manitoba suffrage group who were invited to assist at the founding of the Women's Section of the Saskatchewan Grain Growers' Association (SGGA) in 1913 (Bacchi 1983, 125; Menzies 168, 82). Agnes Macphail (a high-ranking officer in the United Farm Women of Ontario) likewise rarely declined an opportunity to speak to the Women's Institutes (Steward 1991).

While evidence of an overlapping network of formal ties that linked rural women's suffrage and populist organizations exists (Menzies 1968, 87), examples of hostility and competition are relatively rare. Correspondence from Irene Parlby to Violet McNaughton, respective leaders of the United Farm Women of Alberta (UFWA) and the Women's Section of the SGGA, provides one such exception. In private correspondence, Parlby was more critical of the WI than is apparent from formal organizational ties alone: 'I attended the convention of Women's Institutes in Edmonton ... their line of work does not interest me very much – too much of the housekeeping business, and I think the farm women want to be taken out of their housekeeping troubles, and made to realize there are other things of interest in the world' (Parlby to McNaughton, 1916, cited in Rasmussen, Savage, and Wheeler 1976, 138). A letter to the editor in 1915 also complained about the WI: 'Always housework, knitting, and the main women's destination: preparing of dainty side-dishes and salads. Kitchen, kitchen and again kitchen' (*Grain Growers' Guide* 1915, cited in Rasmussen, Savage, and Wheeler 1976, 132).

But regardless of populist leaders' personal impatience with the WI, testimony from surviving members indicates that activities undertaken by any of these women's organizations were identical at the local level. They raised money for community halls, libraries, and rest rooms; sponsored courses; and organized community events in order to improve the quality of rural life (Silverman 1984, 173–83). An analysis by R.G. Marchildon likely voices McNaughton's ambition for such activities: '[WGGA was] part of the larger maternal feminist movement, but this analysis is too simplistic. The key element is that these women were part of an aggressive agrarian movement' (1988, 104). Marchildon thus implies that the WI movement, which was not part of an 'aggressive agrarian movement,' must be 'simplistic' because it was part of the maternal movement. Never mind their actual activities, he argues; once women were involved they could be instructed in and mobilized for populist politics through their affiliations to a larger movement. This basic principle applies to women's auxiliaries in all political movements and parties. Perhaps this strategy, promoted by McNaughton and Parlby, worked, but whether women were actually mobilized at the local level could be verified only by speaking to survivors or reading minute-books, not by relying on the wishful thinking in leaders' correspondence.

With all deference to populist leaders, therefore, the grass-roots activities of the competing organizations must be compared apart from the theory of populist and feminist mobilization. To return to Ontario history, Margaret Kechnie (1985) suggests that the alleged rivalry between the WI and the United Farm Women of Ontario (UFWO) was largely confined to Emma Griesbach's column in the United Farmers' party newspaper. When the UFO government was defeated in the 1923 Ontario provincial election, the party was in disarray and could no longer assist its women's association financially or politically, leaving the UFWO with no basis on which to distinguish itself from the WI. Meanwhile, standing apart from partisan competition, the Women's Institutes had already taken up rural issues such as electrification and improved schools that were paramount at that time and were especially compatible with the organization's domestic focus. Without partisanship to distinguish between women's organizations, some local branches of the UFWO promptly converted themselves into Women's

Institutes, while others survived until 1943 in areas where there were no WI branches (Kechnie 1985, 266–78). Operating subsidies and technical support from the Ministry of Agriculture were probably further incentives for UFWO branches to convert into WI branches. Kechnie concludes that the United Farmers' movement offered women little more than vague and ambiguous phrases that were no substitute for women's traditional methods in improving their situation and reforming society (1985, 276).

The question of partisan-motivated state intervention prompts two responses. The first is to concede that the WI's history indeed intersects with partisan competition and that provincial organizations were, at certain times, partisan-motivated instruments of provincial Liberal and Conservative governments. This is known to be the case in Alberta, where ill will between WI members and those of other groups dates back to 1921, when the United Farmers of Alberta (UFA) defeated the Liberal government; Irene Parlby, who served as minister without portfolio in the UFA government, favoured the explicitly partisan UFWA over the Women's Institutes.[9] Later, in the 1930s, Social Credit women's groups defected from UFWA groups, and the only organization to benefit from the split was the WI, which grew at the expense of the UFWA (Burnet 1951, 147).

During the interwar period, agriculture was not the only partisan grievance on the Canadian prairies to involve farm women. Especially in Saskatchewan, 'the politics of prejudice' were dominant until the governing Liberal party was defeated by the Conservatives in 1929 (Smith 1975). When ties between provincial and national wings of parties were closer, the Saskatchewan Liberal government was committed to Laurier's national policy of immigrant settlement of the West; it maintained power by skilful manipulation and, in fact, exacerbation of antagonisms between Protestant, English-speaking farmers and non-Protestant, Eastern European immigrants (ibid, 136). The Liberal government sought to pacify British and American settlers while protecting immigrants against forced assimilation in the form of English-language education. Organized farmers were among those calling for the immediate 'Canadianization' of immigrants and a halt to further immigration from Eastern Europe. The higher status of English-speaking women – as seen in their noble struggle for prohibition and the franchise – was further proof of British civilization as compared with the virtual domestic serfdom of foreign women (ibid, 126). By the end of the 1920s, the Ku Klux Klan found a receptive audience in rural Saskatchewan; it infiltrated the Conservative party, which defeated the Liberals in the 1929 provincial election on the issue of English-language education.

The archives reveal that women's organizations share some complicity in these events. In 1926-7, Abbie deLury, director of the Saskatchewan WI (Homemakers' Clubs until 1972) and employed by the Extension Division of the university, was criticized for publishing in a journal that accepted liquor advertisements. The campaign against deLury took a nasty turn: she was accused of being the 'ringleader' in a plot to direct Homemaker funds to the Roman Catholic church. This particular division over liquor among women was fuelled by larger divisions, as a prohibitionist anxiously related to her friends: 'Protestants are up in arms – The Orange Lodges here are working more than they have for years and several of our men and women have joined the Ku Klux Klan; so until things cool down some there isn't much use to talk of any Woman's Christian Temperance Union getting started here. You folks do not realize how a community can get divided, and you won't unless a Convent [Coven] slips into your town. The Homemakers' Club is divided now.'[10] Only further research can tell to what extent farm women were implicated in the 'politics of prejudice' on the Canadian prairies.

In sum, WI records relate stories of branches springing up spontaneously across Canada as lonely women picked prairie flowers and pined for their Women's Institutes back in Ontario, but all branches quickly came under the supervision of provincial ministries of agriculture. Since very little primary research has been done on the question of partisan-motivated state intervention in relation to farm women's organizations, it must be laid aside for now.

Even so, any further research along these lines will find that, until the end of the Second World War, provincial bureaucracies rarely had the practical ability to deal with the logistics of manipulating civil society. Hence the second response to the question of partisan-motivated state intervention is simply that the question is moot. In the 1950s, new tax-sharing arrangements were negotiated between Ottawa and the provinces that permitted 'province-building' to begin in earnest (and largely by the wealthier provinces); until then, provincial governments scarcely had the resources, in terms of finances, personnel, or technology, to embark on ambitious programs to manipulate civil society for partisan purposes. In this regard, evidence pertaining to the corresponding organization in Quebec, the Cercles de fermières, is instructive. Examination of the archives of the Cercles de fermières convinced Yolande Cohen that the government of Quebec, even in cooperation with a centralized network of parish priests, was inadequate to control or even direct the Cercles. The Cercles asked for more financial and administrative assistance than the Quebec ministry of agriculture was capable of or willing to give (Cohen 1989a, 133). In the absence of assistance from the Roman Catholic church's bureaucracy, one can imagine that the rural population of English Canada, especially in the newly settled prairies, was even more difficult to regulate.[11]

Whereas the issue of partisan-motivated state regulation of the 'passive' WI movement is moot, inquiry into the WI's active contribution to the process of province-building during the first half of the twentieth century is more promising. Caroline Andrew seized on a signal political achievement of first-wave feminism: 'In pushing for and organizing services and programmes designed to improve social conditions, women played an important role in setting the stage for the development of the welfare state' (1984, 673). One can take Andrew's argument farther and say that the WI not only set the stage but also operated as a rural arm of the state. In terms of providing services, provincial government bureaucracies could not penetrate the dispersed society that characterized rural Canada, and the WI often filled the administrative gaps:

In the earlier years, the Women's Institutes made arrangements and provided voluntary assistance for health inspection of children, a service which led to the present health services for schools provided by the Provincial governments ... same arrangements were made for dental clinics. In more recent years, WI members have been active in the establishment of County and District Health Units. All programs to provide information and promote clinics for the control of major diseases have relied greatly upon the active involvement of Institute members. (Federated Women's Institutes of Ontario 1972, 51)[12]

Provincial governments administered rural life through the vehicle of the WI, whose chief task was to 'improve the quality of rural life.'

THE WI AND THE WOMEN'S MOVEMENT

The Women's Institute movement is an example of first-wave social or maternal feminism.[13] Most scholars consider this category of feminism to have become obsolete soon after the end of the nineteenth century (Kealey 1979, 14). None the less, the WI has persisted from its beginnings in feminism's first wave of the nineteenth century through to the crest of feminism's second wave. In Canada, especially, organizations such as the WI survived to bridge feminism's first wave at the turn of the century and feminism's resurgent second wave in the late 1960s (Prentice et al. 1988, 337).[14] The WI reached its peak of prestige and influence during the interval between the two waves. Membership did not decline after the First World War as drastically as it did in other first-wave women's organizations such as the National Council of Women (NCW, founded in 1893) or the Woman's Christian Temperance Union (WCTU, founded in 1874). However, despite the fact that the Federated Women's Institutes of Canada (FWIC) had 47,177 members in 1982, compared with 3,787 WCTU members (*Canadian Encyclopedia* 1986, 622, 1956), it did not grow successfully into second-wave feminism like, for example, the Young Women's Christian Association (YWCA, founded in 1870) did. In Ontario, WI membership has declined from a provincial peak of 36,481 in 1962–3, as branches have collectively aged and died along with their members. A minor crisis ensued in 1984–5, when a Canadian Press item publicly ridiculed the WI, and the Ontario Ministry of Agriculture and Food (OMAF) cut back funding, an act that reinforced members' doubts about the organization's purpose. The provincial executive of the Federated Women's Institutes of Ontario (FWIO) responded by revising its constitution, paying more attention to public relations, and announcing a program to work on waste-management and recycling projects, which members have taken up with great enthusiasm. Their new-found dedication to environmental issues has revived the WI in Ontario.

Declining membership is typical of institutionalized service and interest groups. Even the province's major agricultural lobby, the Ontario Federation of Agriculture (OFA), which, despite criticism,[15] is presumed to be a somewhat more effective and dynamic organization than the WI, bemoans its declining membership. Neither can one overlook the fact that most of the WI's decline, in comparison with those of urban organizations, is attributable to the depopulation of farming and rural communities, rather than to a failure to update its agenda. With 19,354 WI members and 325 Junior Institute members in Ontario, and 35,000 WI members across Canada in 1989, the Women's Institute movement was still a substantial feature of rural Ontario. After the

OMAF cut off all funding, and membership dues rose accordingly, membership had fallen to approximately 16,000 by 1994 (personal communication, FWIO, Oct. 1994).

The claim that the WI is a relatively intact relic of first-wave feminism is bolstered by its isolation from the contemporary women's movement (Phillips 1991, 766). Although the FWIC was among the original groups who pressured the Canadian government to set up the Royal Commission on the Status of Women (RCSW) in 1967 and, in 1971, was on the National Action Committee on the Status of Women original steering committee, it withdrew soon after (Adamson, Briskin, and McPhail 1988, 52).[16] In its lengthy 1967 brief to the RCSW, the FWIC called for, among numerous recommendations already submitted to government, increased access to abortion and contraception, enforced support payments for divorced and deserted wives, and expanded day-care services. The radical and undeniably feminist content of these recommendations illustrates how, in Canada, well-established service organizations were able to cooperate with the newer women's liberation groups on specific projects and policies at the beginning of the second wave. In its submission, the FWIC further called for legal recognition of and financial compensation for farm women's work and their claims to family assets.[17] Only one other farm women's organization presented a brief, which made no such recommendation, which means that the FWIC deserves credit for the separate section on farm women in the final report (Royal Commission on the Status of Women 1970, 40–4). The FWIC also called for a government agency to research and deal with women's problems, which corresponds to the report's final recommendation to establish a Status of Women Council (ibid, 418).[18]

As was said of agrarian leaders' wishful thinking for populist mobilization, the WI leaders should not be the sole basis for judging the movement. Even today, the discrepancy between ambitious and proactive resolutions passed at provincial councils and less ambitious, and indeed traditional, activities that occur at local branch meetings is striking. During the late 1980s, the Federated Women's Institutes of Canada, for example, was speaking out on pornography, violence against women, reproductive technology, and abortion; meanwhile, local WIs had a hymn and scripture reading at each meeting, and roll-call asking each member to 'name a dessert from a different country or culture' or 'an old implement and what has taken its place.' In 1989, an Ontario branch had members present reports on each of the

WI standing committees on agriculture, Canadian industries, citizenship and legislation, education and cultural activities, family and consumer affairs, and international affairs. In June of that year, the international affairs convener stepped aside to introduce a local Mennonite woman who had been the Concerned Farm Women's delegate on an all-woman, Oxfam-sponsored agricultural tour of Nicaragua.[19] Whereas tour participants were visibly moved by their experience, it was more difficult to generate enthusiasm and sympathy for Nicaragua among women back in Ontario, judging from the sceptical response of local Institute members to a slide-show presentation about the tour. Less constrained by the formal standing committee structure of the senior Institutes, an Ontario Junior Institute had on its 1989 agenda microwave cooking, day care, silk screening, holistic medicine, planting a herb garden, and getting to know your township.

Since withdrawing from the mainstream of second-wave feminism, the WI has had little to do with urban organizations. In 1989 the Federated Women's Institutes of Ontario (FWIO) cooperated with the National Council of Jewish Women, another first-wave service organization that is similarly disassociated from the contemporary women's movement. The Ontario Cancer Treatment Research Foundation assisted the Council of Jewish Women to establish workshops on screening for breast cancer, which WI members attended and then delivered the information to fellow members at branch meetings. In the 1980s, the WI has become involved with the Recycling Council of Ontario. Otherwise, the WI is oriented to the rural community, maintaining interlocking networks with representatives on the boards of directors of the Ontario Federation of Agriculture (OFA), the Ontario Agricultural Hall of Fame, the Ontario Agricultural Museum, and the Royal Winter Fair. It also works closely with 4-H, an educational program for rural and farm adolescents and children, likewise sponsored through Rural Organizations and Services of the provincial government. The WI is not affiliated with the anti-feminist organization R.E.A.L. Women. In view of the WI's dissociation from the organized women's movement, other organizations whose urban linkages are institutionally fixed (United Church Women, for example) are more likely candidates for the dissemination of second-wave feminism in rural communities since the early 1970s.[20]

In sum, a focus on the WI implies that as much is to be learned by decline, stagnation, and persistence as from moments of initiative and innovation. Such a focus serves as a useful corrective to enthusiasm that is not warranted by the historical record. Farm women's groups have come and gone in the past century, each hoping to supersede the WI, but they eventually disappeared, while the WI, apparently oblivious to criticism, plodded resolutely forward. For example, only a technicality prevented Concerned Farm Women (CFW), often cited as a leader in the new wave of activism, from dissolving in 1988 when the group pondered its future:

From that came the motion to dissolve CFW ... but we had to give written notice of a motion to dissolve. The written notice to dissolve went out to about 75 members and supporters. The meeting to discuss the motion to dissolve drew eleven members and eight media representatives. The members voted not to dissolve but to carry on. 'When I thought about it afterwards, it seemed ridiculous to continue, but I think we were reacting to our feelings,' Joy Ward [the president] said. Now is the time for CFW to lie low for a while and recharge their batteries. (Stewart-Kirkby 1988, 8)

This is not to say that Concerned Farm Women failed. According to the logic of new social movements, people should coalesce for action around particular issues at crucial junctures, and then move on to other issues rather than devoting energy to maintaining moribund organizational structures.[21] Even so, critics can still admire the WI's tenacity in having maintained for over a century those moribund structures.

CONTEMPORARY FARM WOMEN'S MOVEMENTS AND THE STATE

In addition to a common policy of non-partisanship, all farm women's organizations belong to the farm women's policy community that is dominated by the Farm Women's Bureau of Agriculture Canada. The agricultural policy community is a network of people and organizations with common and competing interests centred on lead agencies within provincial and national ministries of agriculture; farm organizations, journalists, academics, individual farmers, and interested members of the general public interact with government officials in an effort to influence agricultural policy (Skogstad 1990). Organized farm women keep contact with the Farm Women's Bureau of Agriculture Canada, a specifically female auxiliary of the more mainstream, male-dominated agricultural policy community. Not all organizations are equal within this particular policy community.

Particularly from the perspective of the WI and the National Farmers' Union (NFU), the newer farm women's organizations are rivals that monopolize funding and policy involvement at the centre of the farm women's policy community. According to the NFU's Women's President,[22] the NFU has applied to the Farm Women's Bureau for funding during the 1980s and has consistently been turned down. Without ascribing personal hostility to government personnel, what can explain a perceived bias in state funding that works to the advantage of the new farm women's networks?

Before the earlier Ontario groups (Women for the Survival of Agriculture and Concerned Farm Women) coalesced into a provincial organization (OFWN) in 1989, they were 'autonomous, grass-roots' groups, unlike the WI, which was affiliated with provincial ministries of agriculture (Cebotarev and Beattie 1985, 259). But subsequent events turned that distinction upside down in the 1980s. Just when the federal Secretary of State cut off block funding for the WI, and provincial ministries of agriculture and extension programs of agricultural colleges throughout Canada weaned the WI from state-sponsored courses and workshops (Women's Institutes of Saskatchewan 1988), the new farm women's movement became eligible for a series of grants. Agriculture Canada established the Farm Women's Bureau in 1981 to implement Ottawa's Status of Women policies as they apply to agriculture through three principal means: consultation, research, and funding. Since 1988, the bureau has been principally devoted to the implementation of the Farm Women's Advancement Programme (FWAP); it is designed to highlight women's contribution to agriculture and to promote legal, economic, and political equality for farm women in the agricultural industry. The FWAP provides $150,000 per year in grants for eligible projects (such as conferences, newsletters, and advocacy) that conform to the funding guidelines outlined by Status of Women Canada. The seven-person committee that allocates funds consists of one person from the Farm Women's Bureau, one from the Women's Program in Human Resources Development Canada (formerly Secretary of State for Women), and five from the Communications and Policy Branch of Agriculture Canada. The Farm Women's Bureau deliberately sought to bring people from the Communications and Policy Branch into the selection process in order to raise the profile of the Farm Women's Bureau within the ministry.

State sponsorship begins to explain, in part, the emergence and new-found prominence of the new farm women's movement. The Ontario

Farm Women's Network (OFWN), for instance, credits its very origins to government initiative: 'Government officials, provincially and federally, have been requesting representation and input from this Farm Women's Network. As we had no mandate to represent provincial farm women, we could not reply as a provincial voice ... they definitely wanted a provincial farm women's representative' (OFWN newsletter 1/5, 1989). Originally, the provincial farm women's networks were just that – networks for the exchange of information and mutual support. However, representatives from the Farm Women's Bureau and the Women's Program explained that information and support networks do not qualify for funding. To do so, projects must meet the mandate of the Farm Women's Advancement Programme: 'to eliminate barriers to women's participation or to advance women's equality' (*Western Producer*, 23 Nov. 1989, 23). At the first national conference, in New Brunswick in 1989, the provincial networks became the Canadian Farm Women's Network (CFWN), a formal, national organization, in order to qualify for government funding.

The creation of a new national organization was not uniformly applauded. To begin with, it was argued that the creation and continued maintenance of another national organization, parallel to the national WI and NFU, would further fragment farm women whose energy and money were already strained. Because the new CFWN was based on individual, rather than group, membership, it could not accommodate either the WI or the NFU as an affiliated organization; it allows these organizations (and individuals, including the author) only non-voting memberships acquired by subscriptions to national and provincial newsletters. The NFU, moreover, withdrew altogether because it is opposed in principle to multiple farm organizations; it holds only loose affiliations with umbrella groups such as the Associated Country Women of the World. A second criticism was that Secretary of State funding guidelines prodded reluctant farm women towards the formation of a 'lobby group,' which they initially opposed. At the outset of the new farm women's movement in Saskatchewan, leaders publicly stated their abhorrence of lobbying, and a few privately expressed fears that the group could 'turn into a militant women's liberation style organization' ('Rural women's group find defining role a problem,' *Regina Leader-Post*, 22 Feb., A4, and 2 Mar., A7, 1985). Similar sentiments were repeated at the 1989 national conference; opponents argued that the network's new goals of advocacy and lobbying did not come from the grass roots, but from the top down (*Western Producer*, 23 Nov.

1989, 23). The grass roots, according to critics, wanted only a loose information and support network. The Farm Women's Advancement Programme thus dictates guidelines that strain relations between new farm women's networks, which are currently favoured for funding, and the more established organizations. Whereas the more cynical NFU never expected succour from government, the WI movement is somewhat dismayed at having been abandoned by its traditional sponsors.

The new farm women's networks are uniquely identified with the formal purpose of the Farm Women's Bureau. Accordingly, of the fourteen women invited to the Farm Women's Bureau's annual policy consultation in 1991, twelve represented the provincial and national networks, whereas the WI and NFU had one representative each (*OFWN Newsletter* 4/3 [1991], 8). These provincial networks coalesced nationally to conform to the funding guidelines of the Farm Women's Bureau; their program is to promote the role of women in agriculture, specifically through the appointment of women to executive positions on the boards of commodity and producer organizations. Equity in professional organizations is a clear-cut, non-controversial goal for Agriculture Canada which meshes perfectly with its technical, professional orientation. Agricultural policy communities across Canada tend to be closely knit and consensual circles, in part because government branches and non-governmental organizations are dominated by the professional graduates (agrologists and agricultural economists) of faculties of Agricultural Science.[23]

The National Farmers' Union and the Women's Institutes, unlike the networks, do not fit neatly in the same professional/technical niche. The NFU, in particular, might be a marginal player in the farm women's policy community for the same reason that it is marginal to the agricultural policy community in general – namely, its left-wing ideological program. A description of the WI in a NFU manual illustrates the organization's commitment to making significant social and political change: 'An enormous amount of very good work is accomplished by the [WI], but do they help to shift important decisions to the people and communities which are affected by them? Is this another place where we accept the assumption that a woman's role is to make the best of things as they are, rather than to help shape the way things should be?' (Wiebe 1987, 45) This far-reaching criticism of the WI corresponds to the NFU's formal policy positions. The NFU calls for large-scale government regulation of food production as a remedy to 'economic exploitation' (*Farm policy for the 90's*, NFU Policy State-

ment, 1991, A1–2). Such a program of government intervention is immediately at odds with the free-market orientation of Canadian agriculture. As well, the NFU was founded in 1969 in order to 'promote
integrated policies on a broad range of issues to resolve conflicts of
interest between regions and producers of various commodities'
(*Canadian Encyclopedia*, 1194). The NFU's motto – 'In union is
strength' – clearly expresses the organization's central political insight:
namely, that the free-market system, in conjunction with governments,
fragments farmers into commodity organizations and thereby 'keeps
farmers divided and subject to their manipulation and exploitation'
(NFU Policy Statement, 1991, M-11). The NFU seeks to integrate
farmers' diverse interests before lobbying government as a unified body,
but state officials might well prefer to do the accommodating themselves in order to gain some autonomy or room for manoeuvring in
the design and implementation of agricultural policy.

It is not surprising then, that the National Farmers' Union is at
odds with both state officials and other farm organizations. Like the
Ontario Farmers' Union in relation to the Ontario Ministry of Agriculture and Food, the NFU is marginalized because it 'does not share
the norm of quiet diplomacy, opting for confrontationist lobbying tactics' (Skogstad 1990, 70). The NFU's candour in criticizing government
is exceptional when, for instance, a former women's president, Elaine
Driver, attributes antagonistic motives to the government in its deliberately divisive funding policies: 'Having so many organizations
keeps everyone separated and ineffective and frustrated ... That is why
the government is so willing to fund these small groups. If a single,
powerful and effective group could be formed, the lobbying power
would be impossible for politicians to ignore' (*Western Producer*, 18
Jul. 1985, 24). Cogent insights such as these reveal clearly that the
NFU has an ideological program that is antagonistic to current governments and thus makes the organization an uncomfortable intruder
in otherwise consensual and generally conservative agricultural policy
communities.

The experience of the Women's Institutes, however, reveals that abiding by norms of quiet diplomacy does not guarantee access to the
policy community's centre either. If the NFU women were penalized
for their rebelliousness, the WI women were penalized for their deference. Glenis Joyce, an administrator at the University of Saskatchewan Extension Division, suggests that its formal government affiliation actually disempowered the Women's Institutes in the long term

because bureaucrats fostered a relationship of dependency and deference. When the university began to wean the WI from financial and administrative support in the early 1980s, WI leaders were afraid even to inquire about the status of either their funding or their officials. An explanation of why the positions of the NFU and the WI, although from apparently opposing poles of radical criticism and cautious deference on the political spectrum, are roughly comparable within the agricultural policy community is therefore necessary.

Their positions might be comparable because neither the NFU nor the WI is uniquely centred on agricultural policy; both have overarching programs that do not comfortably fit into the scope of a single line department. The NFU's critique of private property and free-market trade in agricultural commodities, for example, can scarcely be accommodated by ministries of agriculture. Neither can the WI's program to improve the quality of rural life be easily accommodated by ministries of agriculture that increasingly devote their attention to the terms of international trade. An agenda that does not comfortably fit into the purview of a single line department usually means that a group does not relate principally to government. The WI's federal body (FWIC), for instance, barely exists as a national umbrella; the WI's active life is conducted almost entirely on the local level, where it is directed to servicing members and their local community. A public-policy approach that seeks to document the WI's lobbying activity in relation to government would barely scratch the surface of its activities.

From an examination of the funding procedures and structure of the farm women's policy community, it is possible to arrive at this general observation without requiring any proof of hostility on the part of the Farm Women's Bureau towards the more established organizations. The state divides society into narrow functional categories (in other words, line departments) and favours those groups that align themselves most closely with the corresponding structure of government bureaucracy. The state is not amenable to organizations that unify or, to use a very old-fashioned term, 'totalize' spheres of activities. And that is what the Women's Institutes do in their amorphous commitment to the 'rural community' or the 'rural way of life' as opposed to narrowly agricultural and single-commodity issues.[24]

In the end, relations among organized farm women were not historically and still are not entirely cordial, but leading farm women would deny it publicly all the same. For example, relations between the WI and the Ontario network got off to a poor start, but soon after resolving an initial dispute, former FWIO president Peggy Knapp stated publicly: 'There is room for both of us. The Network is raising the profile of farm women. WI is more involved with rural women. Rural issues are a little different than farm issues.'[25] It is more to the point, therefore, to document the common ground that all farm women's organizations share and to inquire why such a public premium is placed on consensus.

Leaders like Peggy Knapp might be quick to make amends because there is abundant evidence of overlapping memberships between the WI and new farm women's organizations. Of four CFW and OFWN members surveyed, only one was not also a WI member. OFWN membership amounts to subscribing to a newsletter, which scarcely interferes with local WI activities. Neither a newsletter nor an annual conference substitutes for sociability, which was the most frequent reason given for WI membership.[26] The OFWN logo was designed by a WI member. At the national level, Saskatchewan's provincial director of CFWN is still active in local and district WIs, and PEI's director credits 'her early involvement in the WI which led to her election to the School Board.' Network women receive WI scholarships and attend WI training courses (*Canadian Farm Women's Network newsletter* 3, 1990, 3-4). In discussions led by Diane Harkin, founder of Women for the Survival of Agriculture (WSA), Saskatchewan farm women decided to 'tie in with' the WI in their new movement.[27] Further evidence of overlapping membership is inferred from the *Western Producer* journalists' practice of quoting NFU women and WI members in their coverage of network conferences. This is likely a calculated appeal on the part of journalists to avoid giving offence to a broad readership, but the point is confirmed all the same: the broad readership of the *Western Producer* wants to know about NFU and WI participation in the new farm women's movement. The practice of covering WI and ACWW events, in fact, dates back to when Violet McNaughton edited the women's section of the *Western Producer* from 1925 to 1950.[28]

Peggy Knapp's resolve to reach an accommodation with the network points, moreover, to farm women's overall preference for avoiding conflict, a theme which is developed at length later in this book. This preference is reflected in overlapping membership and might arise from the geographical distances that characterize rural life. One woman, for example, wanted to attend CFW meetings, but she was too tired after chores to drive thirty miles and back, and so joined her local WI branch instead. In relatively stable but sparsely populated areas, where anonymity is difficult and relations last a lifetime, hostility is less easily dispersed, and the beleaguered farming population feels obligated to put differences aside. Memberships might overlap (and the WI persist) because women reported conflict between wanting to experiment and wanting to remain part of the community; for example, they still feel obliged to participate in bake sales and other traditional tasks in order not to be ostracized.[29] One woman reported just the opposite conflict: 'I feel out of place in my WI branch because I'm not involved or interested in farming. Some of the girls come in, they're so excited about being up all night with some cow giving birth, and on and on about some new calf.' At a formal level, Kathryn Habberfield, president of the Alberta Women's Institutes, urged conciliation thus: 'I see no reason to believe that new groups are causing fragmentation, wasting resources, and causing rivalry. I commend them for forming organizations, and if they wish to study agriculture only, that is their prerogative. Whether we belong to Women's Institute ... or any other organization matters not. What does matter is that we work together to achieve our common goal' (*Western Producer*, 18 Jul. 1985, 24). As a result, the exact state of relations between the Women's Institutes and new farm women's networks cannot be reported because farm women themselves are reluctant to criticize or compete openly with each other.

THE 'OLD' DISCOURSE OF FARM WOMEN'S MOVEMENTS

Leaders of the new farm women's movement articulate a discourse, alternatively called social, maternal, or relational feminism, like that usually associated with the old farm women's movement. The term 'discourse' is used here to stress that socially constructed patterns of speech and knowledge create a person's subjective identity (Alcoff 1989, 312–5; Hekman 1990, 62–104). A domestic-oriented discourse appeals to some women because it resonates with their everyday experience of family life and motherhood; it provides a conceptual, cultural structure with which build a personal identity as a good wife, mother, and neighbour. And directly to the point here, domestic and familial imagery describes and justifies women's political activity in public outside of the home.

Contemporary farm women do not, of course, speak spontaneously in nineteenth-century rhetoric. Such a discourse precedes their birth and can be traced back to a variety of pernicious and not so pernicious sources (chief among them, the social gospel). It is transmitted from generation to generation in women's publications (Dumont-Johnson 1981) and in the sentimental rituals of women's organizations. Several WI members expressed affection not only for individual friends in their branch, but for the branch as a collectivity whose history went back almost a century, encompassing all their married life and their mothers' before them: 'I was born, grew up in WI.' WI friendships are 'special – closer and more enthusiastic,' one woman said, 'compared to women's auxiliaries in the church.' In addition to WI memorial services for deceased members, ceremonies are conducted to commemorate disbanding institutes whose collective property, notably Tweedsmuir histories, is carefully transferred to neighbouring branches.[30] Over and above the WI members, a further 5 per cent of the present survey sample belonged to another, separate women's organization (not including United Church Women, etc., which were coded as religious organizations). From the observation that at least one dimension of many farm women's lives is played out in a separate women's organization follows the claim that women continue to have access to a separate, traditionally female, discourse.

Although it is asserted that "maternal feminism no longer provides an option for contemporary women' and 'our analyses have become much more complex' (Adamson, Briskin, and McPhail 1988, 37; Kealey 1979, 14), politically active and dynamic farm women still echo Nellie McClung or Emily Murphy:

... women are nurturers and are interested in the security and future of their families. If my children want to farm, I am going to do my best to see that they can and that the agricultural industry will be healthy for them.[31]

Women, including farm women, think different than men and this to me is good. Let's take advantage of the way farm women think as opposed to farm men ... appoint more women to Boards and Committees.[32]

I think a woman's influence is good for a community because she can look at things from motherhood and other perspectives, rather than just the dollar and cents perspective.[33]

[On women getting involved in male-dominated agricultural organizations:] It's a lot like motherhood actually, if women waited until they were absolutely sure they were ready, there would be fewer children in this world. Instead we get in there and just do it.[34]

[On being a township councillor:] There is still a stigma to a woman running for office. I took the third baby (born 1981) to council meetings. Women are decision-makers at home which is good experience. There is no room for error at home when you're under pressure to make quick decisions. This carries over to council where women make decisions quickly and accurately. Women are busy and don't have time for nonsense.

Maternal imagery persists in the new farm women's movement: the passing of the OFWN constitution is described as 'being somewhat like giving birth'; the network is 'conceived' and must be 'nurtured' (OFWN newsletter 1/5 [1989], 2).

To what strategic purpose might farm women direct such rhetoric? It holds no persuasiveness with policy analysts, administrators, and agronomists within ministries of agriculture; and it holds even less persuasiveness with academic observers. If such rhetoric serves no purpose with bureaucratic and academic members of the policy community, it must be directed solely to farm wives and husbands. Its purpose is transparent – to articulate and justify women's political activity outside of private households in terms of their familial responsibilities. It justifies political participation in terms that appease husbands left at home to babysit, suspicious neighbours, and fellow colleagues who begrudge women's admission to public office. But it also articulates their sincerely held conviction that the standards and practices of domestic life can indeed improve political life and public policy.

Such a discourse might be persuasive to the extent that an orientation to family and children is grounded in household-based agricultural production. Farm women's greater fertility in comparison with urban women, although diminishing, may be more than a historical artefact of delayed social change. Children are a financial liability in a waged economy – as distinct from a technologically advanced or modern economy – where their labour cannot significantly contribute to household income. It is not simply that children contribute their labour to farming because it is less complex than technologically sophisticated occupations; farming is equally sophisticated, but the conditions of waged-employment contracts exclude other family members. Children cost less, too, under conditions of household production, when parents have access to assets other than wages to cover the full cost of their upbringing. Children's potential and actual value as assets to family enterprises were brought home by the example of a thirteen-year-old boy who was instructed by his (departing) father as to the imminent arrival of a freight truck, payment to its driver, and delivery of grain feed into the appropriate bins. Despite the physical hazards of operating oversized equipment, children learn to master advanced agricultural technology.

Such a discourse, moreover, corresponds to the fact that old and new movements alike centre on farm *wives* or on women as members of families. All these organizations take the family farm as their basis: as the basic membership unit for the NFU, as the basic social unit of the rural way of life for the WI, and as the basic economic unit of production for the networks. None of these organizations represents women who are non-family employees, typically foreign guest-workers or recent immigrants to Canada, on large-scale capitalist farms who are the lowest-paid workers on the entire spectrum of occupations. No organization reviewed here can claim to speak for these women, who are equally 'farm women,' because a family-oriented discourse is inadequate to articulate the class relationship between employer and employee on capitalist farms. This is evidently a blind spot on the part of farm women's organizations, but a word might be said in their defence. Non-family labour is concentrated in the horticultural industries (fruits, vegetables, and tobacco) of Southern Ontario and British Columbia. This type of farming is not only geographically distant from many women, but conceptually distant as well in that these organizations are ideologically committed to families as the economic, social, and moral basis for farming.[35]

The distinction between old and new farm women's movements may be finally addressed. Farm women have never been housewives living on farms, but have always done a good deal of agricultural work. When no new farm women's movement existed to seek legal and financial recognition for their agricultural work, their contribution went unrecognized. The agenda of the new farm women's movement dates back to at least 1967, when the Women's Institute's national executive addressed government agencies on the subject.[36] Since then the political context has changed to emphasize and promote farm women's contribution through an organized movement, principally associated with the Farm Women's Bureau of Agriculture Canada. When the dominant model was housewifery, farm women were conceptualized as housewives living on farms; when that model changed to favour career women, farm women became career farmers. The new farm women's movement is keen to be part of an agricultural policy community that concentrates on complex issues of farm-income protection; it represents a remarkable and ambitious group of individuals. But it is no more accurate today to characterize all farm women as career farmers than it was previously to characterize them all as housewives. No single organization is especially authentic or representative of all farm women. Official divisions among farm women's organizations do not mirror, in a straightforward fashion, social divisions in the grass-roots population. Instead, such divisions may better mirror government policies dating back to the creation of the WI in 1897.

2

A Survey of Farm Women

The Huron peninsula is situated between Lakes Huron and Ontario, roughly two hours' driving distance to the west of metropolitan Toronto. Despite its relative proximity to Toronto and to the cities of London and Kitchener-Waterloo, the peninsula remains distinctly rural and agricultural. This rural character is reflected throughout the profile of the two relevant federal ridings displayed in table 2.1. For example, agriculture employs about 14 per cent of the work force; only light manufacturing, concentrated in the towns of Owen Sound and Hanover, employs more people. For its geographic size, the peninsula displays a remarkable diversity of landscape, agricultural commodities, and associated farm prosperity. Prosperity decreases as one moves north, away from the field grains of corn and soybean in the fertile alluvial Great Lakes basin towards the Saugeen clay plain, whose shallow soils and swamps provide pasture and hay for grazing livestock (Chapman and Putnam 1966, 260–70). The Huron peninsula thus profiles, in microcosm, Ontario's thriving and diversified agricultural industry. The prosperity is evident in the rural landscape. Well-maintained farm buildings and silos painted bright red, white fences, and century-old maple trees align freshly oiled concession roads, punctuated by trim cemeteries and red-brick churches. Towns boast fine brick office buildings built at the turn of the century, and shops well-stocked with merchandise that compares with selections in suburban shopping malls. To anyone who has driven through the Canadian prairie landscape of abandoned farms and near-ghost towns, the Huron peninsula seems lushly pastoral. In comparison with urban Ontario, however, the Huron peninsula is not so prosperous, with average family income being well below the provincial figure (Eagles et al. 1991, 264).

TABLE 2.1   Profile of Bruce–Grey and Huron–Bruce federal ridings, 1988

	Bruce–Grey (%)	Huron–Bruce (%)
A. *Voting profile*		
Conservative	41	43
Liberal	39	35
NDP	19	17
Other	1	6
Voter turnout	72	76
Rural polls	72	78
B. *Ethnic and language profile*		
English home language	98	97
Aboriginal people	–	–
Immigrants	7	10
C. *Socio-economic profile*		
Median family income	$29,000	$31,000
Low-income families	14	14
Average home price	$64,000	$60,000
Unemployed	7	6
Self-employed	15	17
Managerial-administrative	7	7
University degrees	5	4
D. *Industrial profile*		
Manufacturing	19	17
Agriculture	12	17
Forestry	–	–
Government services	5	4
Service sector	13	11
E. *Physical setting characteristics*		
Total population	90,000	88,000
Population density (pop/km^2)	15	17

SOURCE: Eagles et al. 1991, 264–5, 318–19.

The Huron peninsula continues to draw the attention of outside observers because of its political heritage as a hub of agrarian protest since the mid-nineteenth century. It was settled later than most of Upper Canada. After the war of 1812, the Crown gave large tracts of the best land in Upper Canada, closest to Great Lakes ports, to high-ranking officers, Anglican clergy, and various gentry as a form of political patronage. This pushed immigrant settlers to more marginal and isolated areas, where they were physically separated from each other by unsettled Crown land. These factors delayed the development of fully commercialized production (Scott 1966, 6). The delay was further accentuated in the Huron peninsula as a result of its great distance from commercial ports on the St Lawrence River. The peninsula's population hit a peak at the turn of the century, and has been declining since. Nevertheless, descendants of original settlers still farm inland from Lake Huron. In Huron County, 'century farms' (which have remained in the same direct line of ownership for over a century) are common (Scott 1966, 62).[1] Recurring surnames of founding families in each township attest to patrilocal norms by which brides take up resident with or near their husbands' kin.

The Huron peninsula is one of the final holdouts of old rural Ontario: British, Loyalist, Methodist, Calvinist, and Orange. Brown faces are still rarely seen. To indicate just how 'white' this part of Ontario is, in 1986, less than 1 per cent of the population of either Grey County or Huron County had immigrated from Africa or Asia.[2] This part of Ontario is still 'Orange' too in terms of having the lowest percentage of Roman Catholics in the province (MacDermid 1990, 368). The only newcomers have been Dutch and German people who immigrated after the Second World War to work as farm labourers and who are now successful and respected farmers. The demographic figures thus 'appear to indicate the continued existence of small family farms still worked by the ancestors of the original immigrant Scots, Welsh, Irish, and English who settled much of the area' (ibid).

In 1989, I interviewed 117 farm women in Huron and Grey counties (see Map 2.1), using a two-part questionnaire (see Appendix). In the first part, standard questions from rural sociology asked about farm characteristics that are assumed to affect a woman's involvement in agricultural production: its legal title, size, product type, employees hired, capital value, inheritance, and, at some length, the actual as opposed to ideal distribution of tasks and decision making among family members (Ireland 1983, 17–23; Rosenfeld 1985, 28–33). The second part of the questionnaire duplicated questions from Euro-Barometer and Election Study surveys. These questions explore politicization and feminism under categories of political salience, conceptualization, participation, and opinions (Neuman 1986; Sapiro 1983). The result is a juxtaposition of agriculture with politics and feminism, combing the wealth of survey research in rural sociology on women's agricul-

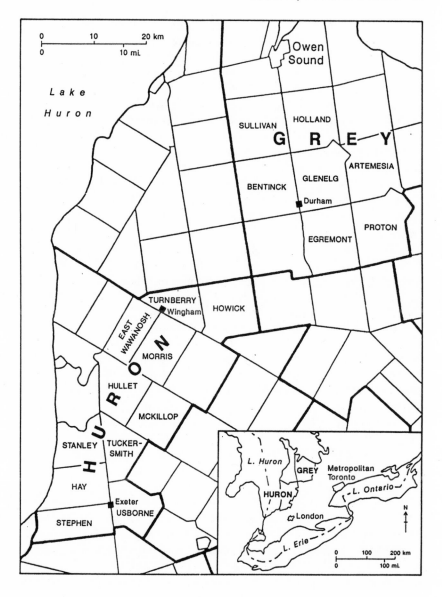

MAP 2.1   Townships in the Huron Peninsula where interviews were conducted

tural work with the wealth of two decades of Euro-Barometer and Election Study research into political behaviour and opinions.

The project proceeded with the approval and assistance of the provincial executive of the Ontario Women's Institutes (FWIO). In February 1989, I presented a research proposal to a meeting of the FWIO executive. Members of the executive stressed that the FWIO was a coordinating body which did not have access to membership lists of autonomous branches. They cautiously decided to pass on the names of six prominent members across Ontario who, on my initiative, might introduce me into the field. I contacted two of these women based on their geographical location and, at their invitation, attended and made presentations to two WI district annuals in May and one branch meeting in June.[3] At these WI events, I talked informally to people in an effort to meet and acquire references to women who were living on agricultural enterprises. Three women provided lists of ten to twenty names of farm members from their Institute. One list, provided by a township councillor, went beyond branch members to include names of non-members in the township. I wrote follow-up or introductory letters and made arrangements over the phone to travel to each respondent's home to conduct a face-to-face interview, which lasted approximately an hour and a half. To gain further access to non-WI members, I asked members to refer me to their nearest neighbours. While conducting interviews for a week at a time, I and my husband and year-old son camped in local conservation areas and thereby entered the life of the community to a certain extent. We were not anonymous; after we had chatted with campsite attendants who knew the women being interviewed, our presence and purpose were public knowledge. I have no idea what my respondents thought of me leaving my husband to babysit (albeit with a laptop computer for company) while I conducted interviews all day.

The scope of the project is restricted conceptually by my focus on household-based commodity production as manifested in family farming. It includes only economically active enterprises; hobby farms and acreages were excluded because those households do not have enough farm in the marriage. It did, however, include enterprises that are only marginally agricultural because the family's main source of income was from self-employed, household-based, and often agriculturally related occupations; for example, eight women listed farm equipment or seed distributorships among the enterprise's commodities. It excludes independent unmarried female farm operators because those households do not have enough marriage in the farm. Membership in this latter group is scarce and scattered. Although in 1986, 5 per cent of Canadian farm operators were female, only 15 per cent of those were truly independent, the other 85 per cent being married (51 per cent) or widowed (34 per cent). Since 1971, married women have increasingly reported 'farm operator' as their occupation, while the number of female farm operators who are not currently married (that is, single, divorced, or widowed) has remained stable or declined (Beyrouti, Dion, and Walsh 1989, 18). In addition the study excludes non-family female workers. Like unmarried female farm operators, their marital relations do not enter directly into their work. Furthermore, as the lowest-paid workers in the agricultural spectrum,[4] non-family female workers require a different sort of class analysis; they are employed by the women being studied here.

I did not deliberately seek feminist farm women at the leading edge of social change in rural communities. Instead, I began with the long-established farm women's movement, the Women's Institutes (WI), and compared WI members with non-members; I interviewed sixty-seven members and fifty non-members. This mix may not be atypical for farm women in the region. Membership in the Women's Institutes is strong throughout rural Southern Ontario. When I asked for names of non-WI farm women in Glenelg Township in Grey County, for example, three respondents said that all the farm people belong to WI; the only non-members were retired people or commuters who had moved up from Toronto. An FWIO president remarked of rural Ontario in general: 'The church is gone, the cheese factory, the school, the general store, even the Orange Lodge. WI is the only thing left, and it's important to keep a community together.'[5] Indeed, as the metropolitan mass surrounding Lake Ontario extends farther into rural areas, WI membership may demarcate parallel communities in a single geographic area, reflecting distinctions between old families who have farmed there for generations and recently arrived urban expatriates.

A plausible alternative to the Women's Institutes might seem to be the Ontario Farm Women's Network (OFWN). The OFWN's commitment (as stated in its constitution) to 'secure social, legal, and economic equality for farm women' might make it seem preferable when investigating the gendered division of labour in household production. There are good methodological reasons, however, for avoiding the OFWN. It lacks the extensive membership, longevity, and familiarity of the WI. In 1991, its 375 members, of whom 75 per cent were estimated to be full-voting farm members,[6] were scattered across the province, thereby precluding a cross-section sample of adjacent townships. A survey of such a small organization might be argued to be justified based on the assumption that OFWN members tend to be the most politically advanced farm women, leading the remaining population down their path. However, I wanted to avoid presupposing a model of modernizing leaders and passive followers. By choosing to begin with the Women's Institutes, I hoped to get a sense of how much following is actually occurring.

In some previous rural sociology research, wives who are active in agriculture have been disproportionately more likely to be interviewed to the neglect of wives less interested in farming. My experience corroborates that of Virginia Fink, who found that two types of farm women were reluctant to be interviewed: women who wanted to be identified by their paid, off-farm occupations; and women who devalued themselves as not being 'real' farm women, that is, unlike neighbours who took on full burdens of traditionally male agricultural responsibilities (1988, 234-8). When such farm women voluntarily exclude themselves from survey samples, researchers cannot help but conclude that *all* farm women are actively committed to and involved in agriculture, even though a good proportion might actually be uninterested in or even hostile to farming. Mail-in surveys of farm women would be particularly prone to this error, catching primarily literate women who are already concerned and knowledgeable about agricultural issues.[7] The dual emphasis of the present survey on community and agricultural involvement avoided this sampling error. As predicted, it was otherwise difficult to convince women that everyone's participation, regardless of her interest in farming, was important to the survey project. WI members were not the only respondents who were eager to have their community service, as opposed to their paid employment or farm work, recognized. And if community service is not a common denominator among all farm women (although the results suggest that it is), the survey's alternative emphasis on farming was certain to appeal to apolitical women focused exclusively on agriculture.

Women were remarkably responsive to requests for interviews. Even though the project's focus on agriculture and politics drew little interest from them, women were eager to have their community service recorded and validated. Only 7 of the more than 120 women approached refused to be interviewed. One of these wanted to meet for an interview but was forbidden to by her husband. Schoolteachers

of all ages were collegial, and younger people were generally less suspicious. When I expressed gratitude to women for helping me out during the busy haying season, their reactions suggested that agreeing
to an interview was a form of self-assertion, taking time for oneself
against husbands' and farms' incessant demands for labour. Babies were
twice thrust on husbands by wives who wanted to have a quiet, un-
disturbed chat. Some women seemed especially pleased to cooperate
in order to gain vicarious access to their children's past, present, or
future experience of university. Women's noted lack of assertiveness
worked to the project's advantage. Even those who refused found it
difficult to reject direct requests for an interview. Instead they were
'too busy'; when called back a month later, one woman was angry:
'I thought I told you I wasn't interested.' When I protested that she
had said only that the previous month was inconvenient, she replied,
'Yes and I'm still too busy.' Even though preceded by a letter on York
University letterhead, the initial phone call seemed to take some by
surprise. For example, one woman seemed hesitant and confused when
setting up an interview over the phone; this was not unusual, but she
had changed her mind by the day of the interview. Explicit refusals
were apparently difficult because women had to work up sufficient
hostility instead of refusing pleasantly and politely. In this regard,
the few refusals were instructive in revealing farm women's discomfort
with conflict and rejection.

While doing the survey in the field, several issues arose which are
relevant to methodological disputes about how to do feminist research.
In general, these feminist disputes centre on power relations and loss
of voice that might be embedded in the research design and interview
procedure itself (Harding 1986). Feminist methodology begins from
the premise that knowledge is a form of power, but some confusion
arose in this regard because the concerns of political science were not
farm women's concerns. For example, I was queried on the absence
of questions on agricultural policy and rural child care. Farm wives
who expected a public-policy orientation may have agreed to cooperate
because they thought that the research project would deal with their
more salient concerns. This same confusion between academic and
public-policy research sometimes caused misunderstanding regarding
my identity. One elderly woman, thinking that I was a representative
of the Ministry of Agriculture or the Women's Institutes' provincial
executive, was frustrated by questions that she couldn't understand:
'What does the Institute want to know all this for?' This woman, in

her confusion, confirmed the theoretical unity of the state; she made no distinction between governments and universities. Seeing that knowledge is a form of power, feminist methodology recommends that research findings should be made available in ordinary language to the people being studied. Accordingly, a four-page summary report was mailed to all respondents in October 1990 and longer reports were mailed intermittently to the provincial Women's Institutes' executive. A final discussion of results was held with the provincial executive in March 1991.

Feminist theory and practice is currently concerned with 'difference,' particularly ethnic, racial, and class differences in opposition to a falsely perceived and imposed unity of 'womanhood.' The relevant difference here is obviously that between urban interviewer and rural respondent. In a previous survey, Ontario farm women reported that they felt more capable, fortunate, and intelligent than urban women, but they thought that urban women perceived farm women as considerably lower in social class and intelligence (Ireland 1983, 59). These findings suggest that, although I claimed to be interested in farm women's lives and opinions, respondents may have suspected my ostensibly favourable motives and interpretation. If one assumes that urban women in general think that farm women are less intelligent, one might conclude that a university researcher should be even more likely to think so. Gruff reticence has been noted as a cultural trait of rural Ontario; pride dictates that one not be too eager to please or to impress pretentious city folk. This passage from a novel by Alice Munro perhaps gives a flavour of the reception given to visitors from Toronto: 'At supper Auntie Grace without saying a word began to do an imitation of his way of eating. "Oh, the *lawyer!*," cried Aunt Elspeth elegantly, and leaning across the table inquired, "Have you always – been interested – in country life?" After their marvelous courtesy to him I found this faintly chilling; it was a warning. *Didn't he think he was somebody!* That was their final condemnation, lightly said' (1971, 32).[8] To a considerable extent, this barrier to egalitarian interviews was overcome. I tried to minimize any authority afforded to me through demeanour and appreciation for subjects' cooperation. I was often mistaken for an undergraduate student, which indicates to me that I was not considered to be pretentious, élitist, or in any way intimidating.

A feminist and egalitarian argument has been made for unstructured discussion and participant-observation. Dorothy Smith favours open-ended conversation, which she anticipates will yield 'stretches of talk that "express" the social organization and relations of the setting' (1987, 189). Smith anticipates that such 'expression' will reveal concepts and perspectives that are indigenous to the people being interviewed. For this reason, I used open-ended questions to allow the women to express their ideas on feminism and community service, the two central themes of this research project. The responses to these questions were abundant and articulate. Most of the women had clearly thought about these issues previously, and merely needed to be prompted by a question. A completely unstructured interview, however, would have limited success among this population. It was gratifying when farm women spoke spontaneously at length on their lives, but I could not rely entirely on its fortuitous occurrence. Except with women my own age and younger, I was rarely able to elicit the intimacy with my subjects reported by other feminist scholars (Edwards 1990; Luxton 1980). Some researchers have reported becoming personal friends with their subjects, but it is doubtful that I could have achieved the same in rural Ontario, even after an extended time in the field, for reasons discussed below.

Patterns of rural sociability might be related to rural social geography. Two of the farm wives interviewed commented on the difficulty of integrating themselves into the community:

Moving from [an urban centre] to here was hard. Joining WI was a way of belonging to the community. There was nothing for women to do in the area; the women were just interested in their own little selves.

I started working [off-farm] because I couldn't handle the isolation on the farm. I was lonely because I didn't grow up here; I didn't fit into the community, and couldn't meet neighbours.

Some survey respondents were indeed lonely and glad of company but, unlike both middle- and working-class urban women, they were not uniformly willing to reveal their private lives to a researcher simply because she was another woman or because she was a feminist (see Edwards 1990, 480–1). Loquacious, easy intimacy may not come as easily to farm wives. Saskatchewan author Sharon Butala attributes her career as a writer to just this trait: 'Life on the land is a lonely life for a woman and more so for me since I was in a strange community, without relatives or friends or compatible people' (1991). In southwestern Ontario especially, people are firmly nestled in family ties extending over several generations, which inhibits the quick inclusion of newcomers in the community.

Another barrier to self-revealing intimacy might also be the abiding influence of evangelical Protestantism in rural Ontario.[9] For example, the Christian dictum on charity, 'let not your left hand know what your right hand does,' might explain one woman's praise for the WI as an 'unassuming' organization which does all the work without promoting or advertising itself. The old evangelical scorn for physical vanity might likewise discourage self-reflection as vanity. Former leader of the New Democratic Party Audrey McLaughlin once farmed near Wingham, and she attributed her privacy to just this cultural background: 'Rural people don't do that [talk about themselves]. I find a lot of that is very phony. I find it easier to talk about ideas than to talk about myself. I think it's just because I was raised as a product of a society where saying, "Look at me, look at me," was not respected' (*Globe and Mail*, 7 Sep. 1993, A6). The factors that made interviewing this population so difficult at times might be rooted in Methodism or Calvinism; that is, the stubborn and sometimes smug pride that women took in their reticence, gruff speech, and secure place in the community as 'good people.' Not every farm wife could speak articulately about the intimate subjects under inquiry, perhaps because some respondents were not given to self-introspection. Although Nancy Cott argues that nineteenth-century evangelical Christianity fostered introspection by its injunction to assess one's state of grace (1977), what she identified as a 'protofeminist' impulse in evangelical introspection is less plausible for contemporary southwestern Ontario. A community leader concluded her speech to a WI event with this admonition: 'The secret to happiness is J-O-Y: put Jesus first, others second, and yourself last.'

The traits may go beyond religion, and stem from traditional culture in general. Some of the older farm women interviewed are indeed traditional if to be modern is to know that nothing is 'natural' and to be entirely 'self-conscious' (Cooper 1984, 283–5). Marx made the same point about modernization but more dramatically: 'Man is at last compelled to face with sober senses, his real conditions of life, and his relations with his kind' (1972 [1888], 476). Survey research is a modern technique because it presupposes the ability to reflect critically on oneself. Many of the older women interviewed seemed to lack a sense of their own self as an object of investigation. They were so immersed in the intimacy of marriage and family that it took some prodding to distinguish themselves (the wife) from husbands and sons. For example, one said, 'Oh yes, we do that all the time,' when actually a male member of the household, representing the farm, negotiated prices with livestock dealers. The 'farm' became a reified thing, personified as an independent actor, when actually whatever the 'farm' does emerges from the cumulative decisions made by individual people. Some respondents were often reluctant to consider that household arrangements are arbitrary and self-conscious choices to be explained and justified. Discussing feminist issues requires just such cognitive skills. To explain and justify their political opinions was easier for many in this sample than to analyse their day-to-day life; explaining one's household arrangements implies knowing that 'the personal is political' or that one's domestic choices correspond to given political values and goals. Farm women are not entirely deficient in this mode of analysis, however, because they regularly make such judgments in their defence of 'farming as a way of life' as superior to urban families and lifestyles.[10] In sum, I asked respondents to separate their individual lives from that of the household, but this was more difficult than anticipated because some women's lives and identities were entirely submerged in the collective life of the household.

Survey research relies on standard questions to produce comparable and reproducible results, but Philip Converse put the enterprise into doubt when he found that the same individuals' responses to the same questions over time are disturbingly random, and hence unreliable (1964). Questions that ask people to evaluate public-policy proposals and legislation are especially vulnerable to Converse's warnings. In this respect, my open-ended questions about the meaning of 'politics' and 'left'/'right' were often experienced as 'exam questions' designed to show up subjects' ignorance, especially after they had just bluffed in answering preceding questions about the same topics. Questions work best when they concern issues that people have already thought about. For instance, most of my respondents had already considered joining or not joining a WI branch, and the meaning of feminism; they merely needed to be prodded to articulate quite fluently their reasons and opinions. The open-ended questions that worked successfully were also, to judge by respondents' behaviour, the most embarrassing and intensely personal questions, precisely because they concerned personally important issues about which the women had thought at length before.

BASIC PROFILE OF FARMS AND PEOPLE

The basic agricultural and demographic information from this survey provide a profile of the sampled population. Some of this information can be directly compared with results from the 1986 Canada Census. According to that census, Huron County is substantially more prosperous than Grey: 18 per cent of Huron farms were worth more than $500,000, compared with only 5 per cent in Grey County; fifty-eight Huron farms were worth more than $1.5 million, accounting for 5 per cent of that category in all Ontario. North–south variation in Huron County is very evident; farm properties ranged in value from an average of $418,000 in Stephen Township in the south, to $288,000 in Howick Township in the northern border with Grey County, where farms were worth, on average, $206,000. The census also reports that, directly opposite to farm capital value, more farm operators take off-farm employment in Grey than Huron (49 to 36.5 per cent) (1986 Canada Census, vol. 96-108, 1–189).

Table 2.2 compares the distribution of farm acreage from the 1986 census to that in the present sample. Median values are 216 acres for Huron census, 152 acres for Grey census, and 242 acres for the present sample. The larger farm size in the present study is accounted for by the exclusion of hobby farms and acreages, as discussed earlier in this chapter. Farms need only report annual gross sales of $250 to qualify as a 'census farm' (Beyrouti, Dion, and Welsh 1989, 44), sales that might easily be earned by a raspberry patch in one's backyard.

An interesting discrepancy is uncovered when reported farm capital value is compared, instead of farm acreage. The median capital values are $166,000 and $270,000 for Grey and Huron (1986) census, respectively, and a whopping $473,000 for the present (1989) sample. Taking into account the much smaller discrepancy in acreage, the capital value per acre is nearly double that in the 1986 census. Several factors may be involved in creating this discrepancy. In Southern Ontario's inflated real-estate market of the 1980s, land values may indeed have risen over the three intervening years. Respondents may also have been caught up in the accompanying exuberance and optimistically overestimated their enterprises' capital value; indeed, 54 per cent of the sample estimated their assets to have increased in value over the preceding few years. Another factor is uncertainty concerning capital value among those interviewed; 21 per cent would not estimate capital value at all, whereas only 1 percent would not disclose acreage.

TABLE 2.2   Farms classified by acreage

Acreage	Huron census (%)	Grey census (%)	Carbert sample (%)
0–69	20	16	4
70–129	21	29	16
130–79	14	14	11
180–239	15	15	19
240–399	18	18	21
400–559	6	6	14
560–759	3	2	7
760–1,119	2	1	4
More than 1,120	1	–	4
Can't say	–	–	1
Median acres	216	152	242
(N enterprises)	(3,416)	(3,358)	(114)

SOURCE: 1986 Canada Census, vol. 96–108, 1–99.

Table 2.3 shows the distribution of commodity types in my sample along with those reported by Statistics Canada for Huron and Grey counties. The red-meat industry predominates (64 per cent of census farms) in the rocky landscape of Grey County because livestock can be grazed on rocky, boggy land that has never been cleared for cultivation. Feedlot operations are the most common; here prairie cattle spend a year putting on extra weight before being slaughtered for the adjacent metropolitan population of Southern Ontario. Livestock is also an important commodity in Huron County, but bigger profits are made from the flat, well-drained fertile fields of the county from Clinton south, which are cultivated for corn and soybean. There are some discrepancies between the census and my sample among the various red-meat industries, but overall general agreement in that category (52 per cent compared with 56 per cent in the census). The only serious discrepancy is the overrepresentation of poultry/egg operations (14 per cent compared with 3 per cent in the census). This group does not comprise a large enough proportion of the sample for this overrepresentation to skew the results substantially.

The farms in Huron and Grey are overwhelmingly family operations as opposed to capitalist enterprises. In the 1986 census, only 3 per cent of farms in Grey and 4 per cent in Huron were legally incorporated; of these few farms, most restricted shares to family members

TABLE 2.3   Farms classified by product type

Product type	Huron census (%)	Grey census (%)	Huron + Grey census (%)	Carbert sample (%)
Cattle	26	51	38	24
Hogs	17	9	14	18
Other animal husbandry	4	4	4	10
Wheat and field grains	28	7	18	12
Dairy	13	16	13	14
Poultry and eggs	4	1	3	14
Equipment, seed distribution	–	–	–	4
Fruit and vegetables	2	4	3	4
Other combinations	6	8	7	–
(N enterprises >$2,500 gross sales)	(3,266)	(2,874)	(6,140)	(114)

SOURCE: 1986 Canada Census, vol. 96–108, 1–219.

(87 and 89 per cent) (1986 Canada Census, vol. 96-108, 1-9). In the present survey, slightly fewer than half (48 per cent) of women interviewed reported hiring paid agricultural labour, and almost all (78 per cent) of this group hired only local people to help out seasonally. Two turnip farms brought in more than ten foreign workers at harvest-time, and seven farms hired two or more full-time employees year-round. Full-time employees were generally adult sons and nephews waiting to inherit. For determining when petty-bourgeois household production becomes 'capitalist,' Parvin Ghorayshi (1987) specifies a minimum criterion of five employees from a reading of Marx's law of value. Using this criterion, only three women surveyed resided on 'capitalist' farm enterprises.[11]

The 1986 census also includes basic demographic characteristics such as age, education, and employment. However, there are no published census data on personal characteristics for farm operators and their spouses at the county level, so the present sample must be compared with the farm population all across Canada. All but nine women interviewed were Protestant (those nine were Roman Catholics); all attended church services regularly, apart from twelve lapsed Protestants and two lapsed Catholics. 'Lapsed' is defined as never attending church except when invited to baptisms, weddings, or funerals. Three Protestant women under age thirty-five years who had married Dutch Catholic men and were raising their children Roman Catholic were recorded as Protestant.

The farming population of Canada is older than the general population. In 1986, a third (34 per cent) of Canadian farm men were fifty-five years or older, but fewer women (24 per cent) were over fifty-five years (Beyrouti, Dion, and Welsh 1989, 37). Women in the present sample tended to be slightly older; 32 per cent of the women were over fifty-five. Roughly half were on each side of the middle age, with a median age of forty-five years, and age ranged from twenty to seventy-nine years. The three eldest women, including the sole widow, lived on farms whose cultivated acreage was leased out; these women were excluded from calculations involving agricultural variables.

On average in Canada, rural families have two-thirds again as many children as urban families (Murphy 1991, 6). Women in the present survey had given birth, on average, to 3.2 children, which is considerably higher than the current total fertility rate of 1.7 children per Canadian and Ontario woman.[12] I did not ask about marital history. Three women volunteered that this was their second marriage. Two of these women shared a similar story: each had been abandoned by her first husband and remarried a disabled farm man whose disability made her responsible for much of the farm work.

In the general farm population, wives are better educated than husbands, but are losing their advantage in younger age groups (Beyrouti, Dion, and Welsh 1989, 38). In comparison with all Canadian farmers, these Ontario couples, and especially the wives, are markedly better educated (see table 2.4). In the present survey, wives' educational advantage is clustered at the level of postsecondary, non-university education; in particular, women over thirty-five years have acquired much more postsecondary, non-university education than men in that category. Higher-than-average education for Canadian farm wives especially marks women aged fifty-five and older. Women in that generation usually achieved postsecondary education by qualifying for teacher certification at Normal School. One might think that this indicates a sampling error, because older Women's Institute members might have been preferentially more educated. The MacDonald Institute for home economics at Guelph College, for example, was affiliated with the Women's Institutes in earlier years. To test for a possible bias in the survey sample, women aged forty-five to seventy-nine were selected, and their level of education cross-tabulated against WI membership. Contrary to this expectation, WI members and their hus-

TABLE 2.4   Wives' and husbands' age by education: Carbert 1989 sample with comparative percentages from 1986 census

Age group	< Grade 9	Grades 9-13	Postsecondary	University	Total
	Education (%)				
20-34 years					
wives	0 (4)[a]	62 (50)	31 (31)	7 (15)	25
husbands	0 (6)	50 (51)	33 (29)	17 (14)	15
35-44 years					
wives	0 (10)	43 (44)	39 (28)	18 (18)	24
husbands	3 (15)	55 (39)	16 (28)	26 (18)	26
45-54 years					
wives	0 (23)	48 (45)	30 (22)	22 (10)	20
husbands	28 (33)	40 (36)	16 (21)	16 (10)	21
55-79 (64) years					
wives	24 (34)	30 (39)	43 (18)	3 (9)	32
husbands	51 (46)	35 (33)	7 (14)	7 (7)	37
Total					
wives	8 (18)	44 (44)	37 (25)	11 (13)	100
husbands	26 (29)	44 (38)	15 (21)	15 (12)	100

SOURCE: Beyrouti, Dion, and Welsh 1989, 38.
a. Figures in parentheses are from the 1986 census.

bands were somewhat less well educated than non-members. Therefore, high levels of education reported here in comparison with farm wives across Canada cannot be attributed to the basic research design of this study, which selected WI members. It might instead be attributed to a well-established network of rural postsecondary institutions, which was historically more accessible to young Ontario women than to rural women in other provinces during the 1940s and 1950s.

The rate of paid employment for farm husbands in this survey (36 per cent) was similar to the rate reported for all Canadian farm operators (39 per cent). Farm operators controlling most of Canada's agricultural capital (76 per cent) were less likely to take paid employment (Beyrouti, Dion, and Welsh 1989, 39, 23-4). The biggest enterprises hire paid employees, accumulate assets over several generations, and can thus afford to keep adult men at home working in the family business.[13]

Half of Canadian farm wives (51 per cent) were in the non-agricultural paid labour force in 1986 (Beyrouti, Dion, and Welsh 1989, 39). In contrast, fewer than half (43 per cent) of farm wives in the present survey held paid employment, of whom only eleven worked full-time. If the census had specified whether at full- or part-time employment, we might know better if this discrepancy is significant. If so, it can easily be explained by the relative dominance of animal husbandry in rural Ontario (see table 2.3). Wives make the least financial contribution from paid employment to dairy enterprises and the most to farms growing field grains (ibid, 40). Dairy enterprises, and animal husbandry in general, are labour-intensive, which means that wives tend to contribute their unpaid labour instead of paycheques from off-farm employment. One infers that, in the dominantly grain-producing prairie provinces, more farm wives should hold paid employment.

The variety of paid occupations reported by farm women can be organized into categories for class analysis of the survey population. To date, the most reliable technique for developing socio-economic scores (SES) generates a score for each occupation reported in the 1981 Canada Census. Each score is based on that occupation's median or middle income and average years of postsecondary education (Blishen, Carroll, and Moore 1987, 469). Perceived occupational prestige is not included because there is no reliable way to measure which jobs are more prestigious than others. Socio-economic scores were calculated for the present sample using formal paid occupations only.[14] The average off-farm-employment SES for farm women was 48.2, while their husbands scored 47.5. The most frequently reported occupations and SESs for women were secretarial (41.8), nursing (55.2), and teaching (63.6 to 70.1). Domestic service was reported once and was the lowest-ranking female occupation. In comparison, university professors score 75.8 and physicians score 101.3. (ibid, 483). Husbands' scores are deceptively high because their most frequently reported occupations are not comparable with urban positions in the same category. A few women's occupations, such as fashion/interior designer, likewise scored deceptively high, but these occurred too rarely to affect statistical averages. Husbands' occupations, however, did skew the results: nine were 'members of a legislative body' (township council) or 'board directors' (Gay-Lea dairy board, Farm Egg Review Board), which scored, respectively, 55.0 and 57.5. They received honoraria for these part-time positions which do not even approach stipends paid to professional politicians or directors of corporations. Otherwise husbands' occupations tended to be in various skilled trades, which scored in the high

30s. The problems encountered in recording and reporting the SES for the survey population affirm the inadequacy of measures of socio-economic status based on full-time occupations in the paid labour market to account for status and wealth in rural communities. Putting aside paid off-farm occupations, one might get a better sense of respondents' class position from SES for farming alone. Scores for live-stock farmers (29.6) and crop farmers (31.3) are just ahead of livestock workers (25.3) and crop workers (22.0), but substantially lower than for many urban occupations.

Farmers' class position is a paradox; they are wealthy in terms of farm assets, but associated with urbanized blue-collar work (Walker 1987, 4). The frequent appearance of self-employed occupations among husbands and fathers in this survey corresponds to the higher proportion of self-employed (non-farm) occupations in rural as opposed to urban Canada (Murphy 1991, 6). Of those adults in the non-agricultural labour force of Huron and Grey counties, between 15 and 17 per cent were self-employed (Eagles et al. 1991, 265, 319). Just next door, in the cities of London and Kitchener-Waterloo, rates of self-employment ranged from 6 to 8 per cent (ibid, 327, 337, 341). The term 'entrepreneur' is too elevated because farm men tend to be manually employed in vocational occupations. Of thirty-two husbands who worked off-farm for paid income, eight were self-employed in construction trades (building contractor, pipefitter, stonemason, carpenter, electrician), and three were self-employed distributors of agricultural products. The same propensity for 'craft' occupations holds true in the United States (Rosenfeld 1985, 174, 318). Members of farm families, if they marry outside of farming, may be especially likely to marry into other self-employed families; for those fifty-two women whose fathers did not farm full-time, seventeen reported self-employed occupations for their fathers, not including six truck drivers who may have also been self-employed. Only nine fathers held white-collar clerical or professional occupations; the rest, self-employed or not, were in working-class labouring, factory, or craft occupations.

There might be relatively straightforward reasons why farming and self-employment coincide. Self-employment, unlike waged labour, is compatible with the seasonal cycle of agricultural work. Apart from teachers, who have the entire summer off, waged workers do not have the option of taking time off for haying and harvesting whenever the sun happens to shine. This point is relevant to the indefinite boundaries of the 'family farm,' which is not always restricted to a single nuclear family; the farm enterprise may depend on members of the extended family for labour, skills, and capital. Further, husbands' self-employed occupations likewise call on wives' unpaid labour; for example, a woman whose husband had just acquired a contract from the Ontario Ministry of Agriculture and Food to weigh cattle took phone calls arranging appointments for the next day while the interview was being conducted. In another marriage, the account books for the husband's building-contracting business were at issue, except that in this case he doubted the wife's ability to handle both the farm and the business accounts. Finally, farm men and women both claim to value 'independence' as a principal reason for farming (Ireland 1983), as do self-employed people in general.

In summary, the foregoing comparisons, along with the historical review in chapter 1, situate the sampled population within the population of Canadian farm women. Major distinctions for the present sample include British ethnicity and Protestant religion, higher levels of education, and, to a lesser degree, lower levels of off-farm employment. These differences limit the direct application of the detailed results to rural Ontario. Even generalizations extrapolated to apply to farm wives of English Canada must be taken with care because the Prairie provinces, in particular, are ethnically much more diverse, having been settled by immigrants from eastern and central Europe.

3

Women's Work

Chapter 1 criticized the often-used categories of 'old' and 'new' farm women as inadequate and artificially divisive. If those categories are inadequate, alternatives must be proposed because all farm women are not alike and the very term disguises their diversity. This survey interviewed women on farms producing a diverse range of agricultural commodities because different commodities are associated with different patterns of mechanization and women's work.[1] Both horticulture, which is associated with a casual non-family work force, and grain cultivation, which is associated with machinery-intensive field-work, reinforce the urban model of domesticity, whereas animal husbandry is associated with intensive agricultural work by all family members. Even among women doing farm work, status within the family may vary according to whether one works on cash crops/products, and thus produces exchange values for the market, or does maintenance chores, and thus produces use values for the farm operation (Blumberg 1981, 52). This chapter classifies women's agricultural work into four categories and investigates how the level of involvement in each category is related to personal and farm characteristics. Subsequent chapters use these categories to discuss the impact of agricultural work on farm women's politicization.

Research in rural sociology began from the assumption that agricultural mechanization excludes women from farming and promotes their domestication. Farm women were supposed to become just like urban housewives. This assumption was revised by subsequent observation that mechanization altered, rather than diminished altogether, women's agricultural work; indeed it appeared that men, rather than women, were withdrawing from agriculture.[2] Much of previous research was strictly descriptive; when a conceptual approach was taken, it tended to apply the 'domestic labour dispute' to agriculture. Just as scholars had earlier demonstrated that domestic labour preceded and made possible waged labour outside the home, thus attesting to the unity of production and reproduction under capitalism (Hamilton and Barrett 1987, 139–254), so too did rural sociologists demonstrate that farm women's apparently domestic and support labour was critical to the agricultural economy (Ghorayshi 1989; Shaver 1989). Women's often sporadic help at haying and harvest times was conceptualized as 'a reserve labour supply' substituting for traditional hired men (Rosenfeld 1985, 25). Women were encouraged to think that 'chatting with sales people is really doing the work of a purchasing agent' (cited in Ghorayshi 1989, 583), or that women's work to maintain family harmony between father and sons or between brothers was critical to day-to-day cooperation among farm workers, and ultimately to the successful transmission of farm capital from generation to generation. Even granting, as Cooper points out (1989, 170), that claims for women's management activities were sometimes exaggerated, research has succeeded in documenting and validating women's myriad contributions to agricultural production.

CLASSIFICATION OF AGRICULTURAL TASKS

Farm women reported involvement in seventeen agricultural tasks. That involvement fell into a pattern of four categories or factors. The groupings are shown in table 3.1, along with the loadings obtained using factor analysis.[3] This pattern duplicates that extracted from the Concerned Farm Women survey data, using the same questions and the same quantitative technique (Cebotarev, Blacklock, and McIsaac 1986, 10). The four factors account for 50 per cent of the variation in women's involvement in the seventeen tasks, and thus the four categories stand in as an acceptable replacement for the seventeen separate tasks. The groupings hold together logically; the factor titles were chosen to express what the associated tasks have in common. The four types of agricultural work were converted into factor scores for subsequent use. Each agricultural task was entered into one of four scales, with a weighted value derived from its loading in the overall factor solution.

The first factor – farm labour relating to animal-husbandry chores – was especially strong, accounting for 32 per cent of the variation

TABLE 3.1   Pattern of agricultural tasks

	Factor 1 Farm labour	Factor 2 Internal admin.	Factor 3 External admin.	Factor 4 Mechanical work
Perform milking chores	.82	.02	.11	−.22
Feed and water livestock	.67	.17	−.07	.22
Attend to animal birth, health care	.66	.07	−.04	.28
Clean barn	.61	−.04	.22	.23
Hours of farm work per week	.49	.16	.21	.18
Decide stocking policy	.04	.91	−.09	.02
Decide cropping policy	−.01	.79	−.05	−.05
Do research	−.09	.40	.28	−.02
Take business calls	.07	.36	.08	.25
Deal with accounts – banking, tax	.08	.25	.03	.02
Supervise hired help	.02	−.02	.80	−.03
Deal with salesmen	−.00	.117	.62	.07
Attend agricultural meetings	.15	−.05	.53	.04
Do field-work	.08	.00	−.12	.73
Drive farm trucks	−.22	.06	.25	.60
Repair buildings/fences	.24	−.03	.01	.53
Repair machinery	.05	.10	.07	.43

in women's agricultural involvement on its own. Roughly half of all women interviewed were responsible, either every day or every few days, for the repetitive chores of farm labour. Roughly a quarter of respondents did these chores regularly: 33 per cent of women regularly attended to animal births and health-care needs, 23 per cent regularly cleaned manure out of the barn, 20 per cent did milking chores, and 34 per cent fed and watered livestock. Roughly another quarter again did the same tasks occasionally: 24 per cent of women occasionally attended to birth and health care, 21 per cent cleaned the barn, 6 per cent did milking, and 28 per cent fed and watered livestock. Since the frequency of women doing regular milking chores (20 per cent) is almost exactly in line with the number of dairy operations in the survey (19 per cent), it seems probable that, if the farm is a dairy operation, women will end up being responsible for a good deal of the chores. Whereas milking was said to be the second most suitable or conventionally feminine task for women in general, respondents were far less keen on it for themselves. They ranked milking as the fifth most suitable task for them in particular.

Considering that actual hours expended on farm work per week load on the first factor, representing animal care and chores, it is better termed a 'farm drudgery' factor. Livestock care and dairying, in particular, are classical labour in the sense of onerous, tedious chores tied to the physical cycle of animal life. Cows must be milked on a regular schedule twice a day, and the barn must be cleaned (removing manure from livestock stalls) almost as often, especially during the winter months when cattle are kept indoors for much of the time. Strict health regulations require that milking equipment be disassembled and disinfected after each milking. Constant vigilance must given to the health of all animals, not just dairy cattle, intended for human consumption, and one is required to determine exactly when and how much medication to give. Attending animal births, too, during the early spring is physically onerous, messy labour which disrupts any attempt to keep regular schedules (Ireland 1983, 18–19).

Animal husbandry is thus very similar to caring for infants and small children. Not only are farm labour and domestic labour conceptually analogous, the house and the barn are located near each other, enabling women to accomplish both tasks simultaneously (Haney 1983, 186; Rosenfeld 1985, 30, 98; P. Smith 1987, 172). One woman had a play-pen set up permanently in the barn and had a sandbox built just outside the barn door, which, she said, was the best money she ever spent. Another woman related proudly how she had obtained her 'artificial insemination papers'; the couple decided that she should acquire this skill because it was so expensive to hire someone. (Artificial insemination is a difficult task requiring skill since it involves inserting one hand up the cow's rectum to seize the cervix while using the other hand to inject sperm.) Pointing out the cows in the pasture by name while standing at her dining-room window, she explained that they are her 'babies,' of whom she's very protective and hence wouldn't want anyone else to inseminate: 'And as a woman, I know what's up there. I can do a better job than a man.' As Tim Ingold (1984, 125) observed of traditional Finnish farm wives, 'the work she did in the [cowshed] was as much a part of the domestic routine as her work in the [house] – in one she would look after the animal component of the family, in the other she would look after its human component. Towards both, she would hold the same affection.' For women in the present study, sometimes cattle even come before children: 'One time during calving, my two little girls were screaming in the window for hours in the early morning. The vet said to me: "Is someone looking after those children?" but what could I do?' This young woman felt guilty and defensive, whereas a middle-aged woman who lived at the other end of the county was nonplussed by such qualms. When the older woman was queried the next day about this story and the problem of farm safety, it drew a blank: 'These young girls [women] are always whining about hard work and wanting day care. So what, that's how it's done, I've always done it that way [leaving small children alone in the house].' Professional and popular standards of child care have changed and are now more rigorous than practices farm women traditionally adopt in caring for children.

Farm labour, in and of itself, does not translate directly into power and status. Productive work for exchange value or profit in the marketplace is a prerequisite for substantial power, but control over commodities produced is more essential in women's equality and well-being (Blumberg 1981) and, argues Janet Bujra, in women's collective solidarity (1979, 35). In other words, producing a commodity probably gives women a voice in deciding how to spend the money earned from that commodity's sale, but we cannot infer that productive work directly guarantees women a voice. These sources suggest that measures related to farm administration may better predict women's relative power and status within farm households.

In the present study, farm administration is divided into two categories of external and internal work. The first is external administration, because its three component tasks refer to dealings with employees, acquaintances, and strangers, who are not intimate members of the farm household. Roughly one-quarter of women reported being involved in three types of external farm administration. Adding together regular and occasional activities, 31 per cent dealt with sales agents about buying farm supplies and equipments, 26 per cent attended and presumably voted at commodity and agricultural meetings, and 22 per cent supervised hired help. Contrary to the expectation noted above, external administration cannot be equated directly with women's control over farm assets. Gregarious women may enjoy these sociable tasks – supervising teen employees, talking to sales representatives, attending auctions, or voting at meetings – without actually being involved in major financial decisions. For a woman to represent the farm enterprise to strangers publicly and formally signifies her personal assertion, but external administration relates more to the implementation of decisions that have already been made between and among the principal players. The locus of power is more directly equated with internal decisions concerning the acquisition of livestock and mix of crops.

The attempt to understand women's power and status in terms of external administration is further complicated because women's control over the sale of commodities also related to farm-enterprise characteristics, and not just to their personal contribution to production. Extended-family enterprises tend to exclude women from farm administration. Almost three-quarters (68 per cent) of couples had acquired the farm through the husband's family. Almost half (44 per cent) could not explain the farm's ownership arrangement without including a family member other than their husband. Roughly a third (27 per cent) answered that, although he might consult her first, the husband made major financial decisions with other partners or shareholders who were fathers, brothers, or adult sons and nephews. In addition to dealing with individual wholesalers, farmers exercise control over the sale of commodities collectively in agricultural organizations. The farms that hold power in commodity organizations are rarely those that enlist wives in farm labour and mechanical work. Higher levels of membership in farm organizations and committees have been reported among men and women on larger, more prosperous farms and ranches (Rosenfeld 1985, 198-201). Status from a successful operation carries over to validate membership and to confer credentials for sitting on agricultural boards and lobbies. A series of findings cumulatively reinforced one another: off-farm work, low education, and less-prosperous farms depressed men's involvement in agricultural associations. These characteristics further reduced the likelihood of women belonging because they became involved in agricultural associations as part of a couple, not wanting to attend meetings unescorted by husbands. A woman who does all her farm's labour and a good deal of mechanical field-work because her husband works full time off the farm, explains why she abstains from agricultural organizations: 'frustrated by [our farm's] limits and embarrassed with the low productivity ... I do not belong to any farm organizations. Our farm doesn't give me much credibility. We need to make a lot of improvements but with little capital, the improvements are slow. Farm organizations are for the elite' (personal correspondence, 8 Aug. 1990). If access to commodity organizations is thus restricted to the 'elite,' the women doing the real physical work of farming might look elsewhere for opportunities to exercise power beyond the farm household.

The component tasks of internal administration refer to dealings inside the farm household. Almost all women personally dealt with business phone calls rather than taking a message so that the 'real farmer' could call back (84 per cent); 57 per cent did so regularly and 27 per cent did so occasionally. When it came to the farm's commodity mix, 23 per cent of women regularly decided on stocking policy, and 11 per cent regularly decided on cropping policy. Relatively more women read (63 per cent regularly and occasionally) the agricultural journals and government publications whose recommendations undergird cropping and stocking decisions. The growing complexity of agriculture seems to have increased at least one type of work that women do: managing farm accounts and bookkeeping. This is usually explained by wives' higher education relative to husbands' and their likely clerical experience –reasons that are accentuated by the introduction of home computers for farm accounts and records (Ireland 1983, 15; Kohl 1976, 56; Rosenfeld 1985, 96). Cebotarev, Blacklock, and McIsaac (1986, 10), whose results were duplicated in table 3.1, found that bookkeeping was a separate factor on its own, consisting of keeping livestock records, preparing tax returns, banking, paying bills, and taking business calls. A similar factor could not be arrived at here because the initial question combined three items (tax returns, banking, and paying bills) as instances of bookkeeping in general. Almost everyone (71 per cent) did one or all of these tasks regularly. As a result, farm accounts and bookkeeping loaded weakly on the third factor of internal administration (.30).

The category of mechanical work is composed of four separate tasks: field-work, operating farm trucks bigger than a pick-up, repairing buildings, and repairing machinery. Roughly half of women surveyed operated farm machinery (combines and tractors) as part of field-work, one-quarter doing it regularly and another quarter occasionally. Regardless of the numbers actually doing mechanized field-work, it was more popular among women than any animal-husbandry chore except birthing calves or lambs, and health care of livestock. Mechanized field-work was women's fourth favourite task; 42 per cent of women thought that field-work was especially suitable for them personally. One woman preferred field-work because, she said, operating a tractor by herself in the empty fields was a time for perfect privacy and freedom away from her children. However much women might prefer field-work, only 6 per cent ever try to repair that machinery. More women (29 per cent) maintain and repair buildings and fences on occasion, but their answers usually referred to painting.

Mechanical work may operate as a surrogate or indirect indicator for women's control over farm-enterprise assets. Respondents may be sensitive about direct questions regarding administrative tasks because such questions invoke perceived and desirable patterns of decision making that are caught up in the personal prestige of family members. Sensitive matters of personal prestige may be tapped more reliably by indirect questions. Mechanical work may actually be the focus of control in farm enterprises; an emphasis on reported administrative tasks assumes a distinction between mental and manual production that is inappropriate for farming. Critical decisions entailing large capital expenditures are undertaken in the course of operating machinery. The bulk of the farm's capital assets might be committed to machinery, and thousands of dollars of damage can be done by the least moment of inattention on a tractor or combine. The same person who operates the tractor when its hydraulic system breaks down will likely decide how to repair or replace it. Or, in other words, 'the pecking order would be established by who got to the tractor first' (Ireland 1983. 39).

Domestic labour inside the farm household is the opposite side of the coin to agricultural work. On average, women reported that housework was nearly a full-time job, at just under forty hours per week. Since child care was included here, hours of housework rises along with the number of people in the household. And since gardening and yard-work were also included, housework fell off by roughly five hours per week during winter. There is, to be sure, a good deal of variation in what was reported as housework. Some women said that all their waking hours were occupied by intensive housework and child care; others said that the same number of hours was 'just puttering.' Reported hours of housework is most accurately understood as a subjective measure of a woman's orientation to homemaking.

A husband's domestic labour relates to the presumed power of wives' agricultural work to reverse the conventional, gendered division of domestic labour and thus effect a more egalitarian marriage. Husband's household activities consistently divided into two categories: housework (meal preparation, cleaning, and groceries) and child care (care for young children and babysit while wife attends an activity of her own choice). These five tasks could be reliably combined into two new scales of husband's housework and child care.[4] The child-care tasks were particularly easy for husbands to fulfil and to avoid. Roughly one-quarter of husbands regularly cared for young children, helped with homework, and attended parent–teacher functions. Half regularly cared for children while wives engaged in a chosen activity. But, with the vague exception of caring for young children, the other tasks (regular help with school projects, attendance at school functions, and babysitting during a monthly WI meeting) are all easy for husbands to fulfil. Regular or even occasional child-care tasks do not amount to the same intensity of work as, say, regular meal preparation three times a day every day. Where there were ample excuses for husbands to avoid child-care tasks – homework that was never assigned, parent–teacher meetings that were never called, and no activities that wives ever attended on their own – there are no excuses for husbands to avoid housework. It is telling, therefore, of entrenched gender roles that wives reported scant cooperation from their husbands in regard to housework. Over half of husbands never (40 per cent) or rarely (19 per cent) prepared meals. Upkeep of the house was even less popular; 80 per cent of husbands never or rarely did laundry or cleaning. The most housework that half of the husbands could be persuaded to do was picking up a few groceries while in town on farm business; only 27 per cent never ran such household errands.

The relationships of the six types of women's agricultural, domestic, and paid labour are shown in table 3.2. The four agricultural factor scores overlap substantially with one another. It makes sense that internal and external farm administration are closely related (.47) to each other; women doing one would likely do the other. Mechanical work is so versatile that it may be the key to total involvement in farming; it goes equally well with farm labour (.50), internal administration (.49), and external administration (.44). Administrative work measures a woman's managerial and decision-making contribution rather than actual hours expended on farm work. Judging from the relatively weaker correlations between farm labour and administration, some women apparently feel confident contributing to decision making within the household, attending formal commodity meetings, or speaking to sales representatives without doing intensive farm labour. If this seems implausible, consider one woman who spent only seven hours a week on farm work; she was the farm's primary operator in her husband's prolonged absence, but they had recently reduced their livestock in a move to get out of farming altogether, thus reducing her farm labour to a minimum. Another woman managed a $4-million enterprise, but several paid employees (including an accountant) reduced her actual hours of farm labour. At the opposite extreme, one woman put in fifty-seven hours of chores a week for forty-five milk

TABLE 3.2   Correlations[5] among types of work

	Farm labour	Internal admin.	External admin.	Mechanical work	House-work	Paid employ.
Farm labour	1.00					
Internal admin.	.33	1.00				
External admin.	.37	.47	1.00			
Mechanical	.50	.49	.44	1.00		
Housework	−.05	−.16	−.03	−.20	1.00	
Paid employment	−.14	−.04	.05	.02	−.24	1.00

cows while leaving managerial tasks to her husband.

Housework is negatively associated with all four types of farm work; when hours of housework increase, involvement in farming goes down. This relationship could operate in two directions. On the one hand, women who've finished their housework earlier in the day may have ample time left for reviewing livestock records or reading farm journals in the evening, and thus their agricultural involvement may increase. Quite the reverse may happen if the prestige conferred by certain agricultural tasks enables wives to get their husbands to help out, and thereby get away with less housework, or if that prestige pressures husbands to tolerate less housework. So which makes room for the other: farm work or housework? Animal-husbandry chores and housework are clearly mutually exclusive in terms of both being labour-intensive; when a wife's domestic labour includes the care of livestock in addition to children, the house is messier. The other agricultural tasks are not so labour-intensive, however, as to reduce housework directly. If we assume that agriculture is given priority over a commitment to housekeeping, we must distinguish between a messy house in which women frantically skimp on housework and a tidy house in which husbands do their fair share. A woman's mechanical work, more so than other types of farm work, had the opposite effect from housework.

In the same fashion, paid employment takes women out of the household and thus reduces their involvement in all types of farm and domestic work. Employed wives do less farm work, but are they doing less farm work because their time is already occupied? Or do wives take paid employment because they are not needed on the farm or because they are not interested in farming? It is not possible to determine, at this point, which comes first.

TABLE 3.3   Determinants of agricultural work scores, hours of housework per week, and paid employment[6]

Determinants	Farm labour	Mechanic. work	External admin.	Internal admin.	House-work	Paid employ.
Husband's housework	–	.08*	.05	.06	−2.34***	–
Husband's education	–	.06	.11**	.16***	1.48	.05
Husband employed	–	–	–	−.29	−6.22	–
Wife's age	−.02**	−.01	–	–	–	.08*
Wife's squared age	–	–	–	–	–	−.00086*
People in household	–	–	–	–	3.49**	–
Farmer father	–	–	–	–	7.27*	–
Dairy farm	1.14***	–	.44**	–	–	−.21*
Livestock farm	.49**	.69***	–	.26	−7.48*	–
Grain/crop farm	–	–	–	–	–	−.24*
Egg/poultry farm	–	–	–	–	–	−.29
Extended family	−.28*	−.23	−.20	−.48**	–	–
Farm acres	–	–	–	–	–	−.38**
Employees hired	–	−.05	–	−.05	–	.04
R Square	.51	.25	.17	.23	.23	.23
Adjusted R Square	.50	.21	.14	.19	.19	.17
(N)	(110)	(110)	(110)	(110)	(108)	(113)

*p < .05   **p < .01   ***p < .001

RELATIONSHIP OF WOMEN'S WORK TO FARM AND DEMOGRAPHIC CHARACTERISTICS

Table 3.3 lists the strongest farm and demographic determinants of six types of women's work explored here. The first column shows that the labour-intensive chores of animal husbandry are almost entirely explained in terms of the commodity being produced (as indicated by the asterisks in the corresponding table entries). While this finding is indeed implicit in the very tasks at hand, it is worth driving home the point that dairy and livestock farms overwhelmingly rely on women's labour. Only extended-family involvement in the farm operation and relative youth have anything to add to the profile of farm labour. Younger couples are especially likely to assign animal-husbandry chores to wives when they are farming on their own. Previous research shows that women are more involved in agriculture when male workers, specifically husbands rather than employees, are scarce, and when agricultural tasks are compatible with child-care responsibilities (Blumberg 1981). Husbands' paid off-farm employment reduces their availability at home, which leaves wives to take up the agricultural slack (Rosenfeld 1985, 98; Sachs 1983). In this study, a husband's paid employment does not appear as a determinant of farm labour. An extended-family enterprise, which was neglected in previous studies, is a significant predictor; the relative availability of male workers may be inferred from this. The fact that an extended-family enterprise emerged when controlling for a husband's employment, and the fact that the two are closely associated, suggest that an extended-family enterprise may have been the real determinant in previous studies as well. Thus when couples cannot rely on extended family for help, it makes financial sense for wives to take responsibility for the day-to-day drudgery of farm labour. Younger women, moreover, probably work at home because farm labour is compatible with responsibilities for young children. These results thus outline the rational calculations made by farm couples in allocating the division of labour. An important point is that women's responsibility for farm labour in men's absence does not amount to a reversal of conventional gender roles. Indeed, such a pattern relies on gender-linked occupations in the work force, where women are paid less than men.

Just like farm labour, women's mechanical work is overwhelmingly associated with livestock operations. Mechanical work is not, however, associated with dairy farms, likely because mechanical work is defined in terms of tractors, fences, and trucks – all of which relate to range cattle out in fields, and not to dairy cows inside barns. A husband's housework predicts a wife's acquisition of mechanical skills, and thus provides significant evidence of substantive gender-role reversal in farm households. In effect, mechanical work thus seems to reverse traditional roles between spouses where it counts most – inside the kitchen. Age, and the number of people at home, are important because, contrary to expectations, younger women's involvement in mechanical field-work is *not* limited by responsibilities for children under six years (Rosenfeld 1985, 88–9).

The third and fourth columns of table 3.3 show that internal administration (decision making and research) and external administration form a pair; this table makes it clear that a husband's higher education and an extended-family enterprise isolate women from the decision-making process. On the same discouraging note, both models of administration are distinguished by the striking ability of a husband's higher education, more so than her own educational skills or personal attributes, to predict a woman's involvement in farm administration. Dairy production predicts external administration. Given women's overwhelming involvement in dairy farming, it is only fair that dairy enterprises should be represented to the public world by women. It might seem odd that a wife's paid employment does not appear in regard to farm administration. Paid employment could reduce a woman's available time for and inclination towards farming, but it is equally plausible that skills, confidence, and networks acquired from paid employment might be transferred to the administration of the farm enterprise. After all, only eleven women worked at full-time jobs, so that most were left with some time for farm administration. Instead, regardless of wives' own credentials, they strike a better deal with better-educated husbands to have a say in farm administration. The same husbands are also slightly more likely to do housework when just the marital couple is involved in farming.

Women's agricultural work is an added burden to their domestic labour unless gender-role reversal indeed occurs inside farm households. A wife's housework is significantly predicted by a husband's housework, the number of people living at home, her having grown up on a farm, and the farm not being a livestock operation. The fifth column of table 3.3 bears out earlier scepticism about a husband's child care. A husband's housework signifies more onerous role reversal than does child care; whereas his housework significantly decreases a wife's hours of housework, a husband's child-care contribution does not reduce her hours in the least. Her child-care responsibilities can be inferred from the number of people living at home, some of whom are likely to be young children. Having a farmer for a father, and thus having grown up on a farm, increases a wife's housework, which may reflect rural traditions of canning and freezing home-grown produce.

The sixth column of table 3.3 further shows that a woman's paid off-farm employment is predicted by altogether different characteristics than are agricultural and domestic labour. Older women take paid employment on smaller farms which are not producing dairy, grain, or poultry commodities. Whatever other commodity produced, these farms tend to hire employees, thus releasing a wife for paid employment. Again, a husband's education, more so than her own, predicts slightly her off-farm employment. The fact that both age and its square are significant in the regression model of off-farm employment means that the relationship between age and employment is significantly non-linear. There is a general tendency for employment to increase with age, but, at the same time, middle-aged women are substantially more likely, and the two extremes less likely, to hold paid employment than a straight linear approximation would imply. This makes sense because women are especially likely to take paid employment after raising children to adolescence and prior to retirement.

To a surprising extent, the gendered division of labour in farm households is very much predicted by demographic and enterprise characteristics. Animal husbandry on livestock and dairy operations overwhelmingly engages women in almost all aspects of farming: physical labouring, skilled mechanical work, decision making and research, and formal business dealings. Women reported that they hold administrative influence with better-educated husbands. Women's influence is muted, however, on extended-family enterprises where they must compete with other family members to have a voice. Younger women stay home to do farm labour, whereas older women leave home to take paid jobs. A good deal about these women's lives – indeed, the overall structure of their day-to-day routine – is mandated by the agricultural commodity produced. What is not mandated by the farm enterprise remains to be mediated through power relations within families (Rosenfeld 1985, 138–9). Even so, two items (a husband's education and an extended-family enterprise) play a consistently significant role in those discussions. A husband's education and his family, rather than a wife's own abilities, limit any ambitions she might have to become involved in management of the family enterprise. It is clear that younger women with young children are bearing the brunt of the actual work, particularly in labour-intensive animal-husbandry and housework chores. The least empowering situation for a woman is to be relatively young and married to a man with little education on an extended-family enterprise. Without understanding exactly how a husband's level of education operates as a power-conferring resource within marriage, it is evident that individual husbands largely decide how marriages and households operate. It cannot be said that a woman's higher education, even in the case of her having paid employment, confers on her status. Noting further that husbands are, except at university level, less well educated than wives, it is more plausible that less or equally well-educated husbands are pulling wives down, thus cancelling out the predictive power of wives' higher education. Thus, a farm woman's choice of husband seems to be more critical to her future than her choice of education or occupation, or her set of skills. The only exception may be mechanical skills, which may carry some weight in the negotiation of egalitarian farm marriages.

4

Political Behaviour

The study of women's political behaviour and opinions, whether farmers or not, begins from the once-conventional truism that women lag behind men in indicators of modernization.[1] These indicators comprise the subjective social-psychological characteristics (self-confidence, inquisitiveness, and absence of religiosity)[2] and the objective resources (literacy, status, and wealth) that are presumed to equip people to be competent, progressive-minded, egalitarian citizens of liberal-democratic countries (Banuazizi 1987; Nelson 1987). Women's supposed conservatism was generally taken for granted in standard academic texts until feminist critiques appears in the 1970s. These critiques initially charged that basic rules of scholarly evidence and rigour had not been observed, and some went on to consider more sympathetic explanations of women's apparently irrational and conservative political behaviour.[3] The more neutral term 'marginality' came to be adopted to describe how women were marginalized from public life because they were confined to the private world of home and family (Githens and Prestage 1977). Research from western Europe and North America came to conclude that the combination of women's increasing education and increasing paid employment outside the home was eroding the gender gap between men's and women's political behaviour (Anderson 1975; Lovenduski 1986, 117–63).

This erosion, however, has its limits. The ambitious seven-nation study of Verba, Nie, and Kim (1978) found that women did not convert socio-economic 'resources' such as education and income into political activity as efficiently as did men with comparable resources. The disparity between men's and women's conversion rates (from resources into participation) suggested that women do not abstain from politics as a result of apathy; instead, 'pervasive inhibiting factors limit the political role of women' (1978, 267). The general thrust of this research is confirmed by another study which found that paid employment had little power to account for women's political participation (Sapiro 1983). Paid employment sometimes even decreased political activity because the double burden of work inside and outside the home restricted women's time and energy for politics. Being a 'wife, mother, and homemaker' is a 'privatized role' that marginalizes or excludes women from public life (ibid, 130, 180–1). Only single mothers are less integrated into political life than women who are simultaneously wives, mothers, and homemakers. Later studies likewise anticipated but found very little evidence that women's increasingly public role in society has had much effect on their political behaviour in Canada and the United States; instead, women's 'roles as wives and mothers' dominated (Kay et al. 1988; Neuman 1986, 122).[4]

Archetypal images of rural life involve isolation and traditionalism; as an early example, Daniel Lerner interviewed a Lebanese peasant woman: 'Asked how she got her news, she replied: 'From the neighbours; at the baker when I go to bake bread, and at the well where I get out drinking water. (Who tells you the news?) All the women who go there. (What do they talk about?) About who is going to marry, who is going to have a baby, who quarrelled with whom and why'' (1958, 177). Lerner commented that her way of life, circumscribed by the daily rounds of women's work and village gossip, has scarcely changed since biblical times. He noted with approval that even destitute shepherd boys, unlike peasant women, poignantly yearn to visit Beirut and to listen to radios. By all the conventional indicators of modernization, rural populations lag behind almost everyone with respect to education, waged labour, and related socio-economic mobilizers; and rural women lag even farther behind than rural men. Empirical studies bear out the applicability of these images to rural communities in industrialized countries. In postwar Europe, for example, farmers ranked lowest – as the most materialist – of all occupational groups on a scale of materialism and post-materialism (Inglehart 1990, 164).[5] Housewives discussed politics least, less often than did farmers, manual workers, and the unemployed (ibid, 352). This research suggested that wealthy, educated urban youths pioneer the way to more progressive personal and political values, leaving rural wives lagging behind down on the farm.[6]

There is a final twist to these discouraging generalizations. When political activity is measured independently of opinions, rural people fare remarkably well. Verba, Nie, and Kim found a strongly inverse impact of community size on political activity (1978, 269–85). It seems that rural people are able to convert scant socio-economic resources into abundant political activity.

Chapters 4, 5, and 6 apply these considerations to the farm women interviewed here, and use standard indicators of politicization and conservatism to measure farm women's political activities and opinions. In this chapter, political behaviour is discussed as a value-free activity. Political behaviour consists of three components: subjective political involvement, political conceptualization, and political participation.[7] Subjective involvement refers to talking about politics and feeling comfortable with the conventional rules of formal partisan politics. Conceptualization represents one's ability to discuss the abstract concepts of politics and left/right, as demonstrated by responses to open-ended questions asking for definitions (Neuman 1986, 191–5). Subjective political involvement and the ability to conceptualize political terms, along with socio-economic characteristics, are 'resources' to be converted into political participation (Verba, Nie, and Kim 1978, 94). Participation refers to women's activities in voluntary organizations, chiefly in the Women's Institutes. Standard indicators of conservatism that measure opinions are substantive political and social issues related to elections, environmentalism, religiosity, sexual morality, and feminism are discussed in chapters 5 and 6.[8]

POLITICAL INVOLVEMENT

Farm women reported subjective political involvement on separate questions relating to salience, efficacy, and partisanship. Political salience involves talking about politics and social issues and being interested in politics. Table 4.1 shows that Canadian women in general are not particularly different from European women in their proclivity to discuss politics; they hovered in the middle, along with Danish, British, and Australian women, and were surpassed by Finnish, Swiss, and American women (Inglehart 1990, 51). This pattern has remained stable across separate surveys: the 1981–2 World Values Survey found that 62 per cent of Canadian women discussed politics often or occasionally (ibid) compared with 58 per cent in the 1984 Canadian Election Study (CES).

TABLE 4.1 Frequency of discussing politics (and social problems)

Frequency	CES 1984 (%)	Europe 1987 (%)		Ont. farm w/neighbour (%)		w/ husband (%)	Quebec farm (%)		France farm (%)	
Often	19	9	(20)	13	(17)	30	7	(23)	9	(25)
Occasionally	39	49	(56)	45	(48)	40	37	(56)	47	(58)
Rarely	25	–	–	24	(21)	16	37	(19)	27	(12)
Almost never	17	41	(22)	18	(14)	14	18	(2)	17	(5)
Can't say	–	1	(1)	–		–	–		–	
(N)	(1,726)	(11,651)		(117)		(116)	(196)		(193)	

SOURCES: Brandt and Black 1989; Canadian Election Study 1984; Commission of the European Communities 1987, 37–8.

Table 4.1 also shows that farm wives in this study reported rates of political salience that are higher than rates reported in Canada and Europe. The frequency of discussing politics with neighbours is similar that of the 1984 Canadian Election Study and mirrors 1987 Euro-Barometer results. Those studies, however, did not ask women to distinguish between discussions with husbands and discussions with friends and neighbours. The equivalent combination for Ontario farm women would be higher than either of the two separate frequencies; a safe underestimate would be the higher of the two – higher than the 1984 Canada Election Study results and the 1987 Euro-Barometer results, and much higher than the 1989 Quebec and France farm results. Farm wives were substantially more willing to discuss politics alone with their husbands because, they said, circumspection was advisable with friends and neighbours: politics 'is too contentious for discussion' and 'is too private to discuss with neighbours.'[9]

It might be that women in general do not talk about 'politics' because they take 'politics' to refer to conventional, partisan politics in legislatures. But since politics encompasses much more than that, women were asked if they discussed social problems such as human rights, poverty, or the third world with friends and neighbours (Commission of the European Communities 1984, 130). Table 4.1 shows that such a distinction appears not to hold among Ontario farm wives; they discussed social issues (65 per cent) at least as frequently as politics (58 per cent) with friends and neighbours. Whereas Ontario farm women did not make any distinction between discussing politics and discussing social problems, such a gap did appear among Quebec and

TABLE 4.2   Interest in politics[10]

Frequency	CES 1988 (%)	CES 1984 (%)	Canada 1987 (%)	Canada 1981 (%)	Europe (%)	Ont. farm (%)
A great deal	8	15	12	10	7	12
To some extent	36	39	38	43	28	53
Not much	44	46	48	33	36	29
Not at all	12	–	–	14	29	5
Can't say	–	–	1	–	–	1
(N)	(1,638)	(1,724)	(1,070)	(1,489)	(11,815)	(117)

SOURCES: Canadian Election Study 1988, 1984; Canadian Charter of Rights Study 1987; Canada Quality of Life Study 1981; Commission of the European Communities 1991, 4.

French farm women, and European women, who much preferred discussing *social* problems to discussing politics. One may only suggest that 'politics' is understood to be more accessible to rural Protestant women in English Canada than to rural Roman Catholic women in Quebec and France.

In this same vein, table 4.2 shows that Ontario farm women reported generally higher interest in politics than did predominantly urban Canadian and European women. It is probably best to combine the categories of 'a great deal' and 'to some extent' because, for instance, one women said that, although she was 'very interested in politics,' she did not qualify for that answer, which she felt was reserved for party activists and politicians. Women's noted modesty and self-deprecation likely have much to do with the reported gap between men and women's political salience (Christy 1986).

The concept of political efficacy is controversial (Lambert et al. 1986b, 705–11; Neuman 1986, 195). Efficacy claims to measure how 'efficacious' or 'effective' people feel about their ability to influence government. It might be included as part of political salience or it might be its own separate concept. If efficacy is part of political salience, it would be considered a subjective resources that increases with education, income, and political knowledge. But this definition neglects people's perception of how responsive government is to their efforts. In what follows, efficacy is taken to be an objective statement of fact about 'perceived system responsiveness' (Barnes and Kaase 1979, 574) that expresses one's alienation from government. For example,

TABLE 4.3 Politics is too complicated to understand

Frequency	CES 1984 (%)	Canada 1981 (%)	Farm wives (%)
Completely agree	33	23	23
Agree to some extent	36	51	32
Disagree to some extent	18	24	36
Disagree completely	10	3	9
Can't say, agree neither way	3	–	–
(N)	(1,693)	(1,464)	(117)

SOURCES: Canadian Election Study 1984; Canada Quality of Life Study 1981.

one respondent was very 'efficacious' in her capacity as a local politician, but she admitted that politics was just too complicated: legislative briefs and policy proposals were written for lawyers and were above her head.

Women's notoriously low levels of political efficacy once led to charges that they failed to understand the basic principle of participatory citizenship – namely, that people are supposed to have an impact on government. But women's low efficacy is now more plausibly seen as an accurate perception of their own and everyone else's very limited ability to understand and influence public policy. Women's notoriously low efficacy is reliably confirmed on only one measure: agreement or disagreement that 'politics is too complicated and one has to be a specialist to understand politics' (Sapiro 1983, 98–101). When this question was posed to Ontario farm wives, their answers indicated remarkable efficacy. Table 4.3 shows that fewer farm wives (55 per cent) agreed that politics is too complicated than did urban Canadian women in 1984 (69 per cent) and in 1981 (74 per cent). By disagreeing with this statement, 45 per cent of farm women affirmed their faith in liberal democracy, and thus demonstrated higher efficacy than did urban women in 1984 (28 per cent) and in 1981 (27 per cent).

Efficacy is further indicated by agreement or disagreement with the statement 'No matter which party wins the election, it doesn't really change the situation in Ontario.' Farm women were split half and half on this measure. This question is evidently about partisanship, but if partisanship does not have an impact on policy, it means that voting in elections does not have an impact either. Only four farm women did not usually vote because 'it's too hard to decide' or because 'it doesn't matter which party is in power.' Contacting elected officials also relates to efficacy because it presumes that personal contact ac-

TABLE 4.4   Occasional and regular political activities

Activities	CES 1984 (%)	Farm wives (%)
Vote in elections	–	95
Give money to a political party	12	12
Work on a election campaign	13	10
Get in touch with an elected official	18	40
Listen to news on the radio	–	93
Watch news/political shows on television	64	91
(N)	(1,723)	(117)

SOURCE: Canadian Election Study 1984.

tually accomplishes something. As table 4.4 shows, farm women were twice as likely (40 per cent, as compared with 18 per cent of urban women) to have contacted an elected official. This suggests that, more so than urban politicians, rural ones are accessible and known personally to constituents. Farm women were also a third more likely (91 per cent, as compared with 64 per cent urban) to watch news on television, which might reflect preferences for the local radio and television stations whose news broadcasts cover rural and agricultural issues at length.

My survey sample happened to include a number of women who had worked in various elections over the years. Ten women volunteered that they had been poll clerks, two had been scrutineers, and three had been deputy returning officers. They were predominantly WI members, but only two held their own party membership, which suggests that they came to partisanship through their husbands rather than through the women's organization.

Liberal theory further presumes that confident, politically efficacious citizens try to persuade others to change their opinions. Many Ontario farm wives, however, abhor this behaviour as rude and aggressive. It is more virtuous, one woman suggested, not to voice one's opinion forcefully: 'People are entitled to their own opinions; I'd like to persuade them, but I don't try to.' Accordingly, as table 4.5 shows, more than half (55 per cent) almost never or rarely persuade other people, not just about politics, but about any issue.

Table 4.5 shows that predominantly urban women share this aversion. The question asked of urban women entailed a more demanding requirement – to persuade others to vote for one's chosen political

TABLE 4.5   Persuade other people

Frequency	CES 1984 (how to vote) (%)	Europe (polit. opinion) (%)	Ontario farm (any opinion) (%)
Often	4	12	7
Occasionally	10	36	37
Rarely	16	27	27
Never or almost never	70	23	28
Can't say	–	–	2
(N)	(1,720)	(11,651)	(117)

SOURCES: Canadian Election Study 1984; Commission of the European Communities 1987, 38.

party. When the question of persuasion is restricted to voting for a particular party, only 14 per cent of Canadian women persuaded people to vote for one's chosen party. This finding is consistent with the observation that suburban housewives refrain from trying to persuade each other: 'political conversation – particularly if the purpose is to influence – may be too dangerous to the well being and maintenance of the social system' (Sapiro 1983, 127). Liberal theorists propose that the ideal of tolerance encourages people to convert others to their own opinions; liberal citizens ought to be pugnaciously aggressive (Vernon and LaSelva 1984, 23). Farm wives, and evidently women elsewhere, mean something quite different and much less argumentative by tolerance.

Previous research suggests that those who identify strongly with a political party are more actively involved in politics (Neuman 1986, 96). The content of 'political life' is left undefined in these studies, but if, as expected, it is defined in terms of electoral and partisan activities, then of course partisan party identifiers are more active. The logic becomes circular and excludes people who are otherwise involved in political protest, or even terrorist, activities. Housewives' low partisanship is inferred from the fact that, compared with that of employed women, housewives' party affiliation is predicted strongly by friends', family's, and especially husbands' party affiliation (Sapiro 1983, 162–3). Housewives are more likely, therefore, to 'vote by proxy' or to cast ballots on the advice of some trusted friend or family member (Neuman 1986, 91).

One Canadian analysis successfully employed partisanship and party identification to predict efficacy. It was concluded that efficacy and trust in government come down to being 'on the winning side.' People who identify with the governing party feel closer to the political action than those who identify with losing parties (Lambert et al. 1986b, 727). But, following Verba, Nie, and Kim 1978, psychological and social characteristics surely have a role because self-confident, well-educated, articulate, and critical people are better equipped to convert such resources into political assets for their chosen party, and thereby come out on the winning side more often than not.

Pursuing this analysis that links efficacy to partisanship, farm women reported considerably less partisanship than would be expected on grounds of efficacy. Fifteen women were members of a political party, but this number is deceptively high because some of these reported their husband's membership as their own.[11] Apart from party membership, another question tested partisanship surprisingly well: 'Do you agree that, if they wanted to, all the political parties could come to an agreement to make good policy for Canada?' A good majority (62 per cent) answered yes. This hypothetical question worked fine for women who agreed completely; they responded quickly and easily, whereas it confused other respondents. Those who rejected this position answered, in effect, that political parties could get together to cooperate if they wanted, but why would they cooperate, since partisan competition is the essence of good government. Not everyone, however, is at ease with or has confidence in the formal rules of partisan politics.

If a good majority (62 per cent) of Ontario farm women favour non-partisan legislatures and only a few are members of a political party, how can they be on the winning side, which, as Lambert and colleagues (1986) found, predicts efficacy? One might well argue that the fact that farmers have always been on the winning side (in overrepresented rural ridings and as recipients of government subsidies) amply explains their high efficacy. Regardless of any final balance of accounts, many farmers would deny being winners in respect to government policies. Pauline Rankin argues for an 'agrarian myth,' which might explain, in part, farm women's surprisingly high sense of efficacy. There are more Muslims or homosexuals in Canada than farmers, whose households form just 4 per cent of the population, but farmers persist in thinking that they are 'grass roots' Canadians and the backbone of society (Rankin 1987, 115). According to Rankin, the religious, ethnic, and occupational traits of Ontario's farming population converge in

TABLE 4.6 Correlations[12] among aspects of political involvement

	Salience	Too complicated	Doesn't matter	See politician	Persuade others	Parties cooperate
Salience	1.00					
Too complicated	−.39	1.00				
Doesn't matter	−.22	.41	1.00			
See politician	.45	−.15	−.22	1.00		
Persuade others	.35	.04	−.16	.30	1.00	
Parties coop.	−.17	.13	.20	−.16	−.03	1.00

the myth of its moral superiority. In sum, farm women reported higher levels of salience and efficacy in comparison to Canadian women in general, higher levels than are warranted by their sparse numbers, levels of education, membership in political parties, and doubts in the merits of partisan competition.

These aspects of political involvement were correlated, as shown in table 4.6. Measures of reliability indicated that it was safe to combine four political discussion and interest questions into a single new item called 'political salience'; similar measures, however, did not allow the combination of the four measures of efficacy listed in table 4.6.[13] Not surprisingly, political salience is positively associated with contacting elected officials (.45) and persuading people (.35). Political salience is negatively associated with the opinion that politics is too complicated (-.39). Two questions demonstrating low efficacy (politics is too complicated and elections don't matter) go together (.41), but the remaining aspects of political involvement are not otherwise associated with each other.

Table 4.7 shows the influence of demographic and agricultural characteristics on political involvement (as indicated by asterisks in the corresponding table entries). As expected, political salience was predicted by increased age, education, husband's education, and not growing up on a farm. Farm characteristics were just as significant and even more intriguing: whereas living on a dairy farm and doing the sociable tasks of external administration increased political salience, doing animal-husbandry chores in the absence of hired help decreased salience. In like manner, contacting elected officials was significantly predicted by farm administration, age, and education. Similarly, the profile of persuasion was positively predicted by internal farm administration, and negatively predicted by farm labour. Women were

TABLE 4.7   Determinants of political involvement[14]

Determinants	Salience	Too complicated	Doesn't matter	See politician	Persuade others	Parties cooperate
Farm labour	−.93*	-	.21	-	−.24*	-
Internal admin.	-	-	−.27*	-	.33**	−.28*
External admin.	.93**	-	−.41***	.39***	-	-
Mechanical work	-	-	-	-	-	.38**
Wife's age	.07**	-	-	.02*	-	-
Wife's education	.43**	−.11*	-	.10*	-	−.11
Wife employed	-	-	-	-	-	−.26
Husband employed	-	−.28	-	-	−.31	−.36
Husband's educat.	.28*	−.09	-	-	-	-
Farmer father	−1.04	.33	-	.23	-	.34
People in house	-	.13	-	-	-	−.11
Housework hours	-	-	−.01*	-	-	-
Dairy farm	1.75**	-	-	-	-	-
Livestock farm	1.44	-	-	−.33	-	-
Egg/poultry farm	-	-	.64*	-	-	-
Farm acres	-	−.43	-	-	−.61*	-
Employees hired	−.24*	-	-	-	-	-
Extended family	−.97	.31	-	−.26	.22	-
R Square	.41	.22	.26	.30	.17	.19
Adjusted R Square	.35	.17	.22	.26	.13	.13
(N)	(104)	(100)	(106)	(109)	(108)	(107)

*p < .05   **p < .01   ***p < .001

also more likely to persuade others on smaller farms, as measured by number of acres.

In regard to efficacy, motherhood and education are expected to pull women in opposing and equally strong directions; motherhood decreases efficacy, while education raises it (Sapiro 1983, 100). That pattern was not entirely repeated in this study. Education did indeed raise efficacy (measured by disagreement that politics is too complicated), but motherhood (measured by the number of people in the household) had only a slight effect. An orientation to homemaking (measured by hours of housework) decreased the belief that elections do not matter. Farm administration had the same positive effect on efficacy as on political salience. Inexplicably, women living on egg/ poultry operations were more likely to think that elections don't matter. In regard to partisanship, women doing internal administration

were significantly less likely to agree that the parties should stop competing and start cooperating. Mechanical work had the surprising ability to convince women that partisanship was bad.

Overall, agricultural characteristics were surprisingly more significant than age and education in this model of political involvement.
Farm administration significantly increased political involvement on
salience, partisanship, and persuasion, whereas the actual physical
work of farming (labour and mechanical work) decreased political involvement on the same three counts. Two women credit farming for
their interest in politics:

I've gotten interested lately in farm policies. Farming has opened up doors
for me because we're touched by so many policies which relate so directly
to my responsibilities for our family and children now.

How government policies affect farm and rural issues is my area of concern.

More so perhaps than other occupations, farming, or specifically farm
administration, enabled some women to draw connections between
public-policy debates, for instance, the future of agricultural trade
under GATT negotiations, and the private situation of their individual
households. So a dairy operation operating under government-
legislated marketing boards predicted political salience. Their ability
to draw these connections between the personal and political might
be further assisted by the fact that the occupation of farming is geographically segregated in rural areas. Under such segregation, the relative dominance of farming in the physical landscape speaks for its
self-evident political dominance in the minds of the inhabitants. In
addition to being expressed at formal agricultural occasions, farmers'
grievances receive a sympathetic hearing at rural churches, fairs, and
family get-togethers. Daily routines and informal patterns of social
interaction among farm families reinforce their common identities and
grievances. This might explain, in part, why farm characteristics predicted so significantly women's reported political involvement, and
why that involvement was higher than among urban women.

POLITICAL CONCEPTUALIZATION

Two opened-ended questions asked farm wives to explain, in their
own words, the terms 'politics' and 'left'/'right.' A third question asked
them to place themselves on a left/right scale. Scrutiny of their

responses reveals traces of an alternative belief system governed by principles of consensus and conciliation.

Respondents' definitions of the term 'politics' related to one or both of two dominant orientations: government and participation. The most interesting element of women's conceptualization of politics that emerged was the unexpected theme of efficacy, both high and low. In order to investigate these concepts quantitatively, two variables were constructed: one describing orientation towards politics defined in terms of government, government policies, and the running of the country, and one describing orientation towards politics in terms of participation, chiefly participation through partisan politics. Table 4.8 summarizes responses for these two conceptualizations. Most women made a stab at trying to conceptualize the meaning of politics. The most frequent response given was in terms of government and the running of the country. Half of all women (52 per cent) showed a positive orientation to a government conceptualization, and a smaller proportion (17 per cent) showed a negative orientation. Roughly a quarter of the responses (26 per cent) related to the theme of participation and partisanship. Of this category, most of the responses were positive, and even enthusiastic, about political participation (22 per cent of the total). Only a few responses (4 per cent) were negative about politics in this sense.

A majority (52 per cent) of women gave conventional, non-controversial definitions of 'politics,' including references to government and the running of the country. To assign responses to either category, a conceptual distinction was made between people as the objects or as the subjects of government policy. In the first category, people were conceptualized as the recipients or objects of politics and policies generated from above by governments. In addition to seeing government as a benign or neutral administrative structure, or 'the powers that be,' other comments conceptualized governments as positively benevolent:

Politics is the general welfare of the common people, not the higher people.

Politics is the government keeping people working together happily.

Politics is the government helping people who need help, looking after the needs of Canadians.

For the most part, a negative orientation criticized government in-

TABLE 4.8   Meaning of 'politics'

Response	Frequency	
Positive orientation to government	59	(52%)
Negative orientation to government	19	(17%)
Positive orientation to participation	25	(22%)
Negative orientation to participation	5	(4%)
Can't say	6	(5%)
(N)	(114)	

tervention, or simply voiced frustration. The following are examples of a negative orientation to politics defined in terms of government:

Politics is a lot of talking about nothing.

Politics is a bunch of baloney. Politicians confuse themselves and the country.

I hate the back-biting and knife-stabbing of politics.

It's just a bunch of overpaid men for what we're getting out of it.

It bamboozles me how politicians carry on like a three-ring circus. They just blow it.

Nothing is as dirty as politics. They're so cruel to each other.

I vote and follow policies, but I don't understand their ruckus.

Politics is a scam. I know because my father was on the local council for years. Why would people want to get involved at all?

You'd have to be a crook to be in politics. You'd have to give up your moral beliefs. There is too much politicking and back-scratching. Governments get too involved.

Despite the vehemence of these comments, relatively few responses were negative or hostile. Overall, farm women gave remarkably positive responses, given that ordinary Canadians are reputed to be experiencing a crisis of confidence in regard to their political institutions. When asked in 1984, almost half of Canadian women, 42 per cent, strongly agreed that people in the federal government were dishonest and 47 per cent strongly agreed that the federal government wastes money (Canadian Election Study 1984). When asked again in 1988, almost half of Canadian women, 47 per cent, agreed that the people running government are crooked and 48 per cent said that they trusted government to do what is right only some of the time.

In the second category, people were conceptualized as agents or subjects who generated politics and policies from the grass roots up. When politics was defined as participation, it was often in terms of partisan politics and elections. More so than the previous category, an enthusiastic sense of personal engagement characterized comments:

Politics is the financial running of a community, from the local level up to the entire country. It's people working together for each other, striving to make things better together. It's communicating and working with other countries.

Politics is representing the people; it's the voice of the people.

People should do more than complain about politics. People should have a hand in it; they should go to a council meeting and do something.

Politics is having a say in running our country, in decision making.

Politics is everything from the Institute up. It includes the Women's Institutes because they have their own scheme of things and mandate, even if they say they're not political.

It's the values and ideas about how things should be done. Politics should involve each person's opinion and what's fair for everybody.

Politics is fighting for people's rights.

Only five comments showed a negative orientation to politics defined in this sense. One woman criticized the excesses of partisan competition: 'As a child, I was taught that politics is about Liberals fighting Conservatives, but I'm not that big on the [Progressive Conservative] party any more, even though I'm still a member.' The request to define politics prompted this woman to reflect on her life before she married a farmer and became a WI leader: 'I never had too much confidence to think I could say anything. I was a single parent. I left my first husband, who was beating me, and I didn't get alimony payments. I asked the police for help, but they didn't help me. I feel alone in this country, but things are changing.' She thus spoke to the barriers preventing her from 'speaking up' as a political agent.

How people conceptualize the meaning of the term 'politics' may be closely related to political efficacy. Farm women's open-ended responses are consistent with the results of a similar exercise conducted in Southern Ontario. In that study, voters defined the meaning of politics negatively or neutrally in terms of remote governments, whereas political activists and partisans defined politics in terms of their own participation in the political process (Burt 1986). In this study of farm women, responses were, for the most part, banal definitions of politics in terms of government and the running of the government. When women did evaluate politics or express emotion in this first category, their responses were positive in conceiving of government as benevolent, 'helping people who need help.' Or their responses were negative in conceiving of government as corrupt. Regardless of whether politics was conceptualized as being in Ottawa or the local township, the hostile comments express a sense of distance from politics. Even a woman whose father had sat on local council for years, for example, was perplexed and repelled by the seamy business of politics. In comments expressing a negative orientation to politics defined as government, low efficacy coexisted with moral superiority and indignation. Responses in the second category defining politics in terms of participation expressed a more personal and active involvement for respondents. Even respondents who identified barriers to their involvement in politics or criticized excessive partisanship conceptualized themselves as agents inside the business of politics.

Although the classic distinction between 'left' and 'right' persists, there is considerable doubt as to its continued usefulness after the end of the Cold War between left-wing socialists and right-wing capitalists. Apart from conceptual debate among academics and journalists, the left/right distinction is judged to have even less empirical currency in the general population, especially among North Americans, and it has been suggested that it should be abandoned for that reason alone. Farm women's responses on this score generally confirm this judgment. Yet it will be seen that an understanding of 'left' and 'right' prevails among farm wives that is entirely appropriate to their common situation in household production.

Two standard questions explored left/right beliefs among Ontario farm women. One asked respondents to locate themselves on a scale of 1 to 10, with 5 being the centre, and the other asked them to define what they mean by left (-wing) and right (-wing). Their responses are compared with more comprehensive data showing that about half of all Canadians could use left and right concepts competently in a political context. Roughly 60 per cent of respondents supplied ideological or partisan definitions of left and right (Lambert et al. 1986a, 561). Better-educated people were able to provide specific policy examples and abstract ideas corresponding to a left/right distinction, whereas less-educated people applied labels to political parties (ibid, 556). Lambert and colleagues concluded that, for a population of political amateurs – about half of all Canadians – left and right are surprisingly useful concepts, especially in regard to partisanship. At very least, the concepts give voters a handle on labelling political parties as 'good guys and bad guys' or 'them *versus* us.' Despite an opposing substantive analysis, another study similarly concluded that left/right labels will increasingly be used in future political discussions among Canadians (Langford 1991, 496). Considerably higher levels of familiarity and competence with this particular concept are reported from Europe. The proportion of respondents giving ideological or partisan definitions ranged from a low of 80 per cent in The Netherlands to a high of 91 per cent in Germany. The proportion of respondents doing so in Britain (81 per cent), the United States (85 per cent), and Austria (87 per cent) ranged in between (Klingemann 1979, 230).

Certainly, this particular population of rural farm wives has been passed over in previous studies of political conceptualization. The terms of the empirical debate on the meaning of left/right in public opinion were first set in the 1960s by academic surveys of university students, among whom future farm wives scarcely figured (Laponce 1970). In subsequent analyses of left/right beliefs, farmers were deleted because they were too few to be an occupational group, and homemakers were deleted to prove that gender was not a significant variable (Lambert et al. 1987, 546). Or, in another case, housewives and 'autonomous wage earners [which presumably includes farmers]' were deleted to see how class position interacts with education on left/right orientation (Langford 1991). In sum, the typical frame of analysis (focused principally on class) excludes farm wives and housewives one way or another. Previous studies of political conceptualization blithely passed over this particular population, among whom a distinct understanding of left and right might be discerned.

TABLE 4.9 Low sophistication U.S. respondents' liberal/conservative, and Canadian
women's and Ontario farm wives' left/right location

Frequency	U.S. low sophistication (%)	CES 1988 (%)	Canada 1987 (%)	Ontario farm wives (%)
Left of centre (liberal)	23	36	18	14
Centre	40	31	50	67
Right of centre (conservative)	39	33	24	19
Proportion of sample placing self on scale	30	12	92	64
(N)	(404)	(214)	(268)	(114)

SOURCES: Neuman 1986, 77; Canadian Election Study 1988; Canadian Charter of
Rights Survey 1987.

As shown in table 4.9, Ontario farm women were less adept with
left/right concepts. Of those willing to place themselves on the left/
right scale, only a third (33 per cent) identified themselves as substantially left or right, and most (67 per cent) preferred the centre. But
those numbers are deceptive because only 64 per cent even placed themselves on the scale; forty-one women could not say or had never heard
of the distinction. In comparison with Canadian women in general,
and even the low-sophistication category of Americans (Neuman 1986,
77), farm women were notably more likely to locate themselves in the
centre. Preference for substantive left/liberal or right/conservative positions, as opposed to the 'middle of the road,' increases with political
sophistication (defined as the sum of salience, knowledge, and conceptualization) and is strongly correlated with university education
(Langford 1991, 480, 493; Neuman 1986, 76–81).[15]

To sort out open-ended definitions, this study employed three standard categories: ideological or conceptual understanding, political parties or classes, and idiosyncratic or affective understanding (Klingemann 1979). The third category, less self-explanatory than the previous
two, collects residual definitions that connect 'left' and 'right' to purely
effective or moralistic states (ibid, 230). These are idiosyncratic, emotional definitions that do not make sense in conventional political
terms because they are peculiar to particular individuals. As such, they
are leftovers consigned to the residual category and often dismissed.

Unlike the term 'politics,' left/right beliefs have correct and incorrect
definitions, so it was possible to separate responses in the first two
categories into usual and reversed definitions. Table 4.10 shows these

TABLE 4.10 Position on left/right scale by meaning of 'left'/'right'

L/R scale	Usual ideology	Reversed ideology	Usual partisan	Reversed partisan	Affective	Don't know	Total
Left	3	3	1	0	2	1	10
Centre	2	7	10	2	20	8	49
Right	6	4	1	0	0	3	14
Don't know	2	0	1	3	3	32	41
Total	13	14	13	5	25	44	114

responses, cross-tabulated with left/right identification. Farm wives' most frequent response was simply that they did not know what 'left' and 'right' meant; 39 per cent had nothing to say on the subject. Only a small proportion of farm wives supplied intelligible ideological definitions (11 per cent) or named specific parties or classes (12 per cent). According to reported finding by Canadians in general, many more Canadians (40 per cent) supplied ideological definitions, and slightly more Canadians (15–20 per cent) supplied partisan or class definitions (Lambert et al. 1987). Of the seventy women who ventured an explanation of their left/right beliefs, twenty-five supplied an idiosyncratic or affective definition.

Table 4.10 shows that the locations of those farm wives who placed themselves on the scale should be taken with caution because some of them were bluffing. It is well established in survey research that respondents are quite willing to locate themselves on this particular scale without being able to explain their position in subsequent questions. Nineteen women invalidated their location on the next question, when they defined left and right in reverse of their meanings in conventional political discourse. A further twenty-five respondents supplied affective definitions that were not conventionally political. These limitations came out in cross-tabulation of left/right location against conceptualization, as shown in table 4.10. Only four of ten 'leftists' and seven of fourteen 'rightists' gave conventionally ideological or partisan definitions. Left/right location was not analysed against social class, party identification, voting, or related political opinions because the results of any such calculations would, of course, be nonsense. Instead, this discussion proceeds directly to the meaning of definitions provided by respondents.

Clearly, Ontario farm wives were unprepared to speak on the subject of left/right beliefs. Fewer than half (41 per cent) were even in the ballpark of conventional definition, even though it was drawn with very generous fences. This percentage includes all the answers referring to ideological contrasts or contrasts involving class or partisanship, even if the contrasts were reversed. It includes even those responses that saw a polarity more or less correctly, without articulating which pole was left and which was right. One response, for example, drew such a contrast: 'one is free with the money and the other holds the purse-strings tightly. But they all act the same; it doesn't matter.'

Ideological answers spoken broadly in terms of free enterprise as right-wing and socialism or communism as left-wing: 'Right stands for the traditional value of individual responsibility for success and failure. Left stands for the socialist idea of cradle-to-the-grave security.' The concept of change frequently appeared under this first category. The desirability of change and the appropriate rate of change are contested values in society, with impatience being associated with the left and a desire to conserve the past being associated with the right. Farm women sometimes confused the two and were unsure which was which, but they understood that an appraisal of change itself belonged to a left/right belief system. Two women took this conventionally political contrast to describe their own personalities. Their self-descriptions make sense because the right generally stands for the status quo which the left tries to change:

Right is to go along with the norm, to have the standard line. Left is more against the norm, which is what government and people try to force on me. Left is to try to keep to my own opinion.

I'm right-wing because I'm conservative in my own thoughts. I'm tight-fisted in my thoughts instead of being extremist.

The broad concepts of free enterprise as right-wing, and socialist or communism as left-wing, typically correspond to partisan and class loyalties. When those concepts were associated with the Progressive Conservative party and rich people, or the New Democratic Party (NDP) and poor people, they belong to the second category of partisan or class responses:

The NDP is left-wing. I don't like government with their fingers in everything.

The left believes that people should be treated equally, with government health care and social programmes. Wealthy people shouldn't get tax breaks and tax shelters, but right-wing parties like the Conservatives and the Liberals are run by big business.

This category also included responses that understood left and right as extreme partisan loyalties to be avoided because, 'I'm not a party person. I vote for the person.'

The third category collects residual responses. Residual responses do not correspond to conventionally intelligible definitions of left and right. Instead of being political definitions held in common, these are idiosyncratic definitions invented by each particular individual. Since levels of familiarity with left/right belief systems were relatively low among Ontario farm wives, the residual category is, in fact, just as large as the ideological category. An inquiry into the residual 'affective' category of left/right belief systems returns one to perhaps the central question at the heart of public-opinion research – namely, whether or not the public indeed has coherent political opinions to be investigated. Philip Converse, who pioneered efforts to extract belief systems from the mass population by means of quantitative empirical analysis, first warned that the general public does not have stable, meaningful concepts with which to organize their opinions on current political controversies (1964, 245). His ominous warning puts the very idea of democracy into question because he implies that no beliefs held by the mass population are worth heeding. Accordingly, the endeavour to extract belief systems through conceptualization has been tied to the viability of democracy. If democracy is to work, as few answers as possible should be assigned to the residual affective category in conceptualizing left/right beliefs. Converse doubted but did not deny the possible existence of coherent 'folk ideologies' (1964, 255) indigenous to isolated sectors of the population. In what follows, I consider the possibility that a 'folk ideology' of conciliation holds among the Ontario farm women.

The more stringently these residual responses are examined, the less they appear to be entirely 'idiosyncratic.' They certainly are 'affective' responses in so far they arouse respondents' personal emotions, but they have a intellectual coherence of their own, affirming the moral superiority of the centre over the polar extremes of left and right. Some women took the conventional political understanding of left/right and applied it to a personal and domestic context. And, most important, their responses all ran along a coherent line. Being in the centre is a moral stance and a general principle of behaviour rather than a political preference. It is called here the 'centre principle.' To be in the centre is:

To keep my beliefs to myself, keep my mouth shut.

To be tolerant and open-minded, to see that there are two sides to every story. Not in the centre are others who are not tolerant, who are cramming their opinions down people's throats.

To go by the biblical standard of moderation.

Left and right don't have open minds; it's their way or no way.

To not rock the boat in a strong discussion between opinionated people. Left and right are assertive, certain of their own opinions.

To be in the middle is to reconcile and balance people. It's a general principle of behaviour, not just politics. I don't like arguments which are on extremes.

Note too that comments coded exclusively as partisan competition also echo the centre principle: 'left/right is to be partisan extremes; centre is to vote for the issues.' They were in the conceptual ballpark of conventionally defined politics, but abhorred competitive partisanship. Remember, too, that, on an earlier question measuring partisanship, farm women generally wished that their politicians shared the same desire for amiable cooperation. Several responses within this residual category articulated an active–passive contrast, which also echoes a moral preference for the centre principle. This contrast defined 'right' as active and 'left' as passive. Women who gave this type of definition were less eager to suppress arguments and competition among 'rightists,' but they were 'leftists' who just didn't want to get involved or disqualified themselves as inadequate to join the fray:

Right is more dominant and has more say. Left is the prohibited group which may want to get involved, but has no elected position. I'm left because I'm just a farm wife. To rise up in the [PC] party would be to go to the right.

Right is to be more outgoing and to speak up in public. Left is to keep to yourself, to not speak up.

Right feels strongly about the country and government; right is active and interested in politics. Left has no interest at all.

Right is more intelligent. Left is less intelligent. Centre is the average person.

These comments are conventionally political if farm wives are using 'right' in the sense that right-wing parties and opinions did indeed dominate in the 1980s. But the point is that respondents here applied a narrowly political contrast as a general principle to describe human relations and individual dispositions. Like the centre principle, moreover, the active–passive contrast scarcely distinguishes between politics and domesticity. For example, the first woman quoted made no distinction between rivalry among party activists in her local riding association and rivalry at home between her husband and three teenaged sons.

A relatively coherent set of principles about conflict and conciliation may be grounded in the domestic dynamics of farm households. Farm households are vulnerable to particular tensions and stresses – unpredictable weather, financial risk, enormous capital investments, dangerous equipment, and relative isolation from neighbours – which wives/mothers, it has been observed elsewhere, are expected to mediate among family members (Kohl 1976, 107; Rosenblatt and Anderson 1981, 162). They occupy pivotal positions, managing much of the communication in households where the emotional baggage carried by parents, children, and siblings come to bear on the mundane distribution of labour and complex financial decisions. In their conceptualization of the terms 'left' and 'right,' women expressed a preference for the centre as a general moral and political principle of behaviour. What has been called here the centre principle makes sense in terms of women's position in farm households; the dynamics of agricultural production place women at the hub of a family wheel where spokes are flying off in different directions. Respondents' answers bring up images of big belligerent men arguing raucously while women retreat to the kitchen. Along with pride in women's role as conciliator, elements of fear and inadequacy emerge. At its best, the 'centre principle' verges on liberal tolerance, and at its worse it prohibits open conflict and discussion. Although it seems to recognize diversity and promote respect for differences among individuals, it also seeks to dispel dissension in order to produce a desired state of harmony rather than actively assert differences.[16]

TABLE 4.11   Averages of six characteristics by meaning of 'left'/'right'

Characteristic	Usual definition	Reversed definition	Affective definition	Don't know
Housework hours	30	53	41	35
Farm labour score	.23	−.16	.18	−.17
Internal admin. score	.67	−.14	−.10	−.29
External admin. score	.58	−.13	−.07	−.26
Mechanical work score	.31	−.35	−.14	.05
Wife's education	6.8	6.0	5.6	5.3

Calculations were done to see if the left/right categories derived from the open-ended responses were associated with demographic and farm characteristics. In table 4.11, usual partisan and ideological definitions are combined into a single category; reversed definitions are likewise combined. A consistent pattern emerges in table 4.11: women giving usual definitions do less housework (30 hours per week) and overall more farmwork; women giving reversed definitions do much more housework (53 hours per week) and scarcely any farmwork; and women giving no definition do not seem to do much of anything. Women giving affective definitions are somewhat between these two poles; they do considerable housework (41 hours per week) and considerable farm labour. Skill with conventional left/right concepts rises directly with a wife's education.

The same pattern that was seen with political involvement is repeated here: farm administration is associated with political skills, whereas housework is not. When farm women do farm income tax, read farm journals, and decipher government regulations, what they learned about left/right in school is reinforced. The schism between farm administration and housework in regard to left/right shows again that an orientation to homemaking marginalizes women most from conventional politics (Sapiro 1983, 130, 180–1). Women giving affective definitions are not much better educated than those who said nothing, but the combination of intensive housework and farm labour results in, what I have called, the centre principle.

In women's preference for the 'centre' as an ordering principle, we are perhaps witnessing a political correlate of women's household situation whereby they assimilated questions about left/right beliefs (about which they were largely ignorant) into their pre-existing preference for the centre. At a higher level of generality, Jean Laponce's notion of left/right beliefs as 'archetypes' might be able to incorporate the explanation proposed here for farm women's apparently idiosyncratic conceptualizations. One may only speculate that this research has begun to uncover evidence in the mass population of specifically domestic opposition to the antagonistic and combative left/right archetypes that characterize our political affairs (Laponce 1981, 206-9). The centre principle might not qualify as uniquely agrarian but is instead accentuated by the particular features of farm households.[17]

POLITICAL PARTICIPATION

Democratic theory proposes that membership in secondary organizations of civil society is critical to democratic citizenship and participation.[18] The voluntary associations of civil society occupy a middle ground between government and private households. They draw people out from their own private lives to find common ground with their neighbours, where they learn to appreciate the close connection between private profit and the general interest. Apart from associations that directly criticize government legislation, all groups contribute to a 'public space' where people can criticize and debate without fearing social reprisals and where they can build solidarity to resist outside pressures to conform. By thus organizing political participation, civil associations defend the autonomy of diverse communities against the possibly despotic power of public opinion and government (Huntington 1968, 86; Tocqueville 1969 [1848], 690-701).

Farm women do their share for democracy because are great joiners. In her study of Saskatchewan, Seena Kohl found that the majority of farm/ranch wives belonged to at least one organization and many were far more active (1976, 40-1). Rachel Rosenfeld's extensive database revealed that 74 per cent of American farm women belonged to at least on organization; the largest block (61 per cent) belonged to a community organization such as a church group, PTA, or League of Women Voters (1985).[19] The present study's focus on WI members raises the prominence of organizations, since on average WI members were involved in at least three organizations; however, even non-members were involved in at least two organizations. WI averages were: member, 3.6 organizations; volunteer, 2.9 organizations; officer, 1.6 organizations. Non-WI averages were: member, 2.6 organizations; volunteer, 2.3 organizations; officer, 1.2 organizations. On average, WI members gave four to five hours a week to volunteering in comparison with non-members, who gave two to three hours.

The relatively greater participation reported by WI members can be explained in terms of the organization's bureaucratic structure. As its motto claims, the Women's Institutes work 'For Home and Country.' Neighbourhood branches are organized into districts, areas, and provinces. A national coordinating body, the Federated Women's Institutes of Canada (FWIC), belongs to the Associated Country Women of the World (ACWW), founded in 1929.[20] The provincial executive, the Federated Women's Institute of Ontario (FWIO), lobbies government for resolutions that have travelled up, in principle, from individual members. Complex organizational structure, abundance of officers, and adherence to parliamentary procedure are typical of long-established women's service organizations. Rather than intimidating or excluding members, the numerous offices to be filled in the complex WI hierarchical structure exert pressure on everyone to hold almost every position, at the branch and district level, at one time or another. For that very reason, two women decided not to join an Institute:

Nothing critical against them, but it's too time-consuming. I prefer to keep my own house in order. WI expects everyone to be a spokesman and leader. I'm not comfortable with public speaking, which is required in WI. I like to help on my own.

They, especially my mother-in-law, want me to join so that I could be a leader. If I joined, I'd be pushed into all the offices.

The WI's complex hierarchical structure is a evident burden on members, but it at least manages to avoid the opposite problem of 'free riding.' Free riding tends to happen in unstructured groups, where shirkers rely on a few unelected volunteers to do all the work without receiving any formal credit.

Taking volunteering as a more accurate indicator of active involvement than membership, which may be passive, table 4.12 lists organizations in order of popularity among urban Canadian and European women.[21] Whereas European women favoured, in order, churches (16 per cent), sports clubs (14 per cent), and community groups (10 per cent) for membership, Canadian women were active members of, in order, sports clubs (20 per cent), education or arts groups (18 per cent), and churches (16 per cent). Farm women, in comparison, were much

TABLE 4.12   Active membership (CES and farm wives) and membership (Europe)

Membership	CES 1984 (%)	Europe (%)	Farm wives (%)
Churches/religious organizations			
(UCW)	16	16	77
Women's organizations	.2	7	63
Youth groups (4-H, scouts, guides)	5	4	44
Community or service groups			
(Fair Board)	4	10	40
Sports clubs	20	14	13
Education or arts groups	18	6	10
Unions/professional societies	7	8	9
Other (assistance, fund-raising)	10	4	8
Political movements or parties	6	4	3
Animal rights/welfare,			
environment	–	4	2
Entertainment/social groups	13	–	–
Charitable organizations	11	–	–
Ethnic or cultural groups	3	–	–
Volunteer organization	10	–	–
Public interest groups	3	–	–
(N)	(1,724)	(9,790)	(117)

SOURCES: Canadian Election Study 1984; Commission of European Communities 1984, 152.

more involved in organizations. Excluding women's organizations, farm women volunteered for, in order, churches (77 per cent), youth groups (44 per cent), and community groups (40 per cent). Only when it comes to the fourth most popular type, sports groups, are farm memberships on the same scale between 13 and 20 per cent.

Membership in professional organizations was especially passive; thirty-four members quickly reduced to seven volunteers and five officers in professional organizations compared with twenty-seven members, thirty volunteers, and twenty-two officers in community organizations. High involvement in women's organizations reflects the majority's membership in WI and should not be taken as representative. But we can still say that farm wives are far more involved than urban women in their local communities. In comparison, not many Canadian women do volunteer work in religious organizations (16 per cent), youth groups (5 per cent), or community groups (4 per cent).

For many farm wives and local politicians in particular, political participation has qualities other than the instrumental achievement of public-policy goals for private profit. If participation is a useful instrument for achieving personal financial advantages, one can be said to have an 'instrumental' orientation to politics. In contrast, many of the farm wives interviewed here might be said to have an 'expressive' orientation, which is characterized by a lack of conventionally defined 'political motivation' (Barnes and Kaase 1979, 527). In other words, they do not pursue an instrumentalist program for personal or group advantage; if pressed, they might not be able to articulate reasons for participation other than to cite self-expression or sociability. An expressive orientation might be called 'existential' if one wishes to claim that political participation, quite apart from its substantive content, may potentially bring out the very best in people and give rise to specifically political capacities and joys that cannot otherwise be achieved in private households.[22]

The reasons women gave for belonging to the Women's Institutes attest to an expressive orientation to participation in civil associations. Some women acquired very practical and transferable skills such as parliamentary procedure in WI:

WI gave me my start in Fair Board. The WI structure, which includes parliamentary procedure, teaches you to belong to other organizations. The provincial executive of the Fair Board uses it, and I was ready. You can pick out WI women by their skilled use of parliamentary procedure at meetings.

In WI you learn to take responsibility in holding office.

They did not, however, cite financial advantages to learning these skills. Women also reported strictly expressive rewards of self-development and autonomy for membership in a WI. These specific rewards are available only from collective political activities. One middle-aged woman laughed, somewhat perplexed by her own preferences: 'I really enjoy formal meetings. I go to all the rallies, conventions.' Women's responses attest to the emergence of qualities beyond the acquisition of administrative skills; we can speculate with interest as to what the woman cited below can have meant, for instance, by a 'person.'

I learned to be a *person* in WI, to speak up with confidence.

To get out of the house and do something for myself.

WI led to me being poll clerk, enumeration. It helped me to get up nerve to do things. I used to get in a sweat about doing things. You just have to go do it!

Doing the babysitting course was a big accomplishment for me. I had three helpers, but it was me who got the speakers and handed out awards at the graduation ceremony, which was very tense for me. I was forced to do it, but it was good for me.

I didn't think I could do it, but being [WI] president gave me more confidence in myself.

One woman claimed that the government heeded WI policy resolutions, but not one person belonged to the WI in order to achieve specific legislative or policy changes. In contrast, another respondent quit the WI because she was fed up with catering and wanted to become involved in policy issues with the Jersey Club: 'It's a common interest with my husband and relates to the money side of things. After all Jerseys are our livelihood.' Another woman who is active in the Ontario Racing Commission explained: 'the WI just 'chats.' I don't want a women's group. I want to share activities with my husband and prefer mixed groups.' Women get involved in agricultural/commodity organizations as part of a couple; they do not attend these meetings without a male escort, whereas they might attend women's meetings on their own. When membership is joint, as a couple, instrumental activities relating to private financial goals become more salient.

It would be analytically tidy if the quantitative model of organizational involvement corresponded to the distinction made in chapter 1 between 'old' and 'new' farm women – namely, that between WI members and non-members. That distinction can be discerned, to a certain extent, from table 4.13. Two significant features set WI members apart; they are significantly older and less well educated. Their lower levels of education are not simply an artefact of their relative age because the quantitative technique controls for, and thus distinguishes, the unique influence of education apart from age. Even given the preponderance of older WI members, strikingly more WI members had not gone beyond high school. At almost significant levels, WI membership is predicted by farm labour and internal administration. This is worth noting because volunteering works significantly in the opposite direction from farm labour. Unlike the case in the United States, there is no evidence that women who had grown up on farms were

TABLE 4.13   Determinants of Women's Institute membership and volunteering[23]

Determinants	WI member	Volunteer hours/week
Farm labour score	.09	−1.24*
Internal administration score	.09	–
Mechanical work score	–	1.09*
Wife's age	.01**	.05
Wife's education	−.07*	–
Farmer father	–	.92
Dairy farm	–	1.51
Egg/poultry farm	–	2.17
Livestock farm	–	−9.31
R Square	.17	.16
Adjusted R Square	.13	.10
(N)	(110)	(108)

*p < .05   **p < .01

more likely than were urban expatriates to belong to community groups and enrol in domestic-extension courses (Rosenfeld 1985, 214). This suggests that the Women's Institutes, despite similarities, are not exactly Canadian analogues to domestic-extension courses, and have an appeal other than traditional crafts and homemaking. Neither is there evidence that WI members are among the rural and agriculture élite; membership is not predicted by the usual correlates of capital value such as acreage, employees hired, or husband's employment.

Indeed, snobbery may prevent better-educated and wealthier women from associating with WI members. One woman interviewed illustrates tensions and continuities between 'new' and 'old' farm women. She had met her husband at university, where they both had acquired professional graduate degrees. She had married into perhaps the most prosperous and well-respected family in the township. She did not belong to the local Junior Institute, even though its members were all her own age and she admitted to being lonely, because she would be too embarrassed if anyone at university – her former classmates or professors – ever found out. She worked for a major publication and justified her career in terms of the farm enterprise: 'Even though I'm away working, it's for the farm really instead of my career. It's not just the money; it's the contacts and the information that I bring to help out the farm.' Although her primary commitment was to the family enterprise, her options were restricted because she 'wanted to do something which no other [member of her husband's family] in this town had done before' – thereby cutting herself off from farm-related activities, which were monopolized by her father- and brothers-in-law.

The second column of table 4.13 shows that intensity of volunteer work is significantly predicted by mechanical work and not doing farm labour. The results thus identify a particular type of woman who is not tied down to milking cows or watering livestock and who does mechanical work instead. Since volunteer work – whether in rural or urban communities – requires more administrative than mechanical skills, it cannot be that women do volunteer work by donating mechanical repairs. Instead, it is more plausible that mechanical skills give women credentials and prestige for community involvement. What might really count in rural communities is the ability to talk knowledgeably about conventionally masculine subjects – what machinery costs and how to fix it.

In sum, farm wives reported higher levels of political involvement (salience and efficacy) and much greater participation in voluntary organizations than did predominantly urban women of Canada and Europe. Like housewives, they were less partisan than were employed workers. Their ability to conceptualize the meaning of 'politics' was adequate, but they demonstrated less skill with concepts of 'left' and 'right.' Their conceptualization of left/right, however, revealed evidence of a generalized moral preference for conciliation and consensus over polarized conflict. Previous studies found that rural people participate more in political and community affairs, especially after accounting for scant socio-economic resources (Verba, Nie, and Kim 1978, 269–85). Ontario farm women bear this out; their political involvement and participation were higher than warranted by their low levels of partisanship and conceptual sophistication, and by their educational and financial resources. An agrarian myth of farmers' moral superiority was proposed to explain their resolute confidence about being able to understand and have an impact on politics. It is perhaps on these grounds that democratic theorists and activists can locate allies among farm women whose commitment to their local community and whose trust in local, personally known politicians intersects with recent enthusiasm for participatory, non-partisan politics.

5

Conservatism

My mother had grown up in a time and in a place where sex was a dark undertaking for women. She knew that you could die of it. So she honored the decency, the prudery, the frigidity that might protect you. And I grew up in horror of that very protection, the dainty tyranny that seemed to extend to all areas of life, to enforce tea parties and wear white gloves, and all sorts of tinkling inanities. The odd thing is that my mother's ideas were in line with some progressive notions of her time, and mine echoed the notions that were favoured in my time. This in spite of the fact that we both lived in backwaters that did not register such changes. It's as if tendencies that seem most deeply rooted in our minds, most private and singular, have come in as spores on the prevailing wind, looking for any likely place to land, any welcome. (Munro 1990, 22)

Now that the basic forms of politicization have been established, it remains to flesh out the political substance of farm women's participation. As one woman said proudly: 'Women's Institute resolutions give women a voice in changing the community and government policy. Government is very aware of WI resolutions, listens to WI.' What are the goals of farm women's participation? According to liberal modernization theory, the unwelcome spectre of a reactionary rural backlash against urban-based innovation arises to cast suspicion on farm women's enthusiasm for community involvement. This chapter examines four aspects of conservatism from liberal modernization theory – election results, environmentalism, church attendance, and attitudes towards sexual morality and abortion – to see what impact farm women might have on public policy when they lobby government or are elected to public office. Feminism is also related to conservatism and has public-policy consequences; it is discussed in chapter 6.

Respondents were asked for whom they voted in the 1987 Ontario and the 1988 Canadian elections. Fieldwork was concentrated in Grey and Huron counties, whose boundaries overlap conveniently with electoral districts. The units for provincial elections are also named Grey and Huron, and county boundaries are identical with election boundaries. Canadian elections include adjacent Bruce County to form two ridings, Huron–Bruce and Bruce–Grey. Official results from polling stations where interviews had been concentrated were selected for in-depth examination in order to assess how this sample of farm wives voted in comparison with others in their townships.[1]

In the 1987 Ontario provincial election (two years earlier than the survey), the Liberal party, led by David Peterson, won an easy election victory throughout Ontario. In Grey District, the Liberal candidate (Ron Lipsett) won 41 per cent of the vote, which was distributed evenly throughout the townships where interviews were conducted. In Huron District, the incumbent Liberal member (Jack Ridell) was easily re-elected, with 60 per cent of the vote; he was less popular at the north end of the district than in his home area in the south end, where he was given up to 73 per cent of the vote. Although only 58 per cent of eligible voters turned out in selected Grey County townships, and 65 per cent in selected Huron townships, where interviews had been concentrated, almost all farm women (92 per cent) reported voting. Of those who remembered how they had voted two years earlier (20 per cent could not), almost two-thirds voted Liberal, a third voted Progressive Conservative (PC), and only two people voted New Democrat (NDP).

The 1988 'Free Trade' federal election had occurred the previous autumn and was much clearer in people's memories. It was also more closely contested. Bruce–Grey riding gave PC candidate Gus Mitges 41 per cent of the vote, less than a thousand votes over the Liberal candidate. Huron–Bruce riding elected PC candidate Murray Cardiff, with 42 per cent of the vote. Voter turnout was higher for this election, ranging from 70 to 80 per cent in selected townships, compared with 93 per cent of farm wives who reported voting. Of farm wives who remembered (12 per cent could not), a little more than half (52 per cent) voted PC; somewhat fewer (39 per cent) voted Liberal; seven people voted NDP; and two people voted for the Christian Heritage Party. In both Ontario and Canadian elections, therefore, farm wives' support for Liberal and PC candidates roughly corresponded to actual votes cast in those electoral districts and specific polling booths in townships where interviews had been concentrated.

Outside of directly asking, it is impossible to know why people vote as they do, but that Ontario farmers voted PC at all in the 1988 Canadian election is surprising. Indeed, the farm wives interviewed here showed a slightly higher preference for PC candidates (4–5 per cent) than did their fellow constituents in this election. A Conservative vote in 1988 has often been interpreted as a vote for the Canada–U.S. Free Trade Agreement, which the Ontario Liberal government argued would be detrimental to all Ontario agriculture, particularly dairy and poultry sectors currently protected by supply management systems (Ontario Ministry of Agriculture and Food 1988). Despite warnings to the contrary, farmers throughout Canada generally favoured the Free Trade Agreement and voted Conservative in 1988. Debate over Free Trade's consequences for agriculture is not the whole picture because this pattern conforms to an archaic religious cleavage in Canadian partisanship – namely, the Conservative party's tenacious hold on votes in Protestant, and especially rural, Ontario (Johnston et al. 1992, 88, 285n).

Farm wives' lack of support for NDP candidates is way out of proportion in relation to the election districts as a whole. In the 1987 Ontario election, proportionally fewer farm wives voted NDP: whereas NDP candidates actually received 14–17 per cent of the vote throughout the Huron and Grey ridings, only 2 per cent of farm wives voted for either candidate. Likewise, in the 1988 Canadian election, 6 per cent of farm wives sampled voted NDP, which represents only a third of the number of votes the NDP candidates in the two ridings of Huron–Bruce and Bruce–Grey received. In other words, farm women were three times less likely to vote NDP federally and seven times less likely to vote NDP provincially than were voters in the towns and villages of rural Huron and Grey counties, let alone urban voters. This disproportion cannot be attributed to the survey's preponderance of WI members because, of nine NDP votes cast, six belonged to WI members.

Farm wives' apparent aversion to the NDP may not be stable, judging from the 1990 Ontario election, when fourteen of twenty-five genuinely rural ridings went to the New Democrats.[2] In the 1990 Ontario election, NDP candidate Paul Klopp was elected in Huron County, winning 34 per cent of votes cast, evenly distributed throughout the county, including rural townships. Klopp was a local pig farmer who had stood for the NDP in the preceding provincial election in 1987; he had come in third, with a mere 14 per cent of votes cast. Grey County elected Conservative candidate Bill Murdoch (also a farmer), who had come a close second in the preceding 1987 election.

Rural Ontario victories for the provincial NDP in the 1990 Ontario election suggest that antagonism to female candidates, rather than simply antagonism to the NDP, might have been a factor in past Grey County elections. Grey County elected Agnes Macphail, Canada's first woman member of Parliament, a member of the United Farmers of Ontario, and a founder of the Co-operative Commonwealth Federation in 1921, and re-elected her until 1940 (*Canadian Encyclopedia* 1985, 1068-9). But more recent voters in Grey County have consistently rejected female NDP candidates; only women have been recent NDP candidates in this county. As noted earlier, just nine votes among this sample were cast for NDP candidates, disproportionately fewer than expected from the distribution of votes in their particular ridings. Were farm women in particular, and Grey County in general, rejecting the NDP, or were they rejecting Cathy Hird and Peggy Hutchison, who ran unsuccessfully for the NDP in Grey County in the 1987, 1988, and 1990 elections?

ENVIRONMENTALISM

This suggestion that I was not poor any more brought a look of reproach and aloofness into my aunt's face. [The aunts] stared back at me with grave accusing Protestant faces, for I had run up against the simple unprepossessing materialism which was the rock of their lives. Things must be used; everything must be used up, saved and mended and made into something else and used again. (Munro 1968, 206)

Indicators taken from electoral and partisan politics are no longer adequate measures of conservatism because new social movements have broadened the scope of what counts as 'political.' Support for ecological and environmental issues is perhaps the best proof of the new social movements' ability to transcend conventional political categories. From dual poles of left and right, the old order promoted unlimited economic growth through industrialization, be it financed collectively through socialist governments or privately through capitalist corporations. But environmentalism argues that there are limits to economic growth because industrialization, by definition, consumes the earth's finite supply of natural resources.

Farm women display a remarkable enthusiasm for environmentalist

TABLE 5.1 Farm wives willing to get involved in activity

Activity	Frequency (%)
Protecting the environment, fight against pollution	82
Setting up a day-care centre	42
Setting up a birth-control centre	41
(N)	(117)

activities. Table 5.1 shows that respondents were virtually unanimous in their willingness to get involved in environmental projects, and far less willing to get involved in other projects. The relevant questions stressed that one would 'get involved, not just support' and that the hypothetical activity would be in their own community with familiar neighbours. That almost half of women interviewed would get involved in either day-care or birth-control centres is impressive on its own, but this comparison highlights the particular appeal of environmentalist projects broadly defined.

The questions posed to Ontario farm women regarding involvement in environmental activities were specifically project oriented, and hence more demanding than Euro-Barometer questions asking for approval of and willingness to join ecology movements. Table 5.2 shows farm wives' responses to the Euro-Barometer question 'What is your opinion of the current movements who objectives are to protect the environment, to fight against pollution?,' along with responses to a similar question concerning the women's movement.

Again farm women were virtually unanimous in their positive appraisal of environmental movements. Only 9 per cent expressed a poor opinion of environmentalism as a political movement. Those few criticized animal-rights activists and alarmists who panicked about Alar spray on apples and antibiotics given to livestock. These women had a rather poor opinion of the movement which they perceived as an urban, fringe threat to agriculture. Of course, they were all in favour of environmental practices – 'Didn't farmers care more about their land and livestock than anybody else?' – but responded negatively to the political movement. Their astute political judgment highlights that their more enthusiastic neighbours probably did not conceive of environmentalism in terms of alliance with urban social movements, but rather as a program entirely identified with their way of life.

TABLE 5.2   Farm wives' opinion of environmental and women's liberation movements

Frequency	Environmental (%)	Women's liberation (%)
Very high opinion	44	1
Quite a good opinion	46	44
Rather poor opinion	9	41
Very bad opinion	0	3
Can't say	1	10
(N)	(117)	(117)

One might imagine that the present sample's slight majority of WI members would produce a bias because the WI's agenda centred on environmental issues during the late 1980s. A 'call to green' at the Federated Women's Institutes of Ontario (FWIO) 1988 annual conference exceeded the provincial executive's expectation when it prompted about three hundred local recycling and waste-management projects across Ontario.[3] Members of one WI district (one-quarter of a county) collected and sorted from forty recycling bins throughout the area, and in eleven months they netted over 10 tons of steel and 1.5 tons of aluminum; an individual branch collected 0.5 ton of aluminum a month, and almost all branches worked closely with township councils to press for and implement recycling programs.[4] These projects have given the organization new life and prominence.[5] Policy makers credit the WI for contributing to the increased profile of environmental issues and sustainable agriculture throughout the agricultural policy community (Burt 1992). The Recycling Council of Ontario named the Federated Women's Institutes of Ontario 'outstanding organization of the year' for 1991 in regards to promoting ecological activities. Cross-tabulation of WI membership with willingness to get involved in fighting pollution, however, showed no strong relationship. Apparently, the high degree of willingness to get involved corresponds to a genuine conviction among the farm population at large. The FWIO could not have mobilized its cumbersome bureaucracy and membership so easily if concern about the environment was not already widely latent in rural Ontario.

In a relevant analysis, the environmentalist version of social change bypasses the industrial working classes, which are no longer agents of revolutionary change, still preoccupied as they are with the production and distribution of material wealth. Instead, the revolutionary agents of environmentalism are said to be chiefly among the new middle class of professionals preoccupied with personal fulfilment.[6] A subsidiary role is identified for farmers and housewives as potential allies, because they are only peripherally attached to the labour market (Offe 1987, 78). Because neither farmers nor housewives work for wages, their labour is decommodified; their self-employed experience thus stands apart from the dominant feature of capitalist life (being dependent on a hierarchical management system for wage increases and job security).[7] By this logic, contemporary farmers are not roused to bargain for better commodity prices, but rather to ally, for example, with the ecology movement to oppose nuclear power plants and sprawling urbanization (Offe 1987, 130n).

Furthermore, calls for 'sustainable agriculture' bring farming into the mainstream of the environmental movement. The strictest version of sustainable agriculture proposes to replace large-scale, industrial, petroleum-driven agriculture with more traditional forms of husbandry, including a return to draught animals. The general principle of sustainable agriculture is to extend subsistence practices in a self-regulating ecosystem encompassing and recycling waste material among livestock, soil, wildlife, people, and crops (Giangrande 1985, 148–67; Jackson, Berry, and Colman 1984). One organic farmer, 'decommodified' his product by pointing out how an apple is connected to larger environmental concerns: 'People buy food, not a bag of soil, so it's hard for them to connect a bright red apple with the breakdown of the ozone or the village well being polluted with chemicals' ('Integration of the farm,' *Rural Voice*, Mar. 1990, 29). The practice of sustainable agriculture in family enterprise, with its goal of drawing a living wage in equilibrium with the environment's resources rather than accumulating capital for economic growth, implicitly challenges capitalism. As food becomes ever cheaper and more plentiful, the production and sale of commodities become increasingly subordinated to farmers' role as stewards of the rural landscape. This sort of analysis proposes that farmers and housewives might be more critical of the established order than expected, based on their 'decommodified' or 'peripheral' relation to capitalist labour markets.[8]

Farm wives' responses highlight a spontaneous enthusiasm for environmentalism quite apart from alliances with or prodding from urban social movements. One turns, therefore, to the possibility that their particular situation gives rise to support for environmental issues. The ideology and practice of domestic labour might be fundamentally

compatible with environmentalism. It is a small step from the traditional concerns of home economics and women's magazines – hygiene,
sanitation, nutrition, and overall health of family members, particularly children – to an environmental agenda.[9] The same logic that
prompted first-wave feminists to acquire the franchise to implement
temperance and other social reforms is at work here too: to secure
domestic good by political means and to secure political good guided
by domestic values and motives. For example, a FWIC president an-
nounced that women must take the lead in environmental protection
because 'women are gentle, kind, and caring. Women have naturally
been the managers and preservers of the home ... and of our natural
resources' (*Western Producer*, 18 Jul. 1991, 59). The principles of domestic management thus expand to include waste management in the
local community. Environmentalism, moreover, may be especially
compelling for Ontario farm women because it corresponds to a fundamental Protestant materialism that holds thrift to be morally good
for its own sake.

Local recycling and waste-management projects are 'housewife'
issues because housewives, along with farmers, are still engaged in
production of use values – a practice that is at odds with the dominant
capitalist production of disposable consumer goods. Although subsistence production in households varies widely among income groups,
the basic principle is that food produced at home is more likely to
be consumed, and its excess recycled, than is food produced for exchange in restaurants. Very few concrete environmental practices of
everyday life are not simultaneously domestic practices that women
still tend to be responsible for. For example, the concrete practices
that count as environmentalist – buying bottled water or filtering tap
water, buying phosphate-free detergent, using paper rather than plastic
grocery bags, and recycling newspapers – are all domestic decisions
that women, even employed women, still tend to be responsible for.
One wonders what environmental practices men would be especially
likely to do, apart from using a push lawnmower or disposing properly
of discarded oil after changing the oil of one's car at home. Whether
done by women or men, good housekeeping is fundamentally compatible with an environmental agenda. This argument works equally
well for urban women too. An Ontario study found, in fact, that being
female correlated better than did socio-economic status to increased
levels of support for environmentalist movements and practices (Mac-
Dermid and Stevenson 1990, 15).

CHURCH ATTENDANCE

Documentation for farm women's alleged conservatism begins from conventional political indicators and proceeds to social indicators of church attendance and sexual morality, including birth control and attitudes towards abortion. The political significance of women's religiosity only makes sense in the context of European history. Women's religiosity put them on the conservative side of history, alongside the allied forces of the *ancien regime* – the landed aristocracy and the Roman Catholic church – that battled modernizing and secular republicans. In France, for example, women's enfranchisement was delayed until 1945, largely because ruling Republican and Socialist parties feared the partisan consequences of women's religiosity. Successive secular Republic and Socialist governments feared that, if women were enfranchised, they would vote en masse, as directed by the Roman Catholic church, against secular ruling parties (Hause with Kennedy 1984). According to such interpretations, women, for a variety of good and not-so-good reasons, affiliated with the Roman Catholic church and consequently gave their support to religiously linked parties of the right. However, as European women entered the work force and acquired higher education, their religiosity declined and, subsequently, their electoral behaviour has become balanced among all parties (Mossuz-Lavau and Sineau 1981).

This once-standard explanation for women's conservatism should be revised by Mattei Dogan's sympathetic assessment of social Catholicism as 'more responsive to the claims of disadvantaged social groups and more open to social change than [secular] parties' (1955, 165, cited in Black 1989, 169). The connection between religion and right-wing conservatism is even less plausible for Protestant countries where, for example, British working-class women also voted for parties of the right on different grounds than religion (Hart 1989). In English Canada, political parties have had no formal religious affiliation, and the historical impact of the social gospel in the Progressive Movement (similar to that of social Catholicism) at the turn of the nineteenth century, and in the origin of the CCF, reduces the possibility that religion is necessarily equated with political conservatism. Indeed, a classic text on the subject concludes that Protestant sects were probably 'the medium by which the multitude of social programmes making up the Canadian welfare state first found their way into social attitudes' (Allen 1971, 352). Historical evidence from Europe and Canada indeed

modifies modernization theory because religiosity is not always associated with conservative politics. But religion scarcely corresponds any
longer to formal partisanship in North America and Europe; either
every politician claims to be religious (as in the United States) or else
religion is irrelevant. Therefore, this section investigates conservatism
further by seeing if church attendance corresponds to conservative
views on sexual morality.

Although church attendance is a standard measure of religiosity,
and hence social conservatism, it should be revised, as Inglehart suggests, because 'religious practice is shaped by family ties, habits and
social milieu' (1990, 184). For example, Republican Irish whose attendance rates are highest rank average on religiosity when asked,
'Would you describe yourself as a religious person?' (Inglehart 1990,
191). Obviously, people may attend church more from sociability and
habit than from personal spirituality. And if people attend church
often enough, they are bound to pick up that denomination's attitude
to politics, social change, and family, but researchers are better off
asking questions directly about those topics.[10] Keeping those reserva-
tions in mind, therefore, it is noted that all Canadians are remarkably
frequent churchgoers. Canadians report higher attendance rates (45
per cent attend at least once a month) than secular western Europeans.
The United States (60 per cent) and South Africa (61 per cent) are
the only Protestant countries to report higher rates. But Ontario farm
women put other Protestants to shame because they apparently attend
church at the same rate as Mexicans (75 per cent) and not much less
than Republican Irish (88 per cent), both of which are traditional
Roman Catholic populations (Inglehart 1990, 200).[11]

As table 5.3 shows, the combined figure of those farm women who
attended at least once a month (79 per cent) is remarkably high compared with that of all Canadians, of whom fewer than half (45 per
cent or 37 per cent) attended that often in 1980-2, according to either
Inglehart (1990, 200) or Bibby (1987, 76). And Ontario farm wives did
more than just attend church; in addition to universal membership,
77 per cent volunteered for church activities and 30 per cent held office.
On average, only 35 per cent of Canadians held membership in a local
church or group in 1985 (Bibby 1987, 107) and far fewer Canadians
(13 per cent) were at all active in a religious organization (Election
Study 1984).

Billboards along the roads of southwestern Ontario announce sal-
vation and damnation, but the 'social milieu' that fosters church at-

TABLE 5.3   Church attendance

Frequency	Ontario farm wives
At least once a week	47%
Once or twice a month	32%
Occasionally for religious holidays	9%
Only for ceremonies (wedding, funeral)	11%
Never	1%
(N)	(117)
	Canadians
Weekly	28%
Monthly	9%
Yearly	44%
Never	19%
(N)	(1,295)

SOURCE: Project Canada 1980 (Bibby 1987, 76).

tendance as a sociable activity (Inglehart 1990, 184) might also include
the conditions of agricultural and domestic labour. For farmers and
women who do not have paid employment, church is a welcomed opportunity to get dressed up and get out of the house at least once
a week. Church attendance and sabbath observance might also appeal
to farmers and housewives because such religious obligations impose
structured leisure on an unending cycle of self-regulated labour. Inglehart inadvertently justifies these formal observances of religiosity
when he argues that Judaeo-Christian tradition reflects an agriculturalist world view and is thus no longer compelling for post-industrial
societies; by implication therefore, its traditional observances remain
compelling for agriculturalist societies (1990, 179–80).

ATTITUDES TOWARDS SEXUAL MORALITY AND ABORTION

Since Western religions have always placed restrictions on human, and
particularly female, sexuality, strict views on sexual morality also mark
religiosity, and thus political conservatism. In asking respondents to
differentiate between men and women, this study tapped a further element of traditional sexual morality – namely, the 'double standard'
that gives licence to men but not women. The first question here asked
if sexual relations were acceptable for a young man or woman before
marriage or only after marriage. The only available exact counterparts

TABLE 5.4   Premarital and extramarital sexual relations

Frequency	For man (%)	For woman (%)	French man (%)	French woman (%)
	Sexual relations are acceptable ...			
Not before marriage	52	52	23	35
	For husband (%)	For wife (%)	French husband (%)	French wife (%)
	Marital infidelity is ...			
Normal	1	0	5	5
Forgivable	26	27	35	29
Unforgivable	70	69	49	55
Can't say	3	3	11	11
N	(117)	(117)		

SOURCE: Mossuz-Lavau and Sineau 1983, 64–5.

to this study's questions on sexual relations are the views of non-employed French women in 1978. Table 5.4 shows that just over half of farm respondents thought that young couples should wait until marriage to be sexually active. Considering that the French figures in the table represent the opinions of non-employed women voting for right-wing parties, who are themselves notably more strict on pre-marital sex than women voting for left-wing parties, Ontario women are strict indeed by comparison.

The question about extramarital infidelity posed three categories of marriage: open marriage, where infidelity is normal; semi-open confess-and-forgive marriage; and traditional marriage demanding life-long exclusiveness, where it is unforgivable. Overall, respondents' extreme disapproval of marital infidelity is not quite apparent in table 5.4 because respondents who chose the 'forgivable' answer maintained that Christians should forgive all sins, including marital infidelity. Farm wives' judgment was strict compared with that of non-employed French women, who were notably stricter than employed French women. Farm wives' judgment was also strict in comparison with that of 58 per cent of Canadians who, in 1981–2, thought that infidelity was never justifiable; and Canadians were notably strict, exceeded only by respondents in Denmark, Mexico, the United States, and the Two Irelands, in their disapproval (Inglehart 1990, 444). On another measure, this group of farm wives was not exceptionally strict: when Canadians were asked an abstract question of moral principle that

removed the elements of 'forgiveness' or 'justifiability,' 81 per cent of
the total, including 73 per cent of those religiously uncommitted,
thought that extramarital sexual affairs are wrong or almost always
wrong (Bibby 1987, 155). In so far as farm wives' responses displayed
little variation in an overwhelming verdict of 'unforgivable,' they at-
tested to considerable community consensus on the subject of marital
infidelity in rural Ontario.[12]

Birth control is not quite as compelling a matter of sexual morality
among Protestant denominations as among Roman Catholics, but it
is worth noting here that church attendance intersects with birth-
control practices through the common item of age. The same cohort
of older women who attended church more frequently were much the
same women who had relied on natural methods of birth control.
Women over fifty-five were significantly more likely than younger
women to have relied on natural as opposed to artificial (chemical,
surgical, mechanical) birth control. Ontario farm wives presumably
adopted artificial birth control in the 1950s. Their reliance on natural
birth control until so relatively recently is surprising; although dissemination of birth-control information was not legal until the 1960s,
previous research shows that rural Canadian women have practised
a variety of contraceptive methods since the beginning of the twentieth
century (McLaren and Tiger McLaren 1986, 29–30). Edward Shorter
spoke to pharmacists in rural Ontario who routinely administered
'apiol' abortifacients before the 1950s, after which time abortion became a surgical and medical procedure rather than a pharmaceutical
procedure (1982, 214–23).

Results relating to the abortion issue are just as surprising. The public consensus in southwestern Ontario is aggressively against abortion;
posters, talk-show hosts, and politicians denounce the pro-choice
movement as a communal enemy. But in private a number of farm
women do not go along with public consensus; almost half (41 per
cent) agreed that increased access to abortion constituted progress. If
the other 6 per cent who were torn on the issue decided to go over
to the 'abortion is progress' side, opponents would be evenly matched.
Direct comparisons for the abortion question asked here are difficult
to find in the many polls which tend to ask about particular policy
options. The straightforward question asked here puts abortion in the
context of modernization and attitudes to progress instead of, for example, the context of whether abortion should be recriminalized or

decriminalized, or if a hospital committee's permission should be required.[13] Comparable perhaps to those farm women opposing increased access to abortion are 46 per cent of Canadian women who say that abortion should never be permitted (Canadian Election Study 1988). Whereas rural populations (living in communities with populations of under ten thousand) are consistently more opposed to abortion rights, they are also consistently more undecided: indecision decreases as population size increases.[14]

RELATIONSHIPS AMONG ASPECTS OF CONSERVATISM

Church attendance and rural residence have elsewhere been found to correlate to strict views on sexual morality.[15] In these studies, churchgoers and self-identified fundamentalists held strict views, disapproving of both premarital and extramarital sex. This observation does not quite hold true among Ontario farm wives. The four aspects of conservatism were related to each other as shown in table 5.5.

While churches have opinions about all matters of sexual morality, table 5.5 shows that they have influence to repress only the one matter that is, for the churches, the least immoral – namely, premarital sex (-.38). Approval for premarital sex is also associated with increased access to abortion services. We may be seeing not so much the direct influence of church sermons on sexual morality as the indirect influence of age through both church attendance and sexual morality. Whereas farm wives answered without hesitation questions of sexual morality, they equivocated on abortion. Perhaps the question about abortion was difficult for them to answer because it veers into feminism, which these women found acutely embarrassing. Surprisingly, abortion does not correlate to church attendance (-.17); this suggests that the effect of church attendance weakens when the issue strays from sexuality to women's autonomy.

RELATIONSHIP OF CONSERVATISM TO FARM AND DEMOGRAPHIC
CHARACTERISTICS

What predicts such high church attendance among Ontario farm wives, relative not only to other Canadians, but to all Protestants? Contrary to popular belief, rural Canadians as a whole are no longer any more religious than urban Canadians, which leads one to seek a variation

TABLE 5.5   Correlations[16] among aspects of conservatism

	Church attendance	Approve premarital sex	Forgive extramarital sex	Access to Abortion
Church attend	1.00			
Premarital sex	−.38	1.00		
Extramarital sex	.04	−.06	1.00	
Access to abortion	−.17	.37	−.04	1.00

on the role of rural culture in Ontario (Bibby 1987, 92–4). The legacy of evangelical Protestantism and the social gospel in Ontario is found perhaps in the fact that religious habits, more so than convictions, are acquired in one's youth; adults may re-establish but rarely exceed levels of religious participation established in childhood (ibid, 237, 99).

Consistent with Bibby's observation of all Canadians, table 5.6 shows that one's father being a farmer is a very significant determinant of church attendance (as indicated by the asterisks in the corresponding table entries). In this sample of farm wives, attending church regularly is primarily a habit acquired in childhood while growing up in farm families. Paid employment significantly reduces church attendance, but this effect is deceptive. Employed women (most of whom were nurses) apologized and regretted that shiftwork made it difficult to get out to church every single week. When church attendance is recoded to at least once a month, working women attended nearly as often. The effect of agriculture is perplexing; farm labour reduces church attendance, while dairy and livestock operations increase attendance. This suggests that so long as somebody else in the household gets up to do chores on Sunday morning, women are quite willing to go to church. The absence of education further confirms that religion is a habit that is scarcely altered by one's acquired adult characteristics (Bibby 1987, 98).

With regard to sexual morality, one expects to see a generational shift, with women becoming less tolerant of sexual permissiveness, including penalty-free pregnancies, as they grow older. This is true for premarital sex, but not extramarital sex. Increased youth very significantly predicts approval for sex before marriage; increased age very significantly predicts forgiveness for sex outside marriage. In other words, older women 'forgave' infidelity more than did younger women.

TABLE 5.6   Determinants of conservatism[17]

Determinants	Good opinion of ecology	Church attendance	Approve youth sex	Forgive infidelity	Support access to abortion
Farm labour score	–	−.37**	–	–	.14*
Internal admin.	–	−.18	–	–	–
External admin.	−.16*	–	–	–	–
Mechanical work	–	–	−.15	−.13	–
Wife's age	.01	–	−.03**	.02**	–
Wife employed	–	−.67***	–	−.27	–
Farmer father	−.35*	.68***	−.25	–	−.17
Wife's education	–	–	−.08	–	–
People in household	.11	–	.13	–	–
Hours of housework	.00	–	–	–	–
Husband's education	–	.10	–	–	.03
Husband's housework	–	–	–	.06	−.03
Dairy farm	–	.48	−.35	–	−.46***
Livestock farm	–	.49*	–	–	–
Egg/poultry farm	–	–	−.51	–	−.23
Grain/crop farm	–	−.34	–	–	–
Extended-family	–	−.34	–	.40*	–
Farm acres	−.32	–	−.53*	–	–
Employees hired	–	.06	–	−.07*	–
R Square	.15	.32	.28	.22	.18
Adjusted R Square	.10	.25	.21	.17	.13
(N)	(104)	(110)	(112)	(107)	(113)

*p < .05   **p < .01   ***p < .001

A plausible explanation suggests that a romantic or companionate ideal of marriage prevails among younger women, which is compatible with premarital sex but is threatened by marital infidelity. Farming, too, is relevant. Fewer farm acres predicts approval for premarital sex. An extended-family enterprise and fewer employees hired significantly predict forgiveness in older women. Older women are perhaps more committed to the family enterprise than to the marriage itself and can therefore tolerate infidelity. The significance of hired employees might make sense if 'forgiveness' occurs on non-capitalist, extended-family enterprises that rely on family members (sons and sons-in-law) as their primary labour force. In this case, it is more important to secure their labour contribution to the enterprise than to secure romantic or companionate marriages that demand mutual sexual exclusiveness. This point is important because it may be an authentically petty-bourgeois sexual morality. Tolerance of marital infidelity is actually the more traditional pattern historically for families holding collective property to be passed on intact to the next generation. Divorce, which is the logical culmination of not forgiving infidelity, threatens this collective goal by dispersing family assets. Younger women who have not invested a lifetime of labour into those assets have yet to be socialized into this frame of mind. In comparison with urban women, though, it can be concluded that farm women are sexual conservatives. They hold up men and women equally, however, to their strict moral standards. Their rejection of promiscuity might be taken less as a measure of conservatism than as rejection of a sexual double standard for men and women.[18]

Neither does the expected generational shift have a straightforward effect on abortion. Age does not predict support for access to abortion. Instead we see the same pattern as for church attendance, but in reverse: farm labour increases and dairy operation decreases support for access to abortion. To a certain extent, age underlies these farm characteristics (with younger women doing labouring chores), but not significantly so. The relationship between age and abortion was too complicated for linear regression to catch. Approval for increased access to abortion does not increase or decrease as women grow older. Women aged thirty-five to forty-four are allied with older women aged fifty-five or more in opposing increased access to abortion. Younger women, under thirty-four years, and older women tend to favour increased access to abortion. Middle-aged women (forty-five to fifty-four years), who were born between 1935 and 1944 and who would have married and begun families from 1956 to 1965, are the most interesting category: why should women change their minds about abortion as they move into middle age? They may possibly become more critical of community consensus when their children are leaving home as young singles or newlyweds. Or perhaps when middle-aged mothers consider their teen-aged daughters' (and sons') prospects for success in marriage and employment, they might be reluctant to permit an unwanted pregnancy to determine their children's life choices and opportunities.

Public consensus against abortion is thus deceptive; many women lead discreet lives and maintain undisclosed views in superficially conservative rural communities. For example, an immigrant Roman Catholic woman born in 1928 is predicted to be conservative by all the expected indicators: she had eleven children, never used birth control, attended church every week, and was active in the Catholic Women's League. But the question on abortion tapped a fundamental dissatisfaction with her life: 'I never should have had so many children.' Only in her sixties, she said, was she able to acquire some space for herself, away from the children. Because of the social milieu, she could voice her sympathy for abortion rights only at the risk of losing her church community; she's 'not a protestor' and would not get involved in day-care or birth-control issues. Instead, in 1982 she rebelled, it might be inferred, by joining the WI, which is formally non-sectarian but entirely WASP in that neighbourhood.[19] It is not that membership in WI is in general more progressive than membership in the Catholic Women's League; the point is that she disagreed with a fundamental belief and activity of the Catholic women's organization – namely, opposition to abortion. Ontario farm wives superficially look like conservative churchgoers, but the substance of their opinions is more complex. In particular, a certain cohort of middle-aged women was observed to become more critical of conventional ideals of romantic marriage and motherhood with increasing age.

In sum, Ontario farm wives confirm the general rule that political participation flourishes in small, relatively homogeneous communities founded by an interlocking nexus of ancestors or, more correctly, ancestors-in-law. Farm wives report higher levels of political salience and efficacy than is expected by their accompanying socio-economic resources. But salience and efficacy are not accompanied by partisanship. Although political salience contributes to participatory democracy, it cannot be said to be intrinsically progressive until the substantive content of farm women's participation is examined.

Their conceptualization of the meaning of the terms 'politics' and 'left/right' revealed little substantive ideological content. The majority defined politics as 'government or the running of the country' and the remainder split half and half to define politics either negatively with hostility or positively as participation. Apart from noting how few women located themselves as substantively left or right on the scale, self-assigned locations reveal less than the actual definitions provided. Responses that previous researchers may have categorized as 'affective, evaluative, or idiosyncratic,' and hence of no cognitive standing, were discussed as evidence of farm women's preference for the 'centre' as a balancing principle of domestic and political affairs. Their preference for the centre is not conceptually sophisticated, but neither is it immediate evidence of conservatism.

Policy results of their participation are unclear, in part because it is not directed instrumentally to specific policy goals, but rather to community maintenance prompted by diffuse expressive or existential motives. Community maintenance is a public-policy goal of course, but it does not directly correspond to the concerns of this chapter – namely, to assess farm women's activities and opinions by standard indicators of conservatism.

In electoral terms, their propensity *not* to vote NDP is so pronounced as to indicate some collective aversion to the party's program or presumed constituency. The study's most articulate NDP supporter explains her vote: 'The PC and Liberal parties are run by big business. Wealthy people get tax breaks and tax shelters.'[20] NDP supporters may well ask why more farm wives do not share her apparently logical and straightforward assessment of partisan politics.

Farm women's enthusiasm for environmental projects is a clear countervailing indicator for conservatism. It was suggested that farm wives (and perhaps women in general) are potentially a strong grass-roots constituency who, even without critical insight or alliances with new social movements, have embarked on popular environmental activism.

As one moves away from conventional political questions to social indicators of conservatism, the pattern of responses exhibits considerable subtlety, particularly with regard to the relationship between age and sexual morality. Remarkably high church attendance provides a context for well-advised circumspection in small communities. Abortion straddles the line between publicly sanctioned and discussed sexual morality and privately held views about limits to women's autonomy.

6

Feminism

Farm women's conservatism, as seen thus far, must now be discussed with regard to feminism. What do self-assertion and a bid for autonomy look like when privacy and anonymity are nearly impossible because women are deeply embedded in a web of family ties that encompasses simultaneously work, love, and recreation? What do femininity and equality look like when women are already doing hard physical labour with livestock and heavy machinery in addition to their domestic labour? The idea of agrarian feminism remains to be developed further, but it is proposed, at very least, that feminism and the women's liberation movement has had an impact on the female population of rural Ontario.

Survey research is presently at odds with the vast upheavals and controversies regarding feminism and the changing role of women throughout the twentieth century. Specifically, major public-opinion studies have failed to establish robust (insensitive to methods of sampling and analysis) quantitative models of 'feminism' in the mass population based on standard demographic and attitudinal indicators. To explain this failure to date, some researchers have suggested that the positive impact of feminism is generally confined to a small, statistically insignificant segment of the population: a young, urban, well-educated, secular, left/liberal élite (Kay et al. 1988; Wilcox 1991, 538). A conflicting viewpoint is presented by Mayer, who concludes from his survey of Euro-Barometer and British Election Study results: 'The literature up to this point has found that a feminist orientation is growing and spreading among Western publics but that this orientation is not only not predictable from gender but it is not predictable from individual attributes' (1990, 11). This view is corroborated by Banaszak and Plutzer, whose review of previous research likewise observes that, except for education, socio-economic status contributes little to feminist attitudes (1991, 5). A critical review of previous models involving feminism is presented at the beginning of this chapter. The second part of the review summarizes the results of a body of research that has begun to reduce the ambiguity in defining feminism.

The first viewpoint discussed above would entail that feminism has had limited impact in rural Ontario because farm women are in no way part of the 'feminist élite.' The conflicting viewpoint anticipates a stronger impact but still sees only weak relationships between standard demographic and behavioural indicators and feminist attitudes. This study discounts the first viewpoint by reporting on farm women's views on women in electoral politics and their orientation to feminism, as measured by support for women's liberation, changing gender roles, and policy issues. The core of this chapter goes directly to the heart of the matter, by reporting on a question never before asked in major public opinion surveys: 'What do you mean by feminism?' This open-ended question elicited responses which were intelligible and well informed, but fraught with remarkably intense emotion: anxiety, hostility, equivocation, and, sometimes, intimacy. These open-ended responses are outlined in detail in the section on conceptualization of feminism. The strength and diversity of responses suggest that feminism has indeed had a significant impact (both positive and negative) on Ontario farm women. Given the personal nature of these women's responses, it is not surprising that standard indicators would fail to predict their opinions about feminism (and hence the real impact of social change) if feminism were defined using questions primarily designed to measure partisanship as related to national political institutions (as used, for example, in Election Studies). It is shown that farm women's conceptualizations fall into conceptual categories consistent with previous research on definitions of feminism. Furthermore, orientation to the women's liberation movement and to these concepts is shown to be predicted by demographic and agricultural work variables. The seemingly absurd influence of particular agricultural items reaffirms just how little we know about feminism in the mass population. These specific findings may begin to illuminate why feminism is generally so elusive in survey data, and point to a possible improvement.

MODELS AND DEFINITIONS OF FEMINISM IN PREVIOUS STUDIES

As the following review shows, evidence for the identification of feminism in mass populations with particular attention to rural/urban and agricultural questions that are relevant to farm women is limited. The egalitarian mythology of the North American frontier relates that rural and farm women have had a central role in the emergence of the women's movement and feminism in United States and Canada. Canadian scholars, for example, defer to the historical examples of farm women such as Nellie McClung, Irene Parlby, and Violet McNaughton, who contributed so much to the suffrage movement and simultaneously mobilized women for agrarian protest while in and out of elected office. Indeed, contrary to some accounts that locate the women's movement among other new social movements that arose in a surge of university-based protest in the 1960s and 1970s, there is some evidence that rural women have been receptive to feminism all along. Urbanization had a weak and inconsistent impact on support for affirmative action programs in a Canadian study (Kay et al. 1988, 15). Bashevkin found that female party activists from rural areas held no less-feminist views and, on some issues, were more strongly feminist than their urban counterparts: 'Liberal women from rural ridings were substantially more supportive of the contemporary women's movement (77.8 vs. 52.6), more likely to believe that women were discriminated against in the party (77.8 vs. 51.0), and more likely to express strong approval of internal affirmative action programs (55.6 vs. 36.8) than urban activists' (1985a, 416). A U.S. study found that rural women held more traditional beliefs about marriage and family, but they more strongly agreed with equal pay for equal work (Bescher-Donnelly and Whitener-Smith 1981, 182). Banaszak and Plutzer combined six Euro-Barometer questions to find that rural people were as equally feminist as city dwellers, but less feminist than those living in small towns (1991, 19).

In contrast, however, evidence pertaining to the demographic variables that predict 'feminist consciousness,' formally defined, is less encouraging. Analysis of Canadian data found that advanced education, particularly at the university level, and high-status, professional occupations were the strongest predictors of support for the women's liberation movement (Poel 1988, 9). Indeed, women reporting 'farmer' as their occupation were the least favourable to the women's movement (ibid, 10). Among European women, support for women's liberation was likewise strongly associated with youth and with higher education (Commission of the European Communities 1984, 41). Not all scholars associated with this literature included community size or agricultural occupations as variables. Among those who did, Klein postulated an early version of feminist consciousness that was found to increase with community size; she argued that people living in rural communities are sheltered from those disruptive life experiences that violate traditional roles and thus give rise to feminism (1984, 112–14). Cook observed that, from 1972 to 1984, only education and age consistently outranked the strength of rural/urban background in correlations to feminist consciousness (1989, 82), thereby confirming earlier analysis of the same data (Fulenwider 1980, 62). Rural residence, moreover, was strongly associated with women's opposition to the Equal Rights Amendment (Burris 1983, 310). When Wilcox roughly translated Cook's research into Euro-Barometer terms, he found ample evidence of weak feminist consciousness throughout Europe, but, again, a more restrictive and stronger definition of feminist consciousness was associated with youth, higher education, less religiosity, and liberal ideology (1991, 521–2, 538). Cumulative evidence from the United States and Europe is compelling: feminist consciousness (as defined in the studies summarized here) is most likely to be found among employed, well-educated, secular, wealthy, urban women, a profile that excludes farm women. Such a profile also excludes the vast bulk of women worldwide, most of whom are not employed, well educated, secular, wealthy, and urban. By restricting feminism to such a statistically insignificant sector of the population, survey research has managed to discredit feminism as insignificant. In other words, such findings, however internally valid, are at odds with the vast upheavals and controversies concerning the roles of men and women in this century.

The only published Canadian research based (loosely) on the American literature cited above came to a similar conclusion that excludes farm women from feminism (Kay et al. 1988). Working from the suggestion that the women's movement has directly mobilized women or has raised relevant issues that mobilize women, Kay and colleagues employed a 'role-constraint' model (Stoper 1977) to argue that household, and particularly child-care, responsibilities inhibit political involvement. Just as post-partum depression most severely afflicts university-educated women who quit well-paying, managerial jobs to become housewives after giving birth, so too are their expected levels of political participation depressed most severely, even after returning to paid employment. Kay and colleagues could not endorse even the modest proposal that there exists a well-educated, high-income activist élite of feminists. Any such élite had to be further restricted to a core of left-identified New Democratic Party voters. In sum, the women's movement, according to Kay and colleagues, has had limited positive impact on Canadian women's mass political behaviour.

The only bright spot in this otherwise dismal account was the finding that working women with lower education and lower income were least constrained by children. Kay and colleagues thought that they were not likely to participate in any case; in other words, zero political participation minus zero constraints is still zero participation. But they allowed that the data possibly confirm that motherhood orients less-educated women into a community network, leading to political activity and responsibility (Sapiro 1983, 134-8). This finding is exciting because it echoes quantitatively the self-stated purpose of the WI: 'WI has opened the way for a woman, however tied with home responsibilities, to have a part in the great human causes of her time.'[1] Or as one survey respondent explained, belonging to the WI 'fits in with being a mother and a home person.' This is the very premise of a certain variation of feminism (alternatively called 'maternal,' 'social,' or 'relational') in its domestic orientation to political participation.

The references by Kay and colleagues to 'feminist consciousness' are misleading because the full series of items used to identify feminist consciousness among American voters was simply not included in the Canadian Election Studies; the closest item that was included (a version of the feeling thermometer) was disregarded by Kay and colleagues. In other words, they used their own unique definition of 'feminist consciousness' to refer to politicization variables of behaviour. According to Kay and colleagues, the most damning evidence against the impact of the women's liberation movement (and their particular version of 'feminist consciousness') emerged from respondents' failure to list 'women's issues' in general, or specific feminist policies in particular, in response to an open-ended question about the most important issues in the forthcoming election. During the 1984 campaign when party leaders staged a debate on that subject, not quite 5 per cent of women mentioned undefined 'women's issues' as an important election issue. It takes a good deal of self-confidence and prior thought, however, to assert to a telephone interviewer that 'women's issues' were more important than the economy, national unity, or, among this population, agricultural subsidies. These are all, in any case, 'women's issues' in that women feel strongly about and are strongly affected by such economic and constitutional issues. Not only is the terminology misleading adopted by Kay and colleagues, the end result of their research design is to discredit feminism, in part because they used questions that were never meant to test for feminism in the first place.

The preceding criticisms relate to a basic problem in survey-based analysis of feminism to date: everyone tends to define it differently, picking and choosing among the variety of survey questions that seem to relate, in one way or another, to each observer's common-sense understanding of feminism. No wonder that a robust model of feminism is so difficult to achieve when each scholar is stipulating a different definition in the first place. It is time to stop reinventing the wheel or improvising in each study and to focus simply on the survey questions that best operationalize the concept of feminism. To that end, this section reviews previous, primarily factor-based, definitions of feminism.

A consensus has begun to emerge, based principally on U.S. Election Studies from 1972 to 1984, about which survey items best define feminism. The two most relevant terms are: gender consciousness and feminist consciousness. Gender consciousness entails sympathetic identification with women as a collectivity; it is a necessary but not sufficient condition for feminist consciousness (Gurin 1985). Gender consciousness can be measured quantitatively by a 'feeling thermometer.' This device asks respondents to rate which of sixteen groups, including both 'women' and the 'women's liberation movement' among other age, ethnic, and class/occupational categories, they feel closest to (warmest in the thermometer) – 'most like you in their interest, ideas, and feelings about things' (ibid, 149; Conover 1988, 991). One farm woman interviewed expressed gender consciousness thus: 'Women need the fellowship of other women; trouble is women don't have time now that they're working, but they still need it. I enjoy ladies' meetings, but I'm not fond of farm meetings.' Another woman explained why she had attended a WI conference at which seventy women had been present: 'I enjoy it so much, meeting women from all over the province who share the same problems, to realize that you're not alone in your problems. We have a really good time at the hotel without the children.'

There is less consensus regarding the components of feminist consciousness. Fulenwider (1980, 47) defined role equity between men and women as feminism's central ordering principle. Klein (1984, 3, 98–101) defined three stages of feminist consciousness: 1 / recognition of women as a group possessing shared interests (corresponding to gender consciousness); 2 / rejection of traditional gender roles (corresponding to role equity); and 3 / recognition of collective solutions to solve a collective problem of sex discrimination. Only women who reach the third stage, Klein stated, achieve full feminist consciousness. Gurin proposed that system-blaming analysis which identifies structural barriers in society rather than individual inadequacies must intervene between rejection of traditional gender roles and collective action. Gurin thus formulated a fourfold scheme of feminist consciousness: 1 / collective identification with women; 2 / collective orientation to political solutions for women; 3 / power discontent that 'women have too little influence'; and 4 / a willingness to blame institutional obstacles rather than women's personal deficiencies for their lesser power and wealth (1985, 148-9). Finally, Cook notably distinguished between gender consciousness (closeness to women) and feminist consciousness (1989, 77-8).

A few studies have attempted to apply this United States–based terminology to Europeans using Euro-Barometer data (Banaszak and Plutzer, 1991; Morgan and Wilcox, 1991; Plutzer and Banaszak, 1991; Wilcox 1991). The term 'feminist consciousness,' however, does not cross the Atlantic quite so easily because Euro-Barometer poses different questions relating to feminism and women's liberation.

In sum, the detailed, primarily factor-based calculations which lie behind these definitions of feminist consciousness are the most reliable avenue to begin building models of feminism in the mass population. This chapter aims to contribute to that endeavour from its unique focus on the open-ended conceptualization of feminism among farm women.

VIEWS ON WOMEN IN ELECTORAL POLITICS

The present study took a set of three questions about the consequences of women's election to political office from Euro-Barometer. At the end of this series of questions, substantial concern about 'women's issues' emerged. To begin with, farm women were asked to assess if things would go better or worse if more women were elected at each level of government.

Table 6.1 reveals more enthusiasm for women politicians, especially

TABLE 6.1   Would things be better or worse if substantially more women were elected ...

| | Locally? | Provincially? | Nationally? | |
| | | | Ontario farm women | European women |
	(%)	(%)	(%)	(%)
Better	44	35	39	33
Worse	6	7	8	8
Same	44	50	46	47
Can't say	5	9	8	12
(N)	(117)	(117)	(117)	(11,651)

SOURCE: Commission of the European Communities 1987, 35.

at the local level, among these Ontario women than among European women for whom, granted, published preferences are available only at the level of women elected to national parliaments. Farm women's relative lack of enthusiasm for more women at the provincial level can perhaps be attributed to the 'Patty Starr' scandal in Ontario, which broke out exactly when interviews were being conducted.[2]

Awareness of rural/urban differences was voiced by women who preferred that more women be elected only at the local level:

There should only be more women at the local level because I trust local women to solve the right problems, not like supporting abortion.

Woman should be elected to local level only because rich women blow money without understanding the situation of poor women. Rich women have more tendency to be stuffed shirts and I don't trust them.

I don't trust full-time politicians. There should be more local women politicians because local women have more time. They're more responsible and do more work. Local politics is only a part-time job, but men can't devote enough time to politics because they keep up a full-time job.

But others preferred women to be elected only in urban areas:

Women can't do local council because its job is to buy machinery. Women don't want to know how to buy snowblowers and other equipment.

Women aren't better for local issues because women couldn't make much of an impact. For example, they couldn't make much difference in deciding what snow-removal equipment to buy.

Local women don't have the experience, but they're professionals at higher levels.

Local women candidates are too emotional.

Very few women said that it would actually be worse if more women were elected, but those who did made comments that were cruel:

It would be worse because women wouldn't know what to do. They're not qualified for the job.

It would be the same because women would just agree with the men.

Women are too emotional. I don't have much confidence in women in positions like that. They don't see both sides of an issue.

Table 6.2 shows the frequency of response when those women who replied 'better' at any level of government in the previous question were asked about plausible reasons for 'things going better.'

The third and fourth options represent familiar first-wave arguments for women's influence to improve the moral quality and decorum of partisanship.

Things would go better because women are more responsible in getting the job done.

It would be better because women go after a problem and get the job done. Women are hard workers. For example, my husband laughs at my opinions, but it was hard for me to be appointed an elder [in the church]. People criticized me and didn't support me, but I did a good job. All women could do it.

Better because women are more honest and show their feelings.

It's like in the house; a woman's hand is needed everywhere.

TABLE 6.2   How things would go better if substantially more women were elected
(% of respondents)

	Frequency	
Women's problems would get more attention	42	(30%)
Certain problems which have been neglected would finally get some attention	42	(30%)
More women would have a steadying effect on Parliament	30	(21%)
There would be less playing politics for its own sake	28	(20%)
(N responses)	(142)	

Women would bring a new and different outlook on politics.

It would be better because women see more issues more broadly. Women care more about people.

These arguments may not longer be so persuasive because these last two options were preferred less frequently (41 per cent) than the first two options (60 per cent). But, as the next comment shows, there may not be sharp distinctions between altruistic and selfish reasons for women being elected: 'Things would go better because women think differently. Men brush off women's problems.' In regard to the second option, it was not specified what certain neglected problems might be; it is quite possible that respondents themselves could not have articulated their content. If these hitherto ignored problems are a less assertive form of women's problems (what other problems might women politicians solve that men do not?), more than half of the responses given (60 per cent) voiced hope that women politicians could better represent women's concerns.

The same preference for local women candidates (seen in table 6.1) emerged again in regard to paying more attention to women's problems or neglected problems. Those respondents who preferred more women to be elected locally were, overall, more convinced by the first two reasons for things possibly going better (more attention to women's problems) than were respondents who preferred more women elected provincially and federally; the former group's agreement with these reasons ranged from 85 to 93 per cent compared with agreement in the mid-70 per cent range for the latter group.

And finally, table 6.3 tabulates the outcome when all respondents were asked to choose from a list of possible reasons why more women

TABLE 6.3   Why more women aren't elected

	Frequency (%)	N
Too few women are prepared to run as candidates	88	117
The population prefers to vote for a man	77	117
The parties support men instead of women	55	117
The women aren't those one would vote for	31	117

were not elected. Agreement with the listed possibilities declined as blame was pinned more specifically. Almost everyone was inclined to agree to a general lack of willing female candidates (88 per cent), or was inclined to blame the general population for preferring male candidates (77 per cent). Three respondents observed that rural people won't vote for women, and another said that 'the ethnics and immigrant population in Canada won't vote for a woman.' Not nearly so many farm women (55 per cent) were willing to blame party élites. Still fewer (31 per cent) were willing to blame specific candidates who had run for office.

As mentioned earlier in chapter 5, in the section on election results, voters in Grey County have consistently rejected female NDP candidates. This observation may be relevant to respondents' views on women being elected to public office. When farm wives were asked to assess a list of possible reasons why more women aren't elected to Parliament or legislatures, 31 per cent agreed with the anti-feminist possibility, that 'the women who do run for office just aren't the type you'd want to vote for.' Although nobody explained why any particular candidate was so disliked, a few women sighed with resignation during interviews, saying 'Yes, there's one woman around here like that who's always running for election,' and mumbled that she just wasn't suitable at all. Another respondent said, 'The women candidates seem to come out of nowhere; they just don't have the public profile that male candidates do.' When Ontario elected an NDP majority in 1990, Grey County rejected yet another female NDP candidate.

Overall, this series of pointed questions on women and electoral politics revealed substantial awareness of what are usually seen as women's issues and discrimination against women running for political office in rural Ontario. None the less, it may be that researchers cannot grasp feminism's impact by asking conventionally political questions. Instead, its impact might be better grasped by asking farm wives direct questions about changing gender roles, the women's liberation movement, and feminism.

VIEWS ON FEMINISM

A good many women are positively oriented to feminist ideas. In the May 1986 issue of *Chatelaine* magazine (p. 41), 47 per cent of readers identified themselves as feminist. In that same year, a Gallup Poll reported that 56 per cent of American women were self-identified feminists, and 71 per cent observed that the women's movement had done either fairly well or very well in improving their lives (Katzenstein 1987, 9). Over a decade ago, researchers purposely chose an unlikely sample of affluent, conservative, and suburban clubwomen to test possible alliances with the women's movement; 29 per cent were willing to be called a feminist (Bers and Mezey 1981, 741). By contrast, only a quarter (23 per cent) of Ontario farm wives interviewed admitted to being a feminist, a far lower percentage than that for the overall population. The same proportion (24 per cent) could be a member of women's liberation if the opportunity arose in their neighbourhood (which they doubted it ever would).

A positive orientation to feminism can also be measured by respondents' opinions of the 'women's liberation movement' in comparison to predominantly urban Canadian and European women, as shown in table 6.4.[3] The sample of Ontario farm women was less polarized than were those of Canadian and European women. Although only one individual held a very high opinion of the movement, these Ontario women were less likely to report a very bad opinion than were predominantly urban women. Farm respondents' answers clustered in the middle, where they were split half and half between good and bad opinions. A tendency to cluster in the centre and to avoid polar extremes usually marks a question's relative failure in survey research, but farm wives' proclivity to avoid conferring excessive praise or criticism might also confirm the previously discussed 'centre principle.' In 1988, just as many (43 per cent) urban women held a good opinion of the women's movement, as did this group of farm women (45 per cent). Going back to 1984, 60 per cent of predominantly urban Canadian women held a good opinion of the women's movement. During the 1984 election campaign, the National Action Committee on the Status of Women (NAC) lobbied for and organized a nationally televised debate among party leaders on the subject of women's issues.

TABLE 6.4   Opinion of women's liberation movement

Frequency	CES 1988 (%)	CES 1984 (%)	Europe (%)	Ontario farm wives (%)
Very high opinion	13	30	7	1
Quite a good opinion	30	30	40	44
Rather poor opinion	44	27	25	41
Very bad opinion	9	9	8	3
Can't say	4	–	20	10
Mixed feelings	–	5	–	–
(N)	(1,441)	(1,545)	(9,790)	(117)

SOURCES: Canada Election Study 1988, 1984; Commission of the European Communities 1984, 41.

This debate may have lent the women's movement a degree of prominence and prestige that we see reported as a better opinion in the 1984 election study.

Surprisingly, farm women who held a good or high opinion of the women's liberation movement would not generally consider becoming a member of such a movement themselves. There was no correlation (.32) between support for women's liberation and the possibility of being a member. This apparent inconsistency is also true of European women, of whom even those holding a very high opinion of women's liberation refuse to contemplate membership (Commission of the European Communities 1984, 46). Since Ontario women are not unique in this regard, an alternative explanation is offered for their reluctance to become involved. Rural women might reject membership in a women's movement that they perceive as exclusionary, in this case, seeing the movement as dominated by urban women (Rankin 1989, 326). In other situations, the women's movement might be perceived as exclusionary in terms of racial, religious, or class dominance. Rather than criticize the women's movement as exclusionary, however, Ontario women were more likely to criticize their own deficiencies:

It depends. I could be a member if all the women in the neighbourhood joined too.

I could be a member, but I'd feel out of place and put down because I'm at home working.

I'm not opinionated enough to belong.

I'm not educated enough to belong.

We're too far out in the hicks for this.

A feminist wants women's rights to be the same as men's. I agree with their ideas, but I'm too old-fashioned to get involved.

The relatively small proportion, about a quarter, of farm wives who are self-identified feminists or who could be a member of the women's liberation movement is deceptive, therefore, because they disqualified themselves on the grounds that they were not sufficiently sophisticated or educated to be members.

Although respondents were relatively reluctant to be associated with organized feminism, they displayed some support for two specific policy goals of prominent constituent groups identified with the Canadian women's movement (for instance, the National Action Committee on the Status of Women, the Ontario Coalition for Abortion Clinics, or the Ontario Coalition for Better Childcare. That is, whereas roughly only a quarter of farm wives were self-identified feminists who supported women's liberation, almost half would get involved in activities promoting day care or birth control (see table 5.1).

Considering that anticipated involvement is a powerful and demanding question and positive responses are bound to be fewer than those garnered for simple support, farm women were very willing to get involved in day care and birth control. But they were substantially more reluctant to get involved in these feminist issues compared with their almost unanimous enthusiasm for environmental projects, even when it was stressed that participation in collective environmental projects was at stake, not simply individual practices in one's home. Finally, this set of questions highlights how much care must be taken to avoid presuming that indicators (like child-care or birth-control centres) are straightforward proof of 'feminism.' The expressed interested of 41 per cent of farm wives in a birth-control centre is deceptive because some respondents realized that involvement in a clinic might hypothetically lead to their being appointed to the board of directors and thus implementing policies to stop abortion at that clinic. Apart from any deliberate pro-life tactics, day-care and birth-control centres may not be the best indicators of feminism for another reason. Middle-aged and elderly women said, 'I've done my share already' to justify why they would not get involved in issues that they perceived as the responsibility of a younger generation. Instead, their chief concern was more likely prospective widowhood; the imminent death of a WI member's husband came up twice in interviews with other members in anticipation of the support the branch would give collectively to its bereaved member.

A more general indicator of women's orientation to feminism is respondents' appraisal of social change in relation to gender roles. Almost all (95 per cent) of the farm wives interviewed agreed that the role of women was indeed changing, so everyone in effect answered the subsequent question asking farm women to appraise changing gender roles. They were, on the whole, positive and eager for further changes in women's roles. Respondents were largely satisfied (61 per cent) with the present rate of change being 'at the right pace.' A substantial 25 per cent were eager for accelerated change in the role of women. Only a few (9 per cent) thought that women's role was changing 'too quickly.' Women who feared that changes in gender roles were occurring too quickly should be credited for being especially attuned to the consequences of social change and for suggesting that most families could do with a 'breather' from all the upheavals and adjustments:

Change is too quick for men and for me too. There are too many adjustments for a family to handle over jobs and housework. It's happening too quickly because families still have a lot of problems to be sorted out. Like I want to work and my husband wants me to be at home here helping him farm.

Families suffer when women are away working. Women can do what they want, but women end up having to deal with the consequences.

Discussion about the right pace of change led into direct evaluation of changes in conventional gender roles. A majority of respondents (58 per cent) agreed that there should be fewer differences between men and women.[4] In response to this question, women's replies turned to the topic of femininity. Their answers highlight how farm women modify their understanding of 'feminism' by drawing from their own experience. The physically onerous side of farming seems to exacerbate differences between men and women, thus accentuating women's relative frailty and dependence on men:

There should be fewer differences, but women just can't do some heavy jobs.

Women can't do all of men's heavy work on a farm. A woman's crazy to take it all on.

Women can't do men's jobs like construction [repairing buildings and fences] and farming when they're pregnant.

I'm just not able. I'm not like these superwomen. It kills a woman to be throwing bales around.

Feminists think they can do everything as well as a man, but I can't, like changing the tiller. Men beat us in physical strength.

The recurring theme of femininity suggests that feminism indeed hinges on the question of conventional gender roles.

I like to be very feminine as a woman. I like being a woman even if I'm doing heavy field-work.

Girls should be girls; they should be feminine. I like to get dressed up and go out. I like to wear feminine clothes after wearing barn clothes all the time.

I admire Brigid Pyke [former president of the Ontario Federation of Agriculture] as a leader. A sex-pot image isn't appropriate to OFA. I don't think much of sex-pots.

Both hostile and sympathetic responses confirm that agricultural work has important consequences for women's self-perception in terms of femininity. While farm work may physically liberate some women from the constraints of femininity, it may give rise to anxieties about or a premium on their sexual identity among other women.

In addition to agriculture, Ontario's religious and cultural background may also influence women's attitudes to feminism. Hard physical work is the best measure of a person, and the Protestant work ethic condemns urban 'feminists.' The same conditions governing grace extend to women's equality; one cannot *earn* grace through good works because it is given naturally and arbitrarily by God, but the tangible results of hard work are the surest signs of God's grace. Likewise, women are also thought to be naturally equal but, at the same time, must prove their equality through good works: 'A woman is almost equal to a man in rights. But you must provide yourself through life to earn rights, rather than just demanding rights. Some women make it bad for others.' Evangelical injunctions to 'plainness' might persist to condemn urban feminists for their vanity and pretences: 'A feminist wants to be treated like a lady; she is too good for farm work, overly concerned with clothes. I'm a woman, not a lady.' One woman recalled doing domestic service for a town couple to explain why traditional farm households are morally superior: 'Politics is no job for women. Too many women are getting men's jobs when their place is with home and family. The more money women earn, the more they squander it on liquor and cars and the poor kids suffer.' In this case, role reversal between men and women is seen to spell the decline of Protestant virtues of thrift and sobriety.

These above measures of feminism are an improvement on standard questions relating to electoral politics, but they, too, only begin to tap women's complex views on this subject. The inadequacy of previous measures became apparent, in part, through respondents' acute embarrassment with these questions. Not that the questions regarding feminism and women's liberation were intellectually difficult on the surface, but they asked for a degree of honesty and intimacy that had not been anticipated in the research design. Sometimes seeing them admit that they were feminists or could be a member of women's liberation was akin to watching them come out of the closet to admit their deep, dark secret to an anonymous and presumably sympathetic stranger. Given the premium that these women place on harmony and conciliation, no wonder that they are circumspect on feminism. In a separate inquiry, when asked directly about this subject, one farm woman wrote: 'At agricultural college I was involved in campus politics for two years [in mid-1970s]. I used to be outspoken on women's liberation topics. I've learned to back off. I feel you have to be well respected and well know before anyone will listen. In a farm community, it takes years to earn respect and one foolish remark will destroy you' (personal correspondence, 8 Aug. 1990). Judging from women's forthright responses to questions about pre- and extramarital sex, sexual morality apparently is a matter for public discussion, whereas feminism is not. Conventional notions of public and private were reversed when the interviewer asking about feminism was warned: 'You're getting too political now.' This somewhat hostile comment testifies to the continued relevance of an early aphorism of the women's movement: 'the personal is the political.'

Election Studies and Euro-Barometer include questions pertinent to feminism, but have not yet asked people to conceptualize 'feminism' as they have 'left-wing/right-wing' and 'liberal/conservative' belief systems (Converse 1964; Neuman 1986; Klingemann 1979; Lambert et al. 1986a). The present study is unique in asking respondents to explain the meaning of 'feminism' in an open-ended question, just as they previously had been asked to conceptualize 'politics' and 'left/right' belief systems. Given that this question has never been asked before in an empirical study, there is simply no comparable data set for the meaning of feminism as it is understood by the mass population.[5]

The impact of feminism or the women's liberation movement is immediately evident in the contrast among three open-ended questions requesting definitions of the terms 'politics,' 'left-wing/right-wing,' and 'feminism.' Only 12 per cent of respondents had nothing to say about politics, but, of those who did, 74 per cent defined politics mundanely, as government or the running of the country. A plurality (37 per cent) had no idea what left and right were about, and the remaining answers were startlingly idiosyncratic, distinctly non-partisan, and conventionally unpolitical. Farm wives were positively loquacious, however, when it came to defining feminism. Only 9 per cent had nothing to say, and many of the responses included lengthy and intimate anecdotes. The topic of feminism aroused far more intense emotion than did any preceding political question; even active hostility to feminism is more impressive than apathy. In sum, farm wives could speak articulately and intelligibly on the subject of feminism, whereas they could not for more conventionally political topics.

Most responses related to one or both of two dominant concepts: equality and autonomy. In order to investigate these concepts quantitatively, two variables were constructed: one describing orientation towards feminism's perceived goals and actions regarding equality or role equity, and one describing orientation towards feminism's perceived goals and actions regarding autonomy or self-assertion, as follows. For each woman, except two who refused to answer, a value of -1, 0, or +1 was assigned to the equality variable, and a value of -1, 0, or +1 was assigned to the autonomy variable. A non-zero value of the equality variable indicates that the woman's response conceptualized feminism as being related to equality issues and showed discernible approval (positive orientation = +1) or discernible disapproval (negative orientation = -1) for the perceived goals and actions of feminism in that regard. A zero value of the equality variable indicates that the woman's responses either did not relate to equality or did

TABLE 6.5   Meaning of 'feminism'

	Frequency	
Equality, role equity with men		
Positive orientation	25	(22%)
No discernible orientation	56	(50%)
Negative orientation	31	(28%)
(N)	(112)	
Autonomy, self-assertion		
Positive orientation	22	(20%)
No discernible orientation	67	(60%)
Negative orientation	23	(20%)
(N)	(112)	

not show a discernible orientation. Analogous criteria were used to assign the value of the autonomy variable for each woman. The two conceptual categories are not mutually exclusive. The two variables are fairly independent of each other (.14).

Table 6.5 shows frequencies for these two autonomy and equality variables. Responses were fairly evenly divided between positive and negative orientations for both conceptualizations, with approximately half not showing any discernible orientation. On the original survey, this item was preceded by the question 'Would you say that you are a feminist?' A quarter (23 per cent) of respondents agreed to identify themselves as 'feminists,' but that figure proved to be unreliable because when those self-identified 'feminists' were probed on what they meant by feminism, it became clear that some of them did not interpret the question in conventional terms. Seventeen women confused feminism with femininity or femaleness; some of these prized femininity, whereas others scorned it as an effeminate urban affectation. This confusion highlights that researchers cannot take it for granted that they and their subjects are even talking about the same thing when it comes to feminism.

The most frequent conceptualization related to equality, role equity, and traditional gender roles between men and women. These responses discussed feminism in 'relational' terms with a stress on the female/male unit as the basic social unit (Offen 1988). Role equity has been identified as a central ordering principle of feminism (Conover and Sapiro 1992; Fulenwider 1980). Whereas the standard role-equity question asks about equality in the public sphere (business, industry, and government), farm women respondents were evidently answering more in terms of role equity in the private sphere of their individual households.

A feminist thinks that women should have all the say or that everything has to be 50-50; she's very pushy. The man is the head of the households, but women should have 50 per cent of the say.

I've felt liberated all along. My husband never held me back from anything.

I'm not a feminist because I'm happy being a woman and I'm happy to feel protected by a man.

A feminist is a very active person who wouldn't be satisfied with being at home; she wouldn't quite her job to raise a family. She goes for strict 50-50 in relationships and lays down the law to enforce it.

Some women conceptualized feminism specifically in terms of the unique equality of farm marriages.

On a farm, I was never belittled. I was never told that I couldn't do anything. But ... other professions have problems. Women farmers and men farmers are equal competitors because both get the same price for commodities. Women could farm just as well as men.

I never had to right for rights. I was raised on a tractor, I was brought up doing chores. I've been equal since I was a child.

Women can do all these [farm] jobs. You work side by wide with your husband; you take for granted that you'll fill in when needed. It's not like city people. I get disgusted by women's lib. They do some good, but carry things too far. Farm people, we've been women's lib all our lives ... maybe I've been a feminist all my life.

Their praise for the mutuality of farm marriages, of pitching in to help whenever needed without concern for it being men's work or women's work, is consonant with egalitarian and interchangeable gender roles.

Because this category was defined in relational terms, it included a subset of responses that spoke about feminists' evident hostility to men. It was startling to discover just how concerned so many women were that feminism emasculates men. While this concern centred primarily on the reversal of traditional gender roles within households, reference was also made to men's emasculation by affirmative action programs in the paid work force.

Men are losing their identity as men. Women start taking over what used to be men's responsibilities and, as a result, marriages break down. Liberation is good for women, but they should respect men. Feminists want their own way; for example, they're like a domineering wife. I'm very stubborn and stick up for my rights, but I wouldn't be boss.

Feminists put women first and put men down. They must have been badly hurt by a man at one time. Each sex has their strengths and should be respected for their strengths.

Feminists show too much hostility to men. They should be more subtle with men. A feminist is a single woman who is not married and doesn't have any family. She sneers at men.

Feminists are women wanting to be better than a man.

Women who undermine men to take their jobs. Related to Affirmative Action program with school board.

A feminist is a woman who wants to be a man in a skirt, who wants to play a man's role.

The second conceptual category relates to women's autonomy and self-assertion. It speaks to the ability of women to lay claim to their own life; it is the 'heteronomous' capacity to make laws for oneself independently of men's authority and control (de Lauretis 1986, 11). Studies of American women in the 1970s found that a 'sense of internal control and life satisfaction show the strongest consistent association with feminism' (Fulenwider 1980, 71). While women might comment about their relations with men here, they also spoke in 'individualistic' terms about their separate selves apart from husbands and families.

Feminist does what she wants to do. That's me; I do what I want, like doing farm work instead of being stuck in the house.

Men have always been idols to women who cater to men – which has to change. Women should stop putting themselves down.

People should be equal. I have strong opinions and can speak up too. I'm not "Mrs Joe Smith.' I have my own identity.

A person who is assertive on her own behalf and forms her own opinions.

Feminist is to remain a 'lady,' but to have the same power and influence that men have. You don't have to change to somebody else's opinion [in authority]. Just be yourself.

A feminist looks at things from a woman's point of view.

More militant, more outspoken than myself. I believe in women's rights, but I won't campaign for them.

A feminist is somebody who thinks that she's equal to a man and wants to be recognized as an individual.

   Self-assertion also provoked considerable hostility, but even the hostile comments are appealing in their astute grasp of the stakes involved in feminism.

Like my daughter who is so critical of her teachers, pouncing on anything they say as 'sexist.' She gets all riles up and defensive.

Equality is good, but feminists want control. They take privileges they're not qualified for. Feminists give up femininity, which is part of being a woman.

Feminists seem like vultures, forcing their aggressive opinions on women.

Person who thinks that they can do everything, that their way is the only way, autocratic, self-confident, overbearing, opinionated. I don't like women to be so forceful. Women should have no more clout than men, but they should be the same as men.

Women who are for their own selves. They do some good, but carry things too far.

If feminism is the 'heteronomous' capacity to govern oneself autonomously, it indeed refers to women who are 'selfish' or 'pushy,' who 'want too much,' and think too well of themselves.

Even those who confused feminism with femininity spoke in ostensibly feminist terms of activity and self-assertion to criticize their neighbours whom they understood to be 'feminists':

Feminists think that women have their own place, that women shouldn't step beyond their bounds. Feminists cater to their husbands and let husbands make the decision.

A feminist thinks that women should be at home, traditional.

A feminist sits on a pedestal. She's too busy doing housework to get involved in farm or community work. Housework is their first priority.

Finally, even the most parochial women, by measures of age, education, and paid employment, were able to conceptualize feminism, something they were not been able to do for the meanings of politics and left/right. For instance, such comments included:

Connected to language issues, for example, God as a man or a woman. You have to watch what you say.

Does feminism mean pulling away from men, wanting nothing to do with men, to be on your own?

These responses are coherent and intelligible; the first relates to the revision of hymnals to gender-neutral language and the second relates to perceived separatist themes in feminism.

In sum, farm women's articulate conceptualization of feminism is *prima facie* evidence of its impact on them. The variety of their responses corresponds to the diversity of each woman's particular situation; none the less, it conforms to prevailing debates among academics, journalists, and politicians. In the context of those debates, responses were categorized in either or both relational terms of equality with other people (and husbands in particular) and individualistic terms of women's claim to autonomy and self-assertion (Offen 1988).

RELATIONSHIPS AMONG FEMINIST ITEMS

Factor analysis was used to investigate the relationship between the newly created equality and autonomy variables (from open-ended responses) and other presumably feminist items. In contrast to Wilcox (1991, 535, 541), the series of Euro-Barometer items relating to gender-role equity and role attitudes (specifically women in political office and non-traditional occupations) did not fit in with the new variables. Also, it has been proposed that support for the women's movement fosters cross-cutting alliances with other progressive new social movements, such as the environmental movement (Magnusson and Walker 1988; Phillips 1991). Results from this study, however, do not support that proposal. There is a high probability of independence between support for women's liberation and support for environmental movements (p = .83). Table 6.6 further shows that self-identified feminists tended to *dis*approve of the environmentalist movement (p = .02). As discussed in the previous chapter, support for environmentalism may be more conventional than generally thought to the extent that it is compatible with a focus on homemaking.

Five opinions relating to feminism did, however, fit together into a pattern of two categories or factors. The pattern accounts for 30 per cent of the variation in women's opinions. This means that the two categories stand in as an acceptable replacement for the five separate opinions. The 'best' solution obtained involved the two new variables and three others: high opinion of the women's liberation movement, agreement that there should be fewer differences between men and women, and agreement that there should be increased access to abortion. Two factors were extracted and labelled as equality and autonomy versions of feminism. These results are shown in table 6.7, along with the loadings obtained using factor analysis.[6]

The first category is consistent with previous research. A correlation between a policy preference for accessibility to abortion and positive attitudes to feminism and gender equity has been previously documented (Conover and Sapiro 1992, 13; Dodson 1989, 7, 11). Support for the women's liberation movement stands in for the second component of feminist consciousness – an orientation to collective political solutions to solve discrimination against women (Cook 1989, 78). An orientation to collective political action belongs with a conceptualization of feminism in terms of role equity and traditional gender roles. The question of gender-role differences, including the belief that men

TABLE 6.6 Feminist self-identification by the environmentalist movement

	High opinion of environ. movement	Good opinion of environ. movement	Poor opinion of environ. movement	Row total
Feminist	44	33	22	23
Not feminist	44	51	6	77
Column %	44	47	10	100%

TABLE 6.7 Pattern of feminism

	Factor 1: Equality	Factor 2: Autonomy
Orientation to equality/role equity	.59	.10
Good opinion of women's lib movement	.50	.11
Fewer differences between men and women	.45	.03
Increased access to abortion	.32	−.14
Orientation to autonomy, assertion	.06	.61

and women can be 'different but equal,' certainly belongs in this equality factor. This is not a expansive notion of equality, however, because survey items relating to the equal integration of women into elected political office and traditionally male occupations did not fit with items about women's liberation and the meaning of feminism.

Orientation to the autonomy conceptualization of feminism sits by itself as the second category. Unlike the equality variable, it does not belong with an orientation to collective political action through women's liberation movement. Apparently those with a positive orientation to autonomy are more likely to identify individual, idiosyncratic strategies for autonomy in their everyday life rather than through formal organized movements associated with standard policy issues. The results involving the open-ended conceptualizations are thus consistent with the principle that role equity, as opposed to personal autonomy, is the central ordering principle of feminism.

The five items relating to feminism were related to each other as shown in table 6.8. The items relating to feminism were all positively associated with each other, but not with uniform strength. Feminist self-identification (ID) was associated with autonomy, and especially equality orientations to feminism, and less so with a willingness to

TABLE 6.8   Correlations[7] among aspects of feminism

	Opinion of WLM	Join WLM	Feminist ID	Autonomy	Equality
Opinion of WLM	1.00				
Join WLM	.31	1.00			
Feminist ID	.17	.22	1.00		
Autonomy	.16	.01	.32	1.00	
Equality	.30	.22	.52	.16	1.00

becoming collectively involved with the women's movement (WLM). Here again we see evidence that an equality orientation is a central ordering principle of feminism because, more so than other items, it goes both ways – with feminist self-identification and with the women's movement.

RELATIONSHIP OF FEMINISM TO FARM AND DEMOGRAPHIC CHARACTERISTICS

This section first discusses the impact of farm and demographic characteristics on support for the women's liberation movement. A parallel discussion of the impact of those same items on two conceptualizations of feminism (the equality and autonomy variables derived from the open-ended responses) follows.

Table 6.9 shows that internal administration (decision making and research) and youth very significantly predict a high opinion of the women's liberation movement (as indicated by asterisks in the corresponding table entries). Also at a very significant level, external administration lowers one's opinion of the movement. This model for opinion of women's liberation is especially strong. The number of people (that is, children) in the household and a husband's higher education significantly predict a woman's willingness to join women's liberation group in her own area. These results corroborate previous studies in which youth consistently predicts support for the women's liberation movement, but it is surprising that education did not appear. Analysis of Canadian data for the same question found that advanced education, particularly at the university level, and high-status, professional occupations were the strongest predictors of support for the women's movement (Poel 1988, 9). Among European women, support for women's liberation was likewise strongly associated with youth and

TABLE 6.9   Determinants of positive orientations to women's liberation movement and definitions of feminism[8]

Determinants	Good opinion of WLM	Would join WLM	Feminist ID	Autonomy define	Equality define
Farm labour score	–	–	.13*	–	.33***
Internal admin.	.24***	.05	–	–	–
External admin.	−.22***	–	–	–	–
Wife's age	−.02***	–	–	−.02*	–
Wife employed	.20	–	–	−.21*	.25*
Wife's education	−.05	–	–	–	–
People in household	–	.08*	.06	−.15*	, –
Hours of housework	–	–	–	–	.02*
Father a farmer	–	−.12	–	−.18	−.31*
Husband's education	−.04	.06*	−.04	–	−.13***
Husband employed	–	–	.19*	.25*	.22
Husband's child care	–	–	–	−.04	–
Dairy farm	–	–	–	−.11	−.40*
Egg/poultry farm	–	–	.30*	–	–
Grain farm	–	–	.20*	–	–
Farm employees hired	–	–	.03	.06*	–
Farm acres	−.23	–	–	–	–
Extended-family	.16	–	–	–	–
R Square	.30	.18	.19	.20	.23
Adjusted R Square	.24	.15	.12	.14	.17
(N)	(99)	(109)	(100)	(114)	(106)

*p < .05   **p < .01   ***p < .001

with higher education (Commission of the European Communities 1984, 41). Instead, the appearance of a husband's higher education suggests that Ontario farm wives look for their husbands' approval to join women's organizations.

Table 6.9 shows that orientations to two conceptualizations of feminism share one significant determinant in common: a wife's paid employment, but with opposite (negative) effects on autonomy and (positive) effects on equality. The opposite effects of wife's paid employment may imply that the hierarchical structure of paid employment encourages a woman to play by the rules to get her fair share and to resent those who make up their own rules, but this is speculative. Feminist self-identification is significantly predicted by two familiar items; it is like equality orientation in regard to farm labour, and autonomy in regard to a husband's employment. Egg/poultry and grain enterprises also predict significantly feminist self-identification, but this effect probably masks other, more plausible explanations.

An autonomy orientation to feminism has four more significant predictors: being relatively young, but having few or no children (as measured by the number of people at home), having an employed husband, and hiring farm employees. It is not clear what these women do while left alone on the farm all day in their husbands' absence. The effect of hired employees means that they are not doing farm work; that and the absence of housework means they can only be doing their own autonomously defined 'thing.'

An equality orientation to feminism has two very significant predictors: farm labour and a less well-educated husband. At still significant levels, farm labour, increased housework, and not growing up on a farm predict the same equality orientation. The same opposite effect between farm labour and dairy operations appears again in relation to an equality version of feminism. If women do dairy chores, they are more receptive to feminism; if other people (husbands, children, or employees) do those same chores on a dairy farm, women are less receptive to feminism. A husband's higher education very significantly predicts a negative orientation to equality conceptualization of feminism.[9] The inhibiting role of husband's higher education agrees with European results, which likewise found that the best-educated men are least favourable to women's liberation (Commission of the European Committees 1984, 41). At the same time, a husband's education significantly predicts willingness to join a women's liberation group. This last result conforms to previous findings that Canadian men with both lower and higher levels of education are more supportive than men with high school educations, who are least supportive of women's liberation (Poel 1988, 10). Whatever the contradictory effects of a husband's education, the important point is that a woman's own education level dropped out of the model. This shows that farm women's belief systems are more significantly influenced by their husbands' level of education than by their own level of education. A husband's higher education, moreover, lies behind internal administration, which predicts very significantly a higher opinion of women's liberation movement. A woman's choice of husband may be the most important decision of her life because his characteristics thus circumscribe her own.

Farm labour is the next most significant determinant of equality orientation, followed by increased hours of housework. The chores of animal husbandry (milking, attending births, vaccination, insemination, and cleaning stalls) are traditionally associated with women and continue to be especially compatible, practically and theoretically, with domestic labour and the care of small children. It is not so surprising that both farm labour and housework appear as significant and positive predictors when one remembers just which women would be doing so much work – namely, women who said that, apart from sleeping at night (which was interrupted itself by child care), their waking hours were entirely occupied by chores close to home. Perhaps the intensive manual labour involved in farm work and housework gives rise to grievances about the division of labour that these women understand in feminist terms. These women obviously have an interest in establishing reciprocity in gender roles between themselves and their husbands, which expresses itself in approval for equality values of feminism.

These results suggest that the specific conditions of family-based farm enterprises may be the real culprit, inhibiting feminism among farm women. A husband's paid employment at off-farm jobs predicted both equality and autonomy. Feminism did not flourish among these farm women when they worked alongside their husbands as equal partners in egalitarian enterprises; instead, it flourished when their husbands held paid employment in separate off-farm jobs. Furthermore, women whose fathers were not farmers and who did not grow up on farms tended to articulate grievances in terms more positive to feminism.

Two observations can be established. First, feminism has had a substantial impact on farm women in rural Ontario. The most basic evidence is that almost everyone could speak articulately and vigorously on the subject of feminism, whereas many could not about other, more conventionally political matters, such the meaning of the terms 'leftwing' and 'right-wing.' Furthermore, their open-ended conceptualizations fell into two conceptual categories – equality and autonomy – that correspond with previously identified components of feminist consciousness. Specifically, a positive orientation towards feminism in terms of role equity between men and women was associated with a willingness to support the collective women's liberation movement.

Second, socio-economic predictors of orientation to these two conceptualizations were found with some success. Support for the women's liberation movement is connected to an equality conceptualization of feminism through the significance of farm labour and wife's paid employment to both calculations. Farm labour, in particular, is associated with feminist self-identification and a positive bid for role equity and a fairer division of labour expressed in terms that women associated with the concept of feminism. That milking cows could be so significant emphasizes that the route that women take to becoming feminist is more complex and more profoundly grounded in everyday life than has been anticipated.

In sum, farm women's comments remind us to be wary of assuming that urban-based feminism diffuses from the centre to rural peripheries because women who reported 'growing up on a tractor' insisted that they had been feminists all along. Even as they criticized women's liberation, its impact is none the less evident in their thoughtful distinguishing of 'natural' equality, earned through hard work on the farm, from urban excesses. Arriving at an understanding of how agricultural work, politics, and feminism fit together under conditions of household-based farm enterprises is the goal of the next chapter.

7

Marriage, Family, and Happiness

Indeed, the idea was that any manly man would wish to shun women but most of them were caught off guard, and for good. (Munro 1982, 65)

Given that a woman's choice of husband has such significant consequences for her involvement in agriculture, and thence for her personal happiness, one is directed to respondents' testimony concerning their experience of farm marriages and families. If determinants related to husbands and marriage appear again and again in models predicting women's politicization, personal testimony about women's experience of marriage sheds further light on the foregoing quantitative results. An arrangement between a man and a woman that is able to compensate for almost all other deprivations in a woman's life is known as a romantic or companionate marriage. An Alberta study, for example, found that marital satisfaction best predicts life satisfaction among farm wives, compensating even for the absence of social networks on isolated prairie enterprises (Langford and Keating 1987, 54). Debates as to the changing nature of marriage are relevant to the history of North American's western frontier where women acquired the franchise before the urbanized, industrialized east. Historians thus ask: did frontier women win the vote first because they homesteaded alongside their men as equals; did their hard, physical labour knock them off their pedestals onto the hard ground of companionate marriage between equals; or did women domesticate the frontier? Eliane Silverman (1984) posed just such questions to survivors of the 'Last Best West' in North America – Alberta. Because Alberta was settled so recently, she was able to speak to women who began homesteading in the 1920s and 1930s. Silverman found that Alberta farm women 'fell through the sieve' of middle-class domesticity which idealized romantic marriage; instead they viewed marriage as a 'vehicle for economic survival ... which both fed and starved them' (1988, 52, 60). (Although Huron and Grey counties were first settled in the 1840s, they were also isolated, traditional farming communities until at least 1945, when telephones, electrification, and mechanized farming arrived.) To a certain extent, these Alberta farm women may be taken to speak on behalf of all farm women of their generation; in that respect, their testimony stands in for the voices of mothers and grandmothers of the Ontario farm women interviewed in this study.

Several generations later, young Ontario wives, born in the mid-1950s and early 1960s, expressed frustration with marriages that their farm grandmothers and mothers (-in-law) may have taken for granted. Their comments echo tensions and stresses in farm families that have been identified as arising from seasonal variations in work requirements, the daily grind of repetitive labour, unpredictable weather, risk of industrial accident, insufficient cash flow although substantial capital is invested, and considerable financial risk (Rosenblatt and Anderson 1981). The division of agricultural labour is also a source of tension, particularly when a daughter-in-law's lack of skill or interest in farming is interpreted in terms of her perceived loyalty and commitment to her husband's family. Just as farm families have opportunities for unusually great togetherness (which is praised as their virtue), so too do they have opportunities for unusually great apartness arising from the proximity and constant demands of unwaged household-based agriculture. An aggrieved spouse, for example, can avoid intimacy by escaping to the barn or machine shed, where the work day never ceases. Apartness has been explained as a farmers' alternative to divorce without its associated social, religious, or, perhaps most important, financial penalties (Rosenblatt and Anderson 1981, 148).

When asked if they had any particular problems, twenty-one women disregarded the list of possible answers to express spontaneously a cluster of opinions that criticize farm marriages and farm families (labelled farm-family criticism in table 7.1). Those women who spontaneously spoke of personal disappointment in their marriages should be give more credence and significance than their relatively few numbers seem to warrant. They were articulate and intimate with me, and their statements may represent the feelings of more reticent respondents. As op-

TABLE 7.1   Principal problems

Problem	Frequency	
Lack of leisure time	53	(25%)
No particular problems	42	(20%)
Financial difficulties	34	(16%)
Too much hard work (on and off farm)	21	(10%)
Farm-family criticism	21	(10%)
Other (health, disability)	17	(8%)
Isolation, lack of support, rural problems	16	(7%)[1]
Machinery breakdown	8	(4%)
Can't say, refuse	1	(1%)
(N responses)	(213)	

posed to those women making deliberate efforts to preserve more to-getherness in their marriage, others have chosen, or surrendered to, strategies of apartness. Strategies of apartness or a traditional model of separate spheres might be represented by dedicated WI members who gave up to forty hours a week to volunteering, but these women did not speak so intimately.

Under the title 'farm-family criticism,' respondents identified stresses that afflict all farm wives, regardless of education. For example, this self-identified 'new' farm woman of urban origin explained that her chosen job – delivering nursery stock to customers throughout Southern Ontario – is proving difficult because her toddlers will not tolerate being in the truck all day: 'I'm frustrated that farm work isn't compatible with child care. Safety prevents me from taking them along to do the jobs I want. I want to help my husband more, but I can't.' Another self-identified feminist said: 'I wish I could do more farm work, but children prevent me. Farming's not profitable, so I have to go to work instead of farming with my husband. There's just too much work.'

Two women, neither of whom did farm work, openly and articulately criticized farm women's oppressive double load of farm and domestic labour:

When we were farming full-time, it was hard financially and physically. Now he can take time off for the family and I see my husband more. Farming would be all right if the children were older because then I could go out and work with him, which I enjoyed doing when we were first married. For now I must stay at home with the kids.

I hate farming. But it's not the farm work, it's the farm family that I hate. When we were first married in 1967, we were expected to move in with my in-laws. Farm families have no time together because work dominates the family and always comes first. We've chosen to have a particular kind of family and marriage in which there's time together as a couple for leisure, discussion, companionship.

Apart from these two women who had deliberately and successfully avoided 'farm marriages,' others were disappointed at their failure to achieve a companionate or romantic marriage. Strategies of 'apartness' were forced on them through force of circumstance and all in the name of 'family':

My husband is never available in the spring and fall. It's hard with the children when he can't help. You just have to learn to do things on your own.

My husband is a workaholic; I'm not.

We don't have time together as a family. Dad can never join the family because of chores and farm work.

We don't have any freedom because we're tied down to the pigs. We haven't had a holiday together since our honeymoon. The family can't get away together on holidays.

There's no leisure time together as a family. There's no money either for a family holiday.

My husband has no free time. I just got back from an anniversary party in Kitchener, on my side of the family. I took the children and went by myself because he was too busy.

He doesn't help with the children so it's hard for me to get away by myself. I hate to leave the three youngest with the fourteen-year-old too much.

People talk about 'farm widows.' Women do community work because there's nothing else to do. If you're not doing field-work together, there's nothing else to do.

We can't take family vacations. I don't see my husband a lot. Farm tension hits the whole family.

Not all wives, though, desired quite so much togetherness: 'My husband wants me to do more farm work, but I'm too busy and I'm not really interested in just watching things grow. It's a matter of some disagreement between us.'

Others explicitly focused on their fathers-in-law as the cause of their personal problems. Some in-laws discouraged young wives from taking up farm chores, while others, it was told, were virtual slave-drivers; but, in either case, husbands' kin are not likely to tolerate new daughters-in-law encroaching on farm management and the corresponding territory of commodity groups. Some of these women's most intense relationships are with their father-in-law rather than with their husband because their father-in-law supervises and allocates everyone's work assignments:

Farm work comes first before the house and family. When my father-in-law calls, my husband runs off.

My father-in-law is a real tyrant. He refuses to pay me a wage, although my husband gets a wage. In the winter time, he won't even plough out our driveway after a snowstorm, and I've been stuck in the yard up to two weeks at a time.

I'm surrounded by in-laws [from whom she escaped in part-time employment].

I'm under pressure from my in-laws to go back to my old job [clerking at grocery store] to support the farm when I always just wanted to be a housewife.

In contrast, this woman and her (very companionate) husband missed having relatives with whom to share field-work, child care, and machinery: 'We don't have family around for companionship and sympathy and for help with farming. Our parents and family like to come visit the farm, but they're like tourists; they don't understand and they're really no help at all. We're at a competitive disadvantage to the big [extended] families in the neighbourhood.' Farming may be

too capital- and labour-intensive for an individual couple, let alone
woman, to go it alone in one lifetime.

To find out exactly which type of farm women was likely to make
this particular criticism of farm families and marriages, demographic
and agricultural work determinants are presented in table 7.2. An
extended-family enterprise does not appear in the table; this means
that the close involvement of husbands' kin does not predict farm-
family criticism so much as the above entries testimony would suggest.
As indicated by asterisks in the corresponding table entries, younger
women who did not grow up on farms are more critical of traditional
arrangements. Women doing mechanical work do not criticize farm-
family arrangements; this finding suggests that mechanical work has
the ability to alter significantly household arrangements in women's
favour. The role of egg/poultry production cannot be explained.

Rural women may be comparatively happier than urban women.
In 1981, equal numbers of Canadian women reported being 'very
happy' (48 per cent) or 'fairly happy' (48 per cent) and only 4 per
cent were 'not too happy' (Social Change in Canada Study 1981). In
this study, most farm wives (64 per cent) said that they were 'very happy'
and the others (35 per cent) said that they were 'somewhat happy.'
It sounds suspicious that farm wives were so uniformly happy, but
if we bring a cultural value of 'keeping a stiff upper lip' to bear, being
only 'somewhat happy' becomes a more important sign of women's
personal dissatisfaction with life. Only one woman refused to answer
the question of personal happiness and her husband was dying.

The question of personal happiness refers back to a proposal presented in chapter 3. When it comes to improving women's status within
households and communities, it was proposed that the actual labour
of producing commodities is less effective than control over the sale
of commodities (Blumberg 1981; Bujra 1979). In this survey, control
over both the sale of commodities and the financial assets of the farm
operation corresponds to the two types of administrative work, internal
and external. Objectively measured status is not the same as perceived
personal happiness, but happiness surely lies behind any concern with
status.[2] The first half of the hypothesis holds up in table 7.2; the actual
labour of producing commodities significantly depresses status as
measured by personal happiness. The capacity of farm labour to decrease happiness is vividly illustrated by one woman's story of stopping
by in the evening to visit another member of her Institute: 'She was

TABLE 7.2   Determinants of personal happiness and farm-family criticism[3]

Determinants	Personal happiness	Farm-family criticism
Farm labour score	−.11*	–
Mechanical work score	–	−.14***
Wife's age	–	−.02***
Farmer father	.13	−.14*
Husband's housework	.04*	–
Husband's child care	.04	–
Hours of housework per week	.00	–
Egg/poultry farm	−.23	.20*
Employees hired index	–	−.02
R Square	.15	.37
Adjusted R Square	.10	.34
(N)	(115)	(111)

*p < .05   ***p < .001

eight months pregnant and still out milking, not worried about being kicked. She laid down for a nap after supper without washing up dishes. Her husband came in and told her: "Get up and do your chores." They go out together to do chores. He finished his while she was still working out in the barn. He returned to the house leaving her alone. He sat down to watch TV without washing the dirty dishes left over from supper.' In the opinion of the woman relating the story, husbands take advantage of 'gung-ho farm wives'; they neglect farm work, which is properly men's job, to inflict a double load of housework and farm work on their wives. Wives then neglect their children to do farm work – neglect, in this case, being defined as not enrolling children in a full range of classes and play groups.

The second half of the hypothesis, that control of the sale of commodities better guarantees women's happiness or status, does not hold up in table 7.2. Instead, gender-role reversal, measured directly by husband's housework, significantly predicts happiness.[4] Whereas administrative work has a positive impact on politicization, it has no capacity to increase personal happiness. This finding does not seek to rebut the hypothesis that control of financial assets is central to women's personal happiness and status. It merely confirms that questions about farm administration have scant ability to reveal much about power relations within farm families. Although women reported speaking to sales representatives, taking business calls, supervising teenagers, attending commodity meetings, and taking part in decisions, their stated interest likely exceeded their involvement, which, in reality, was probably limited to the periphery of the enterprise's management. In other words, their involvement in external farm administration was not far removed from the social chit-chat that, however important to the farm's standing in the rural community, does not intrude on internal decision-making dynamics.

A consistent pattern emerged from this sample that saw younger women doing the actual work of farming and older women reporting greater farm administration and greater political involvement. Although the tendency for women to be squeezed out of agriculture in middle age by their grown children has been noted with some alarm (Rosenfeld 1985, 31), Ontario women never resented their exclusion and instead expressed pride that their sons [-in-law] were willing to take over the farm. They described an ideal life cycle for farming families that defines success as the ability to retire from the physical work of farming at middle age. Questions about agricultural work prompted nostalgia rather than guilt among middle-aged women: 'Oh yes, I used to do that all the time; I've done it all at one time; I enjoyed the dairy at the time, but I wouldn't want to do it now.' Such self-satisfaction contrasts sharply to the weariness of a fifty-three-year old woman who continued to be responsible for milking chores twice daily; she confessed that she was worn out and fed up: 'I still love my cows, but after thirty or more years, it gets a bit much.' In addition to the sheer physical strain of farm labour, which prompts women to pass chores on adult children or employees with relief, some women feel compelled to downplay or reduce their agricultural work to display prosperity, and thus maintain status in the community (Fink 1988, 238). There are warnings to avoid life-cycle explanations, which, it is argued, confine the complex variety of farm women's lives to family and childcare responsibilities (Cooper 1989, 173). But, in addition to being generated by child-care responsibilities, an ideal life-cycle pattern also conforms to the physical capabilities of individual women and to the collectively held expectations of rural society.

When these findings were presented to a provincial board meeting of the Women's Institute (FWIO), responses were split along generational lines (20 Mar. 1991). Middle-aged women claimed that younger women's complaints came from idleness because they were no more overworked than women a generation before: 'I worked out in the fields all day with my husband and sons, I came in early to get their supper while they were still out there working, and I was happy to feed them, and I was happy to give him a clean shirt.' The suggestion from one participant that perhaps younger women, who had not grown up farming, were doing all the complaining brought a murmur of agreement from her peers. Two younger women, representatives of the Junior Women's Institutes, conceded that their generations' workload was no heavier, but explained that the context had changed: 'When I was growing up on a farm, we were all the same, we were all equal.' They pointed out that farming seemed so much more oppressive now because they and their children, even in ostensibly rural areas, compared their situation to neighbouring families who took annual vacations to Florida and bought consumer household goods. Three middle-aged women sympathetically agreed to this point: younger wives were better educated, had seen more of the world, and hence were frustrated by farming, which offered no challenges or opportunities to develop skills.

The purpose of this chapter has been to establish at minimum that farming does not demonstrably improve women's quality of life, and that labouring is actually deleterious. Except perhaps for those mechanically inclined, women have good cause to avoid farm work and to look elsewhere, beyond the farm enterprise, in paid employment or local community action for opportunities for self-development and autonomy. To this end, one woman, for example, related that her mother-in-law took a job as a concession-booth supervisor to spite her husband, who wanted his wife to help him with farm work. Since paid employment is most likely available to those women with higher education, community service, through the Women's Institutes, may be the preferred option for less well-educated women. Instead of a shared agricultural vocation or an urban capitalist model of dual careers, what may actually prevail in rural Ontario is rather a more traditional separate-spheres model. For instance, one woman had a standard joke: 'I married a policeman, not a farmer,' implying that she'd rather her husband had not switched occupations. Others commented: 'It's his farm, not mine' or 'It's his job, not mine.' Farm women's claims to love 'farming as a way of life' should be taken sceptically because many rightly reject the actual work of farming as 'boring' or too physically strenuous. Even those who sincerely enjoyed farm work sought non-agricultural, often domestic or community, recreations.

8

Towards an Agrarian Feminism

Owning and operating a small family business is a long-standing cultural ideal in Western society that may be an increasingly important economic trend. The tensions that feminists identify within all households are even more pronounced in these households, where the terms of employment are established through the sexual contract of marriage or cohabitation. I have attempted to investigate the consequences for women's politicization, using a case-study of Ontario farm women. This chapter highlights and tries to make sense of the strongest findings from this study. Some of these findings speak to the diversity of farm women and reveal some arresting patterns. Other findings, notably a signal commitment to community service, reveal striking uniformity. This commitment is shown to be a highly successful strategy that addresses simultaneously individual needs of farm women and systemic requirements of the rural community.

Much contemporary research argues for farm women's diversity. Some of the empirical results presented in the foregoing chapters describe differences among farm women; the regression tables summarize how variations in politicization are associated with variations in numerous demographic and farm characteristics. A synthesis can be achieved by comparing these tables and noting which measures of politicization are affected in similar ways by the same demographic and farm characteristics. This synthesis reveals some compelling patterns that demonstrate the perils of invoking a rigid distinction between 'old' and 'new' farm women, as discussed in chapter 1. One pattern combines farm administration with a keen interest in politics among older women who no longer do manual labour. A second pattern combines farm labour with a strong equality version of feminism among younger women, but not politics conventionally defined in terms of partisanship and public affairs. Perhaps the most enviable women are featured in the third pattern that combines mechanical work with personal control.

Table 4.7 shows that both types of administrative work, external (supervision of employees, talking to sales representatives, and attending commodity meetings), and internal (decision making and research), have a positive impact on women's political involvement. Farm labour and mechanical work reduce political involvement on one or more counts, whereas both age and education promote it. In all, farm administration is perhaps the critical element in women's orientation to conventional politics. Women's administrative farm work belongs with a cluster of politicization variables that are found among gregarious and literate political personalities (Kirkpatrick 1974). Whether relating to agricultural or community affairs, the same sort of gregarious people feel confident about and enjoy sitting on committees, making speeches, and reading policy briefs.

Table 6.9 shows that the profile of feminism is very different from that of an administrative/political pattern. Administration is notably absent from a profile of feminism. Whereas labour depresses political involvement and participation, it promotes feminism. Whereas older women are more politically salient, youth significantly predicts feminism. Whereas a wife's education relates positively to her political salience, her husband's education (and not her own) relates to feminism. Feminism is promoted by both spouses' off-farm paid employment and increased housework, neither of which significantly affects political involvement. As would be expected, direct cross-tabulation of feminist indicators with political involvement showed no strong association. This pattern seems to promise the greatest potential for a new farm women's movement in the future because it effectively combines farming and feminism, but these women are not politicized in conventional terms. Women who have taken on the load of caring for children and livestock alike feel that they have earned the right to claim equality with men, but they do not participate in the public realm.

The two patterns coincide in only one respect – namely, one's father *not* being a farmer.[1] This suggests that neither more politically oriented nor more feminist-oriented women grew up on farms, but rather married into farming. This apparent liability did not, however, seem to prevent them from doing either farm management or farm labour.

They just seem to develop stronger feelings about politics or feminism.

If administrative work belongs with politics, and labour belongs with feminism, mechanical work stands by itself. Mechanical work significantly depresses farm-family criticism (table 7.2) and partisanship (table 4.7); it significantly increases volunteer work (table 4.13) and husband's housework, and is neutral to feminism (table 6.9). This third pattern is exhibited by woman who have achieved greater control in their personal lives, but personally empowering characteristics do not have consequences for conventional or organized versions of feminism and politics. Given the surprising ability of mechanical work to effect egalitarian marriages and community involvement, these women may be, unselfconsciously, the real agrarian feminists.

Why do political involvement and feminism not coincide more? Why do the intense feelings provoked by questions on feminism (chapter 6) not translate into political activity? Administration does not preclude labour and mechanical work. Common sense suggests that experience in the gritty drudge work of farm labour confers credentials for farm management. Part of the answer may lie in women's life cycles; the administrative/political pattern and the labouring/feminist pattern involve age in opposite directions. Politically oriented women may have at one time' done their bit for the farm,' and thereby acquired managerial credentials for preferred administrative and community work in middle age. It remains to be seen whether or not the current generation of younger female labourers will retain its feminist critique as the generation ages into an administrative and political pattern. That combination may not occur in the immediate future because many of the women interviewed here conceptualized feminism in terms of domestic and marital relations. Their comments do not directly relate to the public or political, let alone partisan, spheres of activity. This situation may not be uniquely rural; a disjuncture between conventional political behaviour and feminism has also been observed among urban women (Fulenwider 1980, 108). The disjuncture tends to be obscured because 'high participant women tend to be high in socioeconomic standing and high socioeconomic status women tend to be feminist' (ibid, 1232).[2] But once this élite of highly educated and professionally employed politicized feminists is removed, women tend to gravitate to either a conventionally political or an apolitical feminist pattern. Among non-élite women, politicized women's activities lack feminist content and feminist's opinions lack collective political action.

If their understanding of feminism is to cross the chasm into the political (by definition, collective) sphere, farm women must understand how their domestic arrangements and individual marriages are embedded within larger economic and social systems which have often been legislated into existence by government. In short, they must understand how 'the personal is the political.'[3]

Notwithstanding the diversity discussed above, farm women show striking uniformity in some important respects. One of the most compelling and robust results of the foregoing chapters distinguishes unambiguously farm women from predominantly urban women in their strong commitment to community service (table 4.12). They were active volunteers, giving on average more than three hours a week to church, youth, and community groups. Their overwhelming enthusiasm for environmental projects can viewed as an extension of this commitment (table 5.1). Although ideologically inarticulate in formal terms (table 4.10), farm wives none the less articulated overriding principles of co-operation and conciliation (table 4.9) and felt better equipped to participate in politics than their socio-economic resources of education and wealth would generally warrant (tables 4.1–4.4). While not especially receptive to feminism, they uniformly expressed strong feelings on the subject (chapter 6). On a qualitative level, they spoke in very personal and, surprisingly often, negative terms about how farming related to their understanding of feminism and to family life (chapter 7). In what follows, I examine farm wives' commitment to community service as an individual and collective strategy that is simultaneously agrarian and feminist.

On an individual level, the main appeal of community service is organized sociability. Farming is lonely, and sociability does not happen as often and as spontaneously as it does from waged work. Instead of meeting for scheduled coffee breaks, farm households deliberately plan for sociability by scheduling events such as sports days, fairs, or suppers that have little financial cost. Much of this activity is organized through women's groups such as the WI. For women who are unhappy in farming or in their marriages, the Women's Institutes might represent an alternative to divorce. Collective activity outside the home and relatively free from male dominance is attractive for these women. Of their options for collective activity, community service is most compatible with farm women's preferences. Rural women have colonized community service for over a century, infusing it with their values of consensus and conciliation, and putting it on a moral high ground.

Community service may be a relatively accessible, non-élite avenue of political participation. Among the women interviewed in this study, four were local politicians, each of whom was the first woman in her area to be elected to township or county government. Three of the four explicitly gave credit to the Women's Institutes for their political careers. All had been responsible, at one time, for most of the farm work on marginal enterprises; none had a university education. One woman's story was particularly interesting. She began farming in 1966 when she was twenty-six years old, but she is a reluctant farmer. She grew up on a farm in the same township and went to work in Toronto, where she met her husband. After they were married, he decided he'd like to farm. Aiming to put him off, she promised to join him only if their second child was a boy. She laughed: 'There I was on the delivery table and the doctor said, "It's a boy." My first thought was "Damn it; now I gotta go farming."' Her husband has an off-farm job that requires him to be away during the week, leaving her to operate the farm by herself. In his absence, she does all the farm work except maintaining and repairing machinery and buildings; in her words, "I break it and he fixes it.' This was particularly difficult when her children were small. When her back 'gave out' in 1986, they reduced their livestock, and turned to less labour-intensive hay cultivation, supplemented with a few hogs, cattle, and hens. Farming was a struggle during the early years, she said, and was physically hard and lonely. She responded by seeking community involvement in local politics, and was elected councillor and reeve. She enjoys being an elected municipal politician because 'I can do something for the community and for myself. I don't look at things with a farmer's attitude [which] is just to be for myself, for the selfish concerns of farming, always thinking that the poor farmer is so persecuted.' She gave credit to the WI for her successful political career: 'WI led to other groups. WI taught me to stand up and talk, how to organize for a meeting, how to deal with strangers and not be shy. The old women at WI meetings are a little deaf, so this taught me good speaking skills, to speak loud and clear. I practised my campaign speech on my local WI branch. When I was younger, WI was the closest and easiest group for me to attend because my husband was away and I could bring babies and children to WI meetings. The women in my local branch called me up to run. And I topped the polls.' Such praise for WI is not unheard of among local politicians. Another Ontario reeve also credited the WI for her political career: 'I've had the experience of being able to develop leadership.

I credit my ability to do what I'm doing today to WI and to the[ir] short courses and officers conferences I've attended over the years. Getting involved in politics makes women more worldly. It gets them out of their kitchens and out of their homes and they are able to talk about political issues. Still they are wives and mothers and caregivers, and they still find time to make a contribution to issues facing the community.'[4] Apparently, this research stumbled upon a pool of community activists whose interests, and perhaps ambitions, are directed towards local government.

Community involvement does not presently bridge the schism between politics and feminism among farm women, but it might have potential to help. The WI is not explicitly feminist; its principal concern is to promote the rural way of life rather than to promote women's interests in that arrangement. Since farm women are each committed to their own families and to the prosperity of their own family enterprises, their organizations are not likely to propose formal resolutions opposing oppressive farm marriages. Furthermore, the WI does not lobby government effectively in regard to public policy. With the exception of provincial and national executives, which are involved in government-dominated policy communities, local branches are almost exclusively directed to servicing their own membership, municipal agencies, and the rural community at large. However, the WI might qualify in other regards to be called feminist. Women, and women only, hold memberships independently of their husbands' membership in other organizations. Women determine the priorities and day-to-day proceedings – however shortsighted and prejudiced – of these organizations. Rural men recognize the implicit challenge to male dominance. Armed with jokes about 'stitch and bitch' meetings, husbands and sons ridicule women's loyalty. A glowing 1958 article on the movement had ridicule as its theme: 'WI has so thoroughly infiltrated Domain [area] life that farmer Cecil Manness tells his wife, Yvette, "You ought to call yourselves the FBI." Men have been heckling WI for sixty-one years, and living to eat their words' (Collins 1958, 46). Their service work, moreover, corresponds in some ways to standard public-policy goals of the organized women's movement. Since the beginning, the WI has raised funds and distributed a multitude of scholarships for girls of all ages (particularly in 4-H clubs), its own members, and ACWW members overseas[5] – all to promote women's higher education. Examples of support for battered women and single mothers abound. Maple Valley Institute donated eleven home-made quilts for auction on behalf of a new shelter for battered women in Collingwood (*Home & Country* 57/2 [1991], 14). Jaffray Institute donates six baby layettes annually to the maternity ward of the local hospital, for single mothers in need (*Home & Country* 55/2 [1989], 14).[6] The donations are unsubstantial in value compared with funding from provincial social services, but they speak eloquently for the WI's involvement with issues that we normally recognize as feminist. Finally, as discussed above, the WI facilitates some women's integration into public life and political office alongside men, where their concerns can be heard in the process of political decision making.

What kind of 'agrarian' feminism is this when so many farm women reject 'agriculture'? The physical nourishment and growth of crops and animals cannot be separated from the social nourishment and growth of people living in rural communities. The old WI movement represents a continuing link with the tradition of providing services to the local community, including elected office in municipal government. This tradition is elsewhere represented by women's continuing involvement in such organizations as churches, Home and School, or 4-H.

The argument for community service as an integral part of agricultural economies has been made elsewhere. Winnie Lem explained that government subsidies have been less effective in promoting the contemporary commercial success of viticulture or grape cultivation in the Languedoc region of southern France than have more peasant-type reciprocal exchanges of free labour among farmers: 'The networks of cooperation and the constant regeneration of ties based on community, and a similarity of interests as family farmers in the region as a whole, have been critical in informing class actions that have been undertaken to ensure the viability of family-run viticulture' (1988, 524). In other words, family farming is able to compete successfully under advanced capitalism because it operates in communities that preserve substantial remnants of noncapitalist or peasant cooperation (ibid, 526). Networks of cooperation grounded in a sense of community make proven economic sense for these French grape farmers.

In the same spirit, Hansen and Muszynski found that the apparently irrational claims of community survival in rural Saskatchewan work to facilitate individual economic self-interest. For example, the local café in their study was purchased and operated by the mayor and his wife to provide a meeting-place, and only incidentally to make a profit. Even the financial boundaries of the 'family farm' spilled over into the community because relatives operated non-agricultural enterprises in town while continuing to invest labour and capital in extended-family farm operations. In Hansen and Muszynski's words, 'self interest appears to be explicitly embedded in a larger social context ... individuals appear to be subordinating their economic behaviours to larger social claims' (1990, 17). They also observed that multinational franchises and larger corporations had withdrawn from these rural areas because profits were inadequate. In the wake of their withdrawal, independent operators filled the gaps because lower profits were acceptable if they could continue to make a living in their home towns.

Community relations are thus an authentically agrarian object of political action because farmers are, as a class, defined by fixed private property. Unlike waged workers, they cannot transport their assets in pursuit of economic opportunity. Their individual financial livelihood is tied to the collective prosperity of their neighbourhood. Part of this collective prosperity involves the provision of 'social services' that we usually expect formal government or government-funded bodies to provide. The availability of government services in the areas of education, health care, counselling, legal aid, day care, and food banks varies from province to province, but is generally lower in rural areas.

Women have typically assumed the burden of providing social services, whether working as government employees (as nurses, counsellors, and teachers) or as volunteers. The recent curtailing of public expenditures in health, education, and related social services means that rural communities, which were already inadequately serviced, are being abandoned by governments. As the welfare state continues to deteriorate, responsibility for re-creating its services locally may fall to the same organizations, including the WI, that contributed to its creation during the interwar period.[7] When women work in voluntary associations of civil society, their work is less often recognized as providing substantive social services because it appears under the guise of sociability or community service. It is difficult to estimate the net contribution of these groups. The direct donations are rather insignificant; for example, in 1991–2, WI branches across Ontario donated directly a total of $713,511 (*Annual Report* 1992). Direct donations, however, are dwarfed by the value of the volunteer work itself. An average of three hours of volunteer work per week, when applied to the adult female rural population of Ontario, represents a not insubstantial sum compared with government social services in rural Ontario, regardless of the details of the calculation.

Farm women's tradition of local community service signals a potential innovation in the wake of the decline of Canada's centralized, national welfare state. This tradition coincides with a call in democratic theory to 'socialize the welfare state,' by which is meant giving back the provision and administration of welfare services to civil society (Walzer 1988, 20). Michael Walzer identifies women, and housewives in particular, as a skilled 'reserve army of the welfare system' whose traditional service ought to be institutionalized formally (1988, 23). This 'democratization' of welfare services has the potential to exploit women; at very least administrative decisions should be decentralized along with the actual work and volunteer work should be done through formal collective organizations.

As a formal collective organization, the WI is well posed to take part in the devolution of welfare-state services. Its instrumental role in pressing for and implementing blue-box recycling programs is a promising example. Recycling programs are intimately connected to the economic limits of politics, given the fiscal burden of waste disposal on rural municipalities which hesitate to impose still higher property taxes on struggling retail and manufacturing enterprises. To this end, Warwick Women's Institute planned and chaired a meeting between township council and representatives of ratepayers to 'reopen lines of communication and to establish communication' after several confrontations over waste disposal (*Home & Country* 56/3 [1990], 12). Another example involves national child-care policy. In 1989, Health and Welfare Canada asked the Federated Women's Institutes of Canada to conduct, in coordination with local WI branches, a survey of rural families' requirements and preferences for child care. In its report, the FWIC observed that respondents generally preferred that government funding be given directly to assist parents to be at home caring for their own children (*The rural child care survey project*, 1990). Balancing this sentiment against the obvious inadequacy of rural facilities, the report recommended the expansion of less-formal and more-flexible child-care services, operating through Farm Labour Pool offices. The overall thrust of the FWIC report is especially relevant to the analysis being developed here. According to the FWIC authors, 'Rural people are accustomed to solving their own problems and developing low cost, workable solutions,' but their efforts to develop alternative child-care facilities are hindered by 'bureaucratic stumbling blocks [imposing] rigid adherence to overly strict regulations' (1990, 15, 18). In that spirit, Bethesda-Reach Institute had already created in 1988 seasonal child care programmes located in the homes of individual farm families (*Home & Country* 55/1 [1988], 7).

The division between 'old' and 'new' farm women's movements is not rigid, but a broad distinction can be drawn between community-based organizations, such as the WI, directed to the rural community at large, and commodity-based organizations aiming to 'support and strengthen the family farm and the farm family' (OFWN constitution). Commodity-based groups concentrate more on public policy because governments increasingly negotiate the terms of trade in agricultural commodities. The National Farmers' Union notably combines community and commodity issues in an ambitious critique, but for the most part, given that resources (membership dues, government funding, and volunteers) are limited, both routes are competing and, to a certain extent, mutually exclusive. The OFWN, identified here as an agricultural or commodity-based organization, has also called for initiatives to encourage farm women to run for elected office, but Pauline Rankin points out that promoting such community-oriented activities will dissipate members' energies 'on mandates so varied that significant initiatives on specific issues prove problematic,' much as the WI has done (1989, 327). She advised new farm women's organizations to focus strictly on agricultural issues: higher commodity prices, secure farm financing, equal access to government training programs, or legal title to farm assets.

Strictly agricultural organizations represent a perfectly valid route of political participation, but why has their appeal among farm women been limited? To begin with, there are social barriers operating to discourage farm women from commodity-based political activism. For example, one farm woman wrote: "I often find myself frustrated by other women who want to talk only about rural day care not about such vital issues as farm finance and commodity prices' (*Canadian Farm Women's Network Newsletter* 3 [1990], 9). Another woman explained that 'most women I associate with have little involvement in farm management, thus they seem to avoid technical farm conversations preferring to discuss the garden or the children. If I talk about cutting hay or baling I often feel that they think I'm showing them up, or they frown upon me for neglecting my children' (personal correspondence, Aug. 199). Another social barrier involves household arrangements. Women generally begin attending male-dominated meetings only when accompanied by a male escort; this is very much a couples-based recreation and strategy, and so requires as a prerequisite an egalitarian, companionate marriage.

It is a tall order for Canada's relatively few farm women, not only to support local community groups, but also to maintain a specifically female presence in agricultural policy communities directed by government agencies. Such a present requires an enormous amount of volunteer time and intellectual effort to prepare briefs, lobby officials, and organize and attend conferences. Dropping community service is not a valid option because peer pressure makes farm women feel obliged to do their part. And although conventionally female fundraising activities – catering and quilting parties – have their limits, in the end these activities are more fun than what is required to lobby government on agricultural policy – namely, writing formal policy papers.[8]

The object of conventional farm politics, improved commodity prices and terms of exchange, does not benefit wives unless the internal structure of ownership and claim to commodity receipts is addressed within farm households.[9] The women who are doing animal-husbandry chores, especially on extended-family operations, are least likely to benefit from increased commodity prices because they are least involved in decision making and administration. It is not quite clear if increased capitalization, as a result of overall prosperity, will improve their predicament. For example, one woman was responsible for cleaning straw and manure from cattle stalls until the enterprise bought a mechanical loader; her father-in-law subsequently forbade her to use the mechanical loader and redirected her labour into more extensive responsibilities for cleaning and maintaining milking equipment. In this particular case, the farm's capital acquisition, as reflected in this particular purchase, increased, or at least did not decrease, her workload because she did not control administrative decisions. The call for women to strengthen farm organizations and save the family farm[10] (rather than to improve women's particular station) would be more compelling if, on an individual level, administrative/politically oriented women were more receptive to feminism and, therefore, more willing to challenge power relations within individual households.

Furthermore, a commodity-based or generally agricultural agenda plays into a package of international economic restructuring under negotiation, particularly through General Agreement on Tariffs and

Trade (GATT), which is simply too difficult for most farm women (and most people, in general) to understand, let alone have any political impact on. The Ontario government provided material designed to 'familiarize farm and agribusiness leaders' with the Canada–U.S. Free Trade Agreement and sponsored a conference for farmers on the Uruguay Round of GATT negotiations, but only those with a background in economics had a chance of understanding any of it. In comparison, the original populist program from the 1920s that criticized exploitative central Canadian banks and finance capital, and later proposed that 'social credit' fill the gap left by private banking, looks simplistic. Some farm women are able to understand these issues, but they should be identified as an élite. Consider, for instance, this profile of a survey respondent who sat on an Ontario Federation of Agriculture commodity committee, among numerous others. Both she and her husband held degrees in Agriculture and neither did manual labour on their $4-million operation, which employed four full-time employees.

Our limited ability to judge accurately what is the best course of collective, political action has been called an 'epistemic gap' (Dunn 1990b). In the contemporary Western world, domestic political issues (bearing upon secure incomes, mortgages, and taxes) have become international economic issues and, as a result, the extreme complexity of these issues disqualifies the vast bulk of people from judging with any accuracy what their interests really are. The epistemic gap relates not only to understanding such issues as negotiations in international agricultural trade held under the auspices of GATT, but also to putting into political practice that intellectual understanding. Once one understands the enormity of what is at stake for one's family and community, what does one do (politically) with that knowledge? Canada's government is so inscribed within the world system of sovereign states that officials employed by agriculture ministries can scarcely accommodate farmers' grievances. Not even the people we expect to be the most effective in this regard, that is, farmers elected as members of legislatures, are able to do much for their constituents because the debate has been removed from the traditional mechanisms of governing – caucus, cabinet, and parliament – to international conferences where Canada's top negotiators speak as one, relatively weak, voice among many.

The WI appeals in this regard because its local activities produce immediate, concrete results:

I like the local focus on community service. I prefer WI to other 'distant' groups. It's a good balance between yourself and the community.

It's for our own kids and seniors. The money that we raise stays right here in the community rather than being sent off.

WI is for 'home and country' [official motto] – right here. Last year, someone on the line had their barn burn down. We helped them immediately. The money didn't go away through administrative channels. We're made aware of other people's problems, which is difficult because farm people don't talk. But WI members will confide problems to each other and still respect each other's privacy.

Similar sentiments arose at an Institute meeting where a representative from Concerned Farm Women spoke about her recent Oxfam-sponsored tour of Nicaragua for farm women. Although the woman who had made the tour had been deeply and personally moved, her audience remained convinced that charity begins at home and that Oxfam could not be trusted to distribute their charitable donations. Given these discouraging epistemic and social barriers to commodity-based political activism, farm women might well neglect to identify and judge the mechanisms of causation bearing on commodity prices and secure farm financing and, instead, simply try to cope with the local consequences.[11]

In conclusion, farm women's commitment to community service is an individual strategy for personal happiness and a collective strategy for satisfying the systemic needs of rural communities. Farm women's premium on consensus and conciliation is of a piece with their enthusiasm for community service: it secures a public, non-domestic role for women, while offending no one and gaining the moral approval of all. Individual values align with collective characteristics in that organizations such as the WI have historically abided by the same principles of consensus and conciliation. Given the epistemic and social barriers confronting farm women, community service is their most practical political alternative. The political potential of farm women's community service may be limited, but should not be overlooked entirely simply because it is not organized along formal partisan lines of liberal democracy or along Leninist lines of seizing state power by revolution. It is a way of coping at a local level with massive dislocations brought on by the global economy that sheds light on what a household-based, self-employed alternative to the current order could look like.

Survey Questionnaire with Frequencies

This study is based in part on a project conducted by Naomi Black and Gail Cuthbert Brandt that examined the political opinions of Roman Catholic farm wives in Quebec and France. The first part of the survey employed mainly closed multiple-choice questions that are standard to rural sociology. Black and Brandt chose some of the agricultural questions from Suzanne Dion's study (1983), sponsored by the Quebec Ministry of Agriculture. I translated agricultural questions on Brandt and Black's French survey to correspond, as accurately as possible, to the 1980 Farm Women's Survey, sponsored by the U.S. Department of Agriculture (Rosenfeld 1985) and an independent Ontario study (Cebotarev, Blacklock, and McIsaac 1986; Ireland 1983). The present research deliberately included interviews in the same geographic area chosen by a 1983 Ontario mail-in survey (N = 343). Taking advantage of the fact that this 1983 survey, designed and conducted by a local organization called Concerned Farm Women, was a significant political event in the area, the present survey was explicitly introduced as a follow-up project. Hence prospective survey subjects were assumed to be at least somewhat familiar with the basic thrust of this type of research. A few women were interviewed who had completed the original 1983 survey and were, therefore, answering much the same survey for a second time.

The second, political part of the survey took questions from Euro-Barometer and Election Study research. Euro-Barometer surveys are conducted and published by the Commission of the European Communities to measure public opinion in European integration. Election Study surveys are conducted and published independently by academic researchers in each country. English-language versions of questions were generally available for this section. The principal investigators, SSHRC, the Commission of the European Communities, and the Institute for Social Research bear no responsibility for the analyses and interpretations presented here.

Louise I. Carbert
Political Science, York University
North York, Ontario M3J 1P3

Thank you for agreeing to help me with my study. I want to assure you that all results will be confidential. When I have analysed the answers, I will send you a report on the final statistics.

S1. The purpose of my study is to investigate the political opinions of farm wives. To begin with, are you Protestant or not?

	Frequency
Protestant	108 (92%)
Roman Catholic	9 (8%)

S2. Can you tell me if you are currently married or living together or if you have ever been married or lived in a marital situation on a farm?

	Frequency
married, etc.	117 (100%)

S3. What is your current marital status?

	Frequency
married	116 (99%)
widowed	1 (1%)

S4. Now are you a member of a Women's Institute?

	Frequency
member	67 (57%)
non-member	50 (43%)
(N)	117

To begin with, I'll ask about you and farming.

1. Do you now have a job for pay outside home or farm work?

	Frequency
yes	50 (43%)
no	67 (57%)
(N)	117

1a. Do you work full-time or part-time at this job? (50 people)

	Frequency
part-time	32 (64%)
full-time	11 (22%)
seasonally	7 (14%)
(N)	50

2. What is it? This would only be paid, off-farm work.

Wife's current job title	Frequency
office administrator	1
deputy clerk/clerk-treasurer	1
township councillor, warden, reeve	3
director or delegate of agri assoc	1
teacher (no B.Ed.)	3
teacher (B.Ed.)	3
college professor	1
nurse's aide	1
nurse	10
teacher's aide	1
lab technologist	1
magazine editor	1
medical/dental receptionist	2
secretary	7
bookkeeper	3
bank teller	1
store cashier	1
floor manager at shop	1
concession booth supervisor	1
home-care worker	1
hairdresser	1
domestic service	1

2. *(Continued)*

Wife's current job title	Frequency
bus driver	1
factory worker	1
enumerator/poll clerk	2
(N)	50

3. Please tell me how long you have had your current employment outside of farming? (Not same employer, but same type of work)

Mean	11 years
Midpoint	8 years (half below 8 years, half above)
Maximum	40 years

4. Why do you have a job outside of farming? (up to 3 answers each)

	Frequency
financial, individual autonomy	35 (52%)
career development	15 (22%)
sociability	10 (15%)
no work for wife on farm	4 (6%)
to help contribute to farm	2 (3%)
other (not money at all)	1 (1%)
(N responses)	67

5. If you are currently holding a job other than farming, how satisfied do you feel about it?

	Frequency
very satisfied	33 (73%)
somewhat satisfied	9 (20%)
not very satisfied	2 (4%)
not satisfied at all	1 (2%)
(N)	45

6. What is the main reason for your satisfaction or dissatisfaction? (up to 3 answers each)

	Frequency
enjoy the work itself	23 (31%)
sociability	23 (31%)
individual autonomy, career success	12 (16%)
financial	9 (12%)
complementarity – family and farm	8 (11%)
information got from work	6 (8%)
work too hard, painful, debilitating (nursing)	3 (4%)
(N responses)	74

7. IF NO OFF-FARM PAID EMPLOYMENT (67 people)
Do you ever regret that you don't have a paid job outside of farming? Do you regret it often, sometimes, rarely, or never?

	Frequency
often	2 (3%)
sometimes	20 (31%)
rarely	15 (23%)
never	28 (24%)
(N)	65

8. Why is it that you don't have a paid job outside of farming? (up to 3 answers each)

	Frequency
I prefer to work with my husband on our farm	40 (40%)
My family responsibilities made it difficult	31 (31%)
other (ill health, age, prefer volunteer work)	14 (14%)
My husband wanted me to stay home to look after the house	10 (10%)
I haven't been able to find suitable work	4 (4%)
I lost my previous job and haven't found another	2 (2%)
(N responses)	101

9. Before working here at home, did you work at something else?

	Frequency
yes	96 (91%)
no	9 (9%)
(N)	105

9a. Did you work full-time or part-time at this occupation?

	Frequency
part-time	26 (27%)
full-time	67 (71%)
seasonally	2 (2%)
(N)	95

10. What was your previous occupation?

Wife's previous job title	Frequency
office administrator	1
deputy clerk/clerk-treasurer	1
township councillor, reeve, warden	1
camp counsellor	1
drafting clerk	1
teacher (no B.Ed.)	9
home economist	1
computer programmer	1
teacher (B.Ed.)	4
nurse	9
interior/fashion design	2
lab animal technician	1
recreation director	1
medical/dental receptionist	4
secretary	16
bookkeeper	5
bank teller	4
store cashier	11
telephone operator	1
data-entry clerk	2
concession booth supervisor	1
waitress	1
home-care worker	1
domestic service	1
cook	1
tobacco picker	1
assembling computerized components	1
bus driver	1
clerical	3

10. *(Continued)*

Wife's previous job title	Frequency
newspaper clerk	1
type-setter and graphic design	1
factory worker	6
(N)	96

11. How long did you work at this occupation? (Not same employer, but same type of work)

Mean	7 years
Midpoint	5 years
Maximum	40 years

12. Have you ever invested your own money in the farm enterprise? This includes wages, inheritance, and savings.

	Frequency
yes	58 (50%)
no	59 (50%)
(N)	117

13. How did you as a couple enter farming? (up to 2 answers each)

	Frequency
purchase	104 (74%)
inherit	28 (20%)
lease	4 (3%)
other (acquired through labour for parents)	2 (1%)
can't say, refuse	2 (1%)
(N responses)	140

14. [If from a family member] From whose family was the farm inherited, purchased, or leased?

	Frequency
from husband's family	79 (68%)
not from either family	34 (29%)
from wife's family	2 (2%)
from both families equally	1 (1%)
(N)	116

15. What year did you begin farming together with your husband?

Mean	1967	22 years ago
Midpoint	1969	20 years ago
Minimum	1936	
Maximum	1988	

16. Now I have some questions about the kinds of work you may do that contribute to the operation of your farm. If a particular type of work doesn't apply to your operation, please be sure to tell me. Do you do this work never, rarely, occasionally, or regularly? (Of 114 active farms, each row adds to 100%, apart from roundoff error)

	never	*rarely*	*occasionally*	*regularly*	*n/a*
field-work: mechanized (tilling, seeding, harvesting, fertilizing)	27%	21%	26%	25%	0
help with farm animals (doctoring, births, etc.)	20%	11%	24%	33%	12%
maintain or repair farm buildings/fences	40%	31%	23%	6%	0
perform milking chores	9%	1%	6%	20%	64%
clean barn, etc.	40%	13%	21%	23%	3%
maintain or repair farm machinery	77%	17%	6%	0	0
operate trucks as part of field-work	33%	17%	23%	24%	4%
nursery/greenhouse work	0	0	1%	1%	98%
packaging products for market	2%	0	2%	10%	86%
labelling products for market	2%	0	1%	5%	92%
maple sugaring	0	1%	3%	3%	93%
processing products for market (juice, butchery, cheese, wool, honey, maple products)	1%	1%	0	5%	93%
supervise the work of hired help	29%	7%	10%	12%	42%
market products directly to consumers	12%	1%	8%	18%	61%
market products to wholesale buyers	70%	6%	9%	10%	4%

16. *(Continued)*

	never	rarely	occasionally	regularly	n/a
represent the farm at commodity and agricultural associations, not homemaking division	66%	5%	15%	11%	3%
research	24%	14%	31%	32%	0
keep farm accounts, livestock records, pay farm bills, do farm banking, prepare the farm income tax forms	16%	1%	12%	71%	0
decide stocking policy	55%	6%	6%	23%	10%
decide cropping policy	73%	11%	4%	11%	1%
farm management (e.g., answer the phone to attend to business calls)	3%	12%	27%	57%	1%
deal with salesmen about buying farm supplies and equipment	56%	14%	19%	12%	0
pruning/tieing grape vines	1%	0	0	0	99%
work on the grape harvest	1%	0	0	0	99%
wine-making	0	0	0	0	100%
feed and water farm livestock	13%	13%	28%	34%	11%
harvest fruit	0	0	1%	3%	96%
raising geese for pate	1%	0	1%	1%	97%
other (running errands)	0	0	4%	11%	85%

17. Here is a list of household tasks. Does your husband do the following
tasks never, rarely, occasionally, or regularly? (Of 114 active farms, each
row adds to 100%, apart from roundoff error)

	never	rarely	occasionally	regularly	n/a
meal preparation	40%	19%	35%	6%	0
upkeep of the house (laundry, cleaning)	58%	22%	18%	2%	0
care for young children	12%	12%	38%	27%	11%
run errands, purchase household goods	27%	24%	39%	11%	0
help children with homework and school projects	19%	16%	26%	19%	19%
attend parent–teacher functions	25%	18%	19%	25%	13%
take care of children while you attend an activity of your choice	3%	7%	33%	48%	10%

18. Does your husband now have a job for pay outside home or farm work?

	Frequency
yes	41 (36%)
no	73 (64%)
(N)	114

18a. Does he work full-time or part-time at this job?

	Frequency
part-time	17 (42%)
full-time	22 (54%)
seasonally	2 (5%)
(N)	42

19. What is your husband's current job for pay outside of farm work?

Husband's current job title	Frequency
AgRep for county	1
deputy clerk/clerk-treasurer	1
vice-principal	1
township councillor, reeve, warden	6
seed distributor	1
automotive sales	1
director or delegate	3
fertilizer and other sales	1
crop insurance sales	1
factory foreman	1
teacher (B.Ed.)	2
weighing cattle	1
insurance investigator	1
sales manager	1
herd manager for a stock dealer	1
livestock worker	1
tool & die maker	1
self-employed building contractor	2
tire repair service	1
installing milking machinery	1
Bell Canada technician	1
electrician	2
stonemason	1
pipefitter	1
carpenter	1
truck driver	3
bus driver	3
factory worker	1
(N)	42

20. Please estimate how many hours per week you normally spend on farm work. (Include books, chores, field-work)

	Midpoint	Mean	Maximum
spring	8.5 hours/wk	16 hours/wk	70 hours/wk
summer	8	17	84
autumn	8	15	72
winter	8	13.5	84

20. *(Continued)*

WI mean		Non-WI mean
spring	15 hrs/wk	18 hrs/wk
summer	17	16
autumn	15	16
winter	13	14

21. Please estimate how many hours per week you normally spend on house-work. (Include child care, gardening, freezing, meals)

	Midpoint	*Mean*	*Maximum*
spring	38 hrs/wk	38 hrs/	97 hrs/
summer	39	41	97
autumn	39	38	97
winter	35	37	97

	WI mean	*Non-WI mean*
spring	38 hrs/wk	39 hrs/wk
summer	40	42
autumn	37	39
winter	36	38

22. Please estimate how many hours per week you normally work at paid employment.

	Midpoint	*Mean*	*Maximum*	*WI mean*	*Non-WI mean*
spring	21 hrs/wk	22 hrs/wk	44 hrs/wk	22 hrs/wk	22 hrs/wk
summer	20	19	44	18	19
autumn	22	23	44	23	22
winter	22	23	44	23	21

23. Are you a member of any of these organizations?

Total mean	3.1 organizations
WI mean	3.6
non-WI mean	2.6

24. Do you currently do unpaid volunteer work for any of these organizations?

Total mean	2.7 organizations
WI mean	2.9
non-WI mean	2.3

25. Are you an officer in any of these organizations?

Total mean	1.5 organizations
WI mean	1.6
non-WI mean	1.2

23–5. Membership, volunteer work, and office held (% is of 117 people, more than one answer each; %s add to more than 100%

	Member	Volunteer	Officer
women's organizations (WI)	62%	63%	46%
community groups (Fair Board)	34%	40%	25%
churches or religious organizations	86%	77%	30%
education or arts groups	17%	10%	9%
trade unions or professional societies	40%	9%	6%
political movements or parties	13%	3%	–
organizations concerned with human rights	2%	–	–
animal rights/welfare, environmentalist	4%	2%	2%
youth groups (4-H, scouts, guides)	33%	44%	25%
consumer organizations	–	–	–
sports clubs	21%	13%	5%
other (hospital, assistance, fund-raising)	3%	8%	1%

26. Apart from WI, are you a member of any other women's organization?

	Frequency
Concerned Farm Women/Women in Support of Agriculture	2
Ontario Farm Women's Network	2
Other (Eastern Star, Rebekah's Lodge, Legion Aux.)	7
(N)	11

27. What year did you join a Women's Institute? (67 respondents)

Mean	1968	21 years ago
Midpoint	1973	16 years ago
Minimum	1925	
Maximum	1988	

28. Why did you join a Women's Institute? (up to 4 answers each)

	Frequency
sociability	49 (35%)
information, education, crafts	30 (21%)
invited by friends, family	20 (14%)
community service	19 (13%)
self-development, autonomy	17 (12%)
other (criticism of WI)	7 (5%)
(N responses)	142

29. How many of the following events did you attend last year? (67 respondents)

Number of events attended	Mean	Midpoint	Maximum
Branch meetings, district annual, Fall rally, area	9	10	20
Convention, provincial convention	2	2	9

Number of people attending	Frequency	N
Branch meetings, district annual, fall rally, area	66 (99%)	67
Convention, provincial convention	53 (79%)	67
workshops	26 (39%)	67
day outings	25 (37%)	67
overnight events	13 (19%)	67
other (board meetings for 3 women)	3 (4%)	67

30. Why aren't you a member of a Women's Institute? (50 respondents, up to 3 answers each)

	Frequency
too busy or inconvenient to belong	24 (37%)
hostile, critical of WI	21 (32%)
WI is too demanding of one's time or money	11 (17%)
I prefer other community work (church mostly)	5 (8%)
not interested in women-only groups	3 (5%)
other (never heard of WI)	1 (2%)
(N responses)	65

31. Please estimate how many hours per week you usually spend on volunteer work. [Not WI branch meetings, 4-H is 30 hrs/project]

	Midpoint	Mean	Maximum	WI mean	Non-WI mean
spring	2 hrs/wk	3 hrs/wk	20 hrs/wk	4 hrs/wk	2/wk
summer	1	2	20	3	2
autumn	3	4	40	5	3
winter	2	4	40	5	2

33. How are you remunerated for the work that you do on your farm? (114 respondents, up to 3 answers each)

	Frequency
I take what I need	70 (47%)
weekly, monthly, or annual salary	22 (15%)
other (cheques come in my name)	21 (14%)
RRSP from farm income	16 (11%)
percentage of farm's profits	10 (7%)
increased share in the equity of farm corporation	5 (3%)
gifts	3 (2%)
hourly wage	2 (1%)
can't say	1 (1%)
(N responses)	150

34. Would you say that you are very satisfied, somewhat satisfied, not very satisfied, or not satisfied at all with your remuneration for farm work?

	Frequency
very satisfied	64 (59%)
somewhat satisfied	31 (29%)
not very satisfied	7 (7%)
not satisfied at all	5 (5%)
can't say	1 (1%)
(N)	114

35. IF NOT PAID A WAGE FOR FARM WORK

Why aren't you paid a wage for your farm work? (77 respondents, up to 3 answers each)

	Frequency
The financial situation of the business doesn't permit it	29 (25%)
I never asked to be paid	23 (20%)
I don't need to be paid	22 (19%)
It wouldn't change the family's income	18 (16%)
It wouldn't be advantageous for the business	8 (7%)
My husband does not think it's necessary	6 (5%)
Other (prefer that my children be paid wages instead)	4 (4%)
My husband doesn't want to be disadvantaged concerning taxes	2 (2%)
I don't want to disadvantage my husband concerning taxes	1 (1%)
can't say	1 (1%)
(N responses)	114

36. IF NOT PAID A WAGE

Do you think you should be paid a wage for your agricultural work?

	Frequency
yes	16 (21%)
no	59 (76%)
can't say	3 (4%)
(N)	78

37. What factors are most influential in dividing up agricultural work? (114 respondents, up to 4 answers each)

	Frequency
my abilities	75 (22%)
my responsibilities for my children	52 (15%)
the time that I'm able to devote to farming	39 (12%)
a joint/collective decision after discussion	37 (11%)
my preferences	37 (11%)
my husband's commitments outside farming	20 (6%)
my husband's preferences	17 (5%)
women traditionally responsible for certain tasks	15 (4%)
my husband's decision	14 (4%)

37. *(Continued)*

my husband's abilities	11 (3%)
the profitability of the activity	6 (2%)
can't say	5 (1%)
my children's preferences	3 (1%)
the other shareholders' preferences	3 (1%)
the other shareholders' abilities	2 (1%)
(N responses)	336

38-9. In this list, are there certain agricultural tasks which are more suitable for men in general? ... more suitable for your husband?

	Frequency	
	men	husband
maintain or repair farm machinery	69	72
maintain or repair farm buildings, fences, etc.	57	57
field work: mechanized tilling, seeding, harvesting	45	81
decide cropping policy for the coming year	31	58
deal with salespeople about buying supplies and equipment	27	40
clean barn, etc.	25	28
decide stocking policy for the coming year	25	41
help with farm animals: doctoring,births, etc.	19	51
operate trucks as part of farm work	17	37
can't say, can't distinguish husband from all men	15	–
supervise the work of hired help	11	32
deal directly with wholesale buyers in marketing products	8	29
represent the farm enterprise at meetings	8	25
milking chores	–	20
research	–	20
feed and water farm livestock	–	20
market products directly to consumers	–	17

40-1. In this list, are there certain agricultural tasks which are more suitable
for women? ... more suitable for you?

	Frequency women	self
keep farm accounts, banking, and prepare tax forms	63	79
performing milking chores	42	36
nursery/greenhouse work	41	35
labelling products for market	39	16
help with farm animals: doctoring, births, etc.	36	48
packaging products for market	35	15
farm management, e.g., taking business calls	30	48
deal directly with consumers in marketing your products	23	18
processing products for market: juice, butchery, cheese	19	–
supervise the work of hired help	13	20
research	12	16
maple sugaring	11	10
harvest fruit	10	13
raising geese for pâté	10	–
field-work: mechanized tilling, seeding, harvesting	–	42
feed and water farm livestock	–	34
operate trucks as part of farm work	–	21
represent the farm enterprise at meetings	–	21
operate trucks as part of farm work	–	21
deal directly with wholesale buyers in marketing products	–	14
clean barn	–	13

42. Do you have your own income from any of the following activities?

	Frequency
other (calf, Avon, teaching, cream cheque)	24 (31%)
craft production	15 (19%)
egg production	13 (17%)
fruit or vegetables	12 (16%)
jams, preserves, baked goods	7 (9%)
poultry	6 (8%)
farm vacation, bed and breakfast	0
(N responses)	77

43. When a big decision is necessary, (e.g., large expenditure, new production), how it is usually made? (114 respondents, 3 answers each)

	Frequency
My husband consults me and takes into account my opinion in making his decision	38 (30%)
My husband consults me, then makes the decision (alone or with the other shareholders)	31 (24%)
I make the decision with my husband	18 (14%)
My husband makes the decision	11 (9%)
I just influence the decision	11 (9%)
We make the decision with other shareholders	10 (8%)
I take no part in the decision making	6 (5%)
other	2 (2%)
can't say	1 (1%)
(N responses)	128

45-6. If your farm is a cooperative, legal partnership, or corporation, what percentage of the total do you and your husband own?

	Frequency	
	wife	*husband*
less than 40%	6 (20%)	4 (13%)
40%	3 (10%)	2 (7%)
50%	9 (30%)	19 (63%)
more than 51%	– –	3 (10%)
not a partner or shareholders	12 (40%)	– –
can't say, refuse	– –	2 (7%)
(N)	30	30

47. Choose the main product of your agricultural enterprise. Indicate only the products which contribute income to the farm. Do not indicate products destined for family consumption or use on the farm.

Product type	Huron census	Grey census	Huron + Grey census	Carbert sample
cattle	26%	51%	38%	24%
hogs	17%	9%	14%	18%
other animal husbandry	4%	4%	4%	10%
wheat and field grains	28%	7%	18%	12%
dairy	13%	16%	13%	14%
poultry and eggs	4%	1%	3%	14%
equipment, seed distribution	–	–	–	4%
fruit and vegetables	2%	4%	3%	4%
other combinations	6%	8%	7%	–
(N enterprises >$2,500 gross sales)	3,266	2,874	6,140	114

Source: 1986 Canada Census, vol. 96-108, 1-219.

48. Altogether, about how many total acres are there in your farm? Please include acres you own or lease or rent from other people.

	Huron census	Grey census	Carbert sample
0–69 acres	20%	16%	4%
70–129 acres	21%	29%	16%
130–79 acres	14%	14%	11%
180–239 acres	15%	15%	19%
240–399 acres	18%	18%	21%
400–559 acres	6%	6%	14%
560–759 acres	3%	2%	7%
760–1,119 acres	2%	1%	4%
over 1,120 acres	1%	–	4%
can't say	–	–	1%
Median acres	216	152	242
(N enterprises)	3,416	3,358	114

Source: 1986 Canada Census, vol. 96-108, 1-99.

49. In rough figures, what is the total value of your farm operation today?
    Please include the value of all land, animals, machinery, and other assets.

Capital value	Huron census	Grey census	Huron + Grey census	Carbert sample
less than $ 199,999	40%	64%	51%	8%
$ 200,000 to $ 499,999	42%	31%	37%	35%
$ 500,000 to $ 999,999	14%	4%	9%	18%
$ 1 million plus	4%	1%	3%	18%
can't say	–	–	–	21%
Median value	270,000	166,000	194,000	473,000
(N enterprises)	3,416	3,358	6,774	114

Source: 1986 Canada Census, vol. 96-108, 1–189.

50. In the last two years, do you think the approximate value of your farm
    assets (e.g., livestock, buildings, equipment, land, etc.) has ...

	Frequency
stayed the same	32 (28%)
decreased	16 (14%)
increased	62 (54%)
can't say	4 (4%)
(N)	114

51. Can you estimate what percentage of your family income comes from
    jobs (not investments) held off your own farm?

	Frequency
less than 10%	9 (14%)
10–49%	19 (30%)
50–74%	11 (17%)
75–100%	18 (29%)
can't say	6 (10%)
(N)	63

52. What is the most appropriate title for what you do? (2 answers each)

	Frequency
farm wife	36 (30%)
partner in an agricultural enterprise	31 (25%)
country woman	20 (16%)
housewife	17 (14%)
co-owner and operator of a farm	13 (11%)
other(politician, community worker, teacher)	4 (3%)
farmer	1 (1%)
(N responses)	122

53. Would you say that you are very satisfied, somewhat satisfied, not very satisfied, or not satisfied at all with your present agricultural work?

	Frequency
very satisfied	69 (61%)
somewhat satisfied	35 (31%)
not very satisfied	10 (9%)
(N)	114

54. What are your principal problems?

	Frequency
lack of leisure time	53 (25%)
no particular problems	42 (20%)
financial difficulties	34 (16%)
too much hard work (on and off farm)	21 (10%)
farm family criticism	21 (10%)
other (health, disability)	17 (8%)
isolation, lack of support, rural problems	16 (7%)
machinery breakdown	8 (4%)
can't say, refuse	1 (1%)
(N responses)	213

Now we're going to talk about politics

55. Did you vote in the provincial election in 1987?

	Frequency
yes	107 (92%)
no	8 (7%)
can't recall	2 (1%)
(N)	117

56. Can you tell me which party you voted for?

	Frequency
Liberal party	55 (51%)
Conservative party	30 (28%)
New Democratic Party	2 (2%)
can't recall	22 (20%)
(N)	109

57. Can you tell me why you didn't vote?

	Frequency
It's too hard to decide who to vote for	3
It doesn't matter which party is in power	1
other (childbirth, no citizenship)	4
(N non-voters)	8

58. Did you vote in the federal election in November 1988?

	Frequency
yes	109 (93%)
no	7 (6%)
can't recall	1 (1%)
(N)	117

59. Can you tell me which party you voted for?

	Frequency
Liberal party	37 (34%)
Progressive Conservative party	50 (46%)
New Democratic Party	7 (6%)
other (Christian Heritage)	2 (2%)
can't recall	13 (12%)
(N)	109

60. Can you tell me why you didn't vote?

	Frequency
It's too hard to decide who to vote for	3
It doesn't matter which party is in power	1
other (childbirth, no citizenship)	4
Total non-voters	8

61. Do you completely agree, agree to some extent, disagree to some extent, or disagree completely that, if they wanted to, all the political parties, from left to right, could come to an agreement to make good policy for Canada?

	Frequency
completely agree	37 (32%)
agree to some extent	35 (30%)
disagree to some extent	15 (13%)
disagree completely	26 (22%)
can't say	4 (3%)
(N)	117

62. Some say that politics is too complicated and one has to be a specialist to understand politics. Do you completely agree, agree to some extent, disagree to some extent, or disagree completely with this view?

	Frequency
completely agree	27 (23%)
agree to some extent	37 (32%)
disagree to some extent	42 (36%)
disagree completely	11 (9%)
(N)	117

63. It is sometimes said that 'politics should be left to men.' How do you personally feel about this? Do you completely agree, agree to some extent, disagree to some extent, or disagree completely with this view?

	Frequency
completely agree	1 (1%)
agree to some extent	1 (1%)
disagree to some extent	25 (21%)
disagree completely	90 (77%)
(N)	117

64. Generally speaking, would you have more confidence in a man or a
    woman ... (% of 117 across each row)

	man	woman	same	can't say
to drive your bus	30%	7%	64%	0
to drive your train	47%	2%	47%	4%
as the surgeon to operate on you	26%	3%	69%	2%
as a doctor to deliver your baby	14%	15%	69%	2%
as a lawyer to defend you in court	22%	6%	68%	3%
as your member of Parliament	15%	8%	75%	2%

65. In general, are you interested in politics a great deal, to some extent, not
    much, or not at all?

	Frequency
a great deal	14 (12%)
to some extent	62 (53%)
not much	34 (29%)
not at all	6 (5%)
can't say	1 (1%)
(N)	117

66. Can you tell me what you mean by 'politics'?

	Frequency
Government, running of the country	
Positive orientation	59 (52%)
No discernible orientation	36 (32%)
Negative orientation	19 (17%)
(N)	114
Participation, partisanship	
Positive orientation	25 (22%)
No discernible orientation	84 (74%)
Negative orientation	5 (4%)
(N)	114

67. Do you talk about politics with your family, neighbours, or people you
    work with often, occasionally, rarely, never or almost never?

	Frequency
often	15 (13%)
occasionally	53 (45%)
rarely	28 (24%)
never or almost never	21 (18%)
(N)	117

68. Do you talk about politics with your husband often, occasionally, rarely,
    never or almost never?

	Frequency
often	35 (30%)
occasionally	46 (40%)
rarely	19 (16%)
never or almost never	16 (14%)
(N)	116

69. Does your husband talk about politics with his family, neighbours, or
    people he works with often, occasionally, rarely, never, or almost never?

	Frequency
often	25 (22%)
occasionally	56 (48%)
rarely	21 (18%)
never or almost never	10 (9%)
can't say	4 (3%)
(N)	116

70. When you get together with your friends, do you ever discuss important
    social problems [for example, human rights, poverty, the third world,
    sexual equality]? Does this happen often, occasionally, rarely, never, or
    almost never?

	Frequency
often	20 (17%)
occasionally	56 (48%)
rarely	25 (21%)
never or almost never	16 (14%)
(N)	117

71. When you personally hold a strong opinion, do you manage to persuade your friends, relatives, or fellow workers? If so, does this happen often, occasionally, rarely, never, or almost never?

	Frequency
often	8 (7%)
occasionally	43 (37%)
rarely	31 (27%)
never or almost never	33 (28%)
can't say	2 (2%)
(N)	117

72. Which of the activities on this list do you participate in never, rarely, occasionally, or regularly? (each row adds to 100%, apart from roundoff error)

	never	rarely	occasionally	regularly
vote in elections	3%	2%	3%	92%
give money to a political party	79%	9%	4%	8%
work on a election campaign	79%	11%	7%	3%
get in touch with an elected representative or govt. official	28%	31%	35%	5%
listen to news on the radio	2%	6%	8%	85%
watch news on television	3%	7%	14%	77%

73. Based on their views, one can class Canadians on a left/right scale. As you can see, one can class people as more or less left-wing or more or less right-wing. Where are you personally on this scale?

left	centre	right

	Frequency
left of centre	10 (9%)
centre	51 (44%)
right of centre	15 (13%)
can't say, never heard of it	41 (35%)
(N)	117

74. Can you tell me what you mean by 'left' and 'right'?

	Frequency
Ideological	
Usual definition	13 (11%)
Not included in definition	87 (76%)
Reversed definition	14 (12%)
(N)	114
Political parties or classes	
Usual definition	14 (12%)
Not included in definition	94 (83%)
Reversed definition	6 (5%)
(N)	114
Idiosyncratic or affective definition	26 (23%)
Not included in definition	88 (77%)
(N)	114

75. How do you feel about the following opinion: 'No matter who wins the election, it doesn't really change the situation in Ontario.' Do you completely agree, agree a little, disagree a little, or disagree completely?

	Frequency
completely agree	26 (22%)
agree a little	33 (28%)
disagree a little	36 (31%)
disagree completely	22 (19%)
(N)	117

76. In your opinion, if the right to strike was abolished, would it be very serious, somewhat serious, not very serious, or not serious at all?

	Frequency
very serious	13 (11%)
somewhat serious	46 (39%)
not very serious	20 (17%)
not serious at all	37 (32%)
can't say	1 (1%)
(N)	117

77. Here is a list of group activities that could take place near your home. Which of these activities would you be willing to participate in? (row is % of 177 people)

	Frequency
protecting the environment, fight against pollution	96 (82%)
setting up a day care centre	49 (42%)
setting up a birth-control centre	48 (41%)

78. Would you find it perfectly acceptable, somewhat acceptable, not really acceptable, or not acceptable at all for a woman to be prime minister of Canada?

	Frequency
perfectly acceptable	94 (80%)
somewhat acceptable	16 (14%)
not really acceptable	3 (3%)
not acceptable at all	4 (3%)
(N)	117

80. Would things go better or worse if there were substantially more women elected ... ? (row is % of 117 people)

	better	worse	same	can't say
locally	52 (44%)	7 (6%)	52 (44%)	6 (5%)
provincially	41 (35%)	8 (7%)	58 (50%)	10 (9%)
federally	45 (39%)	9 (8%)	54 (46%)	9 (8%)

81. How would things go better? Answer as many as you like.

	Frequency
Women's problems would get more attention	42 (30%)
Certain problems which have been neglected would finally get some attention	42 (30%)
More women would have a steadying effect on parliament	30 (21%)
There would be less playing politics for its own sake	28 (20%)
(N responses)	142

82. With the aid of this list, can you tell me the reasons why there aren't more women are elected to Parliament or legislatures? (row is % of 117 people)

	Frequency
Too few women are prepared to run as candidates	103 (88%)
The population prefers to vote for a man	90 (77%)
The parties support men instead of women	64 (55%)
The women aren't those one would vote for	36 (31%)
(N responses)	293

83. The role of women in society, compared to that of men, is a popular topic of discussion at present. In your opinion, is the role of women beginning to change?

	Frequency
yes	111 (95%)
no	5 (4%)
can't say	1 (1%)
(N)	117

84. In your opinion, as far as the role of women is concerned, are things changing too quickly, not quickly enough, or at the right pace?

	Frequency
too quickly	10 (9%)
not quickly enough	28 (25%)
at the right pace	70 (61%)
can't say	6 (5%)
(N)	114

85. What do you think of women who claim there should be fewer differences between the roles of men and women in society? Are they right or wrong?

	Frequency
they are right	68 (58%)
they are wrong	41 (35%)
can't say	8 (7%)
(N)	117

86. What is your opinion of the movements which have come about recently and whose aim is the liberation of women?

	Frequency
very high opinion	1 (1%)
quite a good opinion	52 (44%)
rather poor opinion	48 (41%)
very bad opinion	4 (3%)
can't say	12 (10%)
(N)	117

87. Do you belong to such a movement, could you see yourself becoming a member, or are you against being a member of such a movement?

	Frequency
is a member	2 (2%)
could be a member	26 (22%)
against being a member	87 (74%)
can't say	2 (2%)
(N)	117

88. What is your opinion of the current movements whose objectives are the protection of the environment, the fight against pollution?

	Frequency
very high opinion	51 (44%)
quite a good opinion	54 (46%)
rather poor opinion	11 (9%)
very bad opinion	0
can't say	1 (1%)
(N)	117

89. Would you say that you're a feminist?

	Frequency
yes	27 (23%)
no	79 (68%)
can't say	11 (9%)
(N)	117

90. Can you tell me what you mean by 'feminist'?

	Frequency
Equality, role equity with men	
Positive orientation	25 (22%)
No discernible orientation	56 (50%)
Negative orientation	31 (28%)
(N)	112
Autonomy, self-assertion	
Positive orientation	22 (20%)
No discernible orientation	67 (60%)
Negative orientation	23 (20%)
(N)	112

91. Do you or did you practice a method of birth control?

	Frequency
natural	33 (29%)
artificial (chemical, surgical, mechanical)	82 (70%)
can't say	1 (1%)
(N)	116

92. The policy on abortion has become more lenient lately. In your opinion, does access to abortion constitute progress?

	Frequency
yes	48 (41%)
no	62 (53%)
can't say	7 (6%)
(N)	117

93-4. In your opinion, when is it acceptable for a young man/young woman to have sexual relations?

	Frequency	
	young man	*young woman*
before marriage	48 (41%)	49 (42%)
not before marriage	61 (52%)	61 (52%)
can't say	8 (7%)	7 (6%)
(N)	117	117

95-6. In your opinion, if a married man/married woman is occasionally un-
faithful to their spouse, is this normal, forgivable, or unforgivable?

	unfaithful man	*Frequency* unfaithful woman
normal	1 (1%)	0
forgivable	30 (26%)	32 (27%)
unforgivable	82 (70%)	81 (69%)
can't say	4 (3%)	4 (3%)
(N)	117	117

And now we'll finish up with some questions about your own situation.

97. How would you describe the ownership arrangement of your farm? (4 answers each for multiple farms per family)

	Frequency
joint ownership by husband and wife	69 (52%)
solely owned (spouse)	26 (20%)
legal partnership	17 (13%)
family corporation	11 (8%)
solely owned (wife)	6 (5%)
leased by husband or husband and wife	2 (2%)
cooperative	1 (1%)
other corporation	1 (1%)
(N responses)	133

Ownership arrangement – % of 117 people

	Frequency
Arrangement with extended family, adult children	50 (43%)
Can't say	3 (3%)
(N)	117

98. Please tell me your year of birth.

Mean	1943	46 years
Midpoint	1944	45 years
Minimum	1910	79 years
Maximum	1969	20 years
WI mean	1940	49 years
non-WI mean	1946	43 years

99. What education do you have?

	Frequency
elementary school completed	9 (8%)
secondary school begun but not completed	16 (14%)
secondary school completed	36 (31%)
post-secondary education, other than university begun but not completed	3 (3%)
post-secondary education, other than university completed	40 (34%)
university begun but not completed	4 (3%)
university completed	9 (8%)
(N)	117

100. Please tell me your husband's year of birth

Mean	1940	49 years
Midpoint	1940	45 years
Minimum	1906	83 years
Maximum	1964	25 years

101. What education does your husband have?

	Frequency
elementary school begun but not completed	3 (3%)
elementary school completed	27 (23%)
secondary school begun but not completed	29 (25%)
secondary school completed	22 (19%)
post-secondary education, other than university · begun but not completed	3 (3%)
post-secondary education, other than university completed	15 (13%)
university begun but not completed	6 (5%)
university completed	12 (10%)
(N)	117

102. Was your father a farmer?

	Frequency
yes	80 (68%)
no	37 (32%)
(N)	117

103. Was your father a full-time farmer?

	Frequency
full-time farmer	64
part-time farmer	16
(N)	80

104. NOT FARMER'S DAUGHTER What was your father's (primary) occupation?

Father's occupation	Frequency
hospital administrator	1
township councillor, reeve, warden	2
fertilizer and general sales	1
teacher (B.Ed.)	1
lawyer	1
doctor, optometrist	2
chiropractor	1
merchant	2
gas-station owner/operator	1
farm-equipment/feedmill dealership	2
milkman	1
custodian	1
funeral director	1
livestock worker	1
federal turnip inspector	1
supervisor on government farm	1
miner	1
feedmill or gristmill operator	1
sawmill operator/supervisor	3
worked in warehouse/lumberyard	1
car-man for CN Rail	1
millwright	1
line worker at Ontario Hydro	1
stonemason	1
plumber	1
carpenter	3
plasterer	1
truck driver	6
labourer	4
cab driver	1

104. *(Continued)*

Father's occupation	Frequency
maintenance engineer	1
factory worker	5
police/customs officer	2
(N)	54

105. What was your mother's (primary) occupation?

Mother's occupation	Frequency
teacher (no B.Ed.)	3
teacher (B.Ed.)	1
university professor	1
nurse's aid	1
nurse	4
mailroom clerk	1
secretary	4
bookkeeper	2
store cashier	3
telephone operator	1
waitress	1
cook	1
truck driver	1
clerical	2
labourer	1
newspaper clerk	1
factory worker	2
housewife, farmwife	85
farmer	1
disabled	1
(N)	117

105a. Did you grow up around here?

	Frequency
same or neighbouring township	68 (60%)
Ontario	40 (35%)
Holland, United States, England	6 (5%)
(N)	114

106. Do you have children?

	Frequency
yes	115 (98%)
no	2 (2%)
(N)	117

107. What are the ages and sex of your children? Do they live at home with you?

Children born:	mean	3
	maximum	12
	minimum	1
Children living at home:	mean	1.7
	maximum	6
	minimum	0

108. How many people live in your household?

_____ people

109. Does the farm hire any non-family employees?

	Frequency
yes	54 (48%)
no	58 (52%)
(N)	102

110. Who does the farm hire? (3 answers each from 54 employers)

	Frequency
local people hired seasonally	42 (60%)
regular part-time employees	7 (10%)
multiple full-time employees	7 (10%)
multiple regular part-time employees	6 (9%)
full-time employee	6 (9%)
multiple foreign workers hired seasonally	2 (3%)
(N responses)	70

111. How often do you usually go to church?

	Frequency
at least once a week	55 (47%)
once or twice a month	37 (32%)
occasionally for religious holidays	11 (9%)
ceremonies (wedding, baptism, funeral)	13 (11%)
never	1 (1%)
(N)	117

Finally, the last question.

112. Overall, how would you say things are going for you at the moment? Are you very happy, somewhat happy, or not very happy?

	Frequency
very happy	75 (64%)
somewhat happy	41 (35%)
not very happy	0
refuse	1 (1%)
(N)	117

Do you have any questions for me? Thank you for having participated. I hope to send you a summary of the results by the end of 1989.

Notes

1 The terms 'farm wife' and 'farm woman' are used interchangeably. The category 'farm women' is outlined more precisely in chapter 2 to mean married women living on commercial, agricultural enterprises, whether they do farm work or not. Similarly, farm men are referred to as 'farm husbands' and the term 'farmer' is gender-neutral.

2 See Buttel and Newby 1980; Ghorayshi 1987; Goodman and Redclift 1986; Havens et al. 1986; Holland and Carvalho 1985; Mann and Dickinson 1978; and John Wilson 1986.

3 This turning-point is articulated from several perspectives. We are said to be at the end of the 'Fordist' era of full employment, legislated protection for and collective bargaining with unionized workers, and a centralized welfare state, and at the beginning of a new era of global competition (Drache and Gertler 1991). Or, we are at end of the 'first industrial divide,' characterized by mass-production manufacturing, and at the beginning of the 'second industrial divide,' characterized by flexible specialization and artisanal craft production organized through kinship (Piore and Sabel 1984). Or, from the perspective of the informal sector in Asia and Latin America, the 'proletariat' is replaced by the 'housewife' as whole sectors of production are shifted into the home, where they become an unrecognized and unregulated part of women's domestic labour (Bennholdt-Thomsen, and von Werlhof 1988). Or, we are at the end of organized capitalism as fragmented production processes are contracted out to self-employed units (Lash and Urry 1987). The present study does not assume the burden of proof for arguing that such a transition is, in fact, occurring. It further avoids the burden of moral justification for whether such

changes are desirable or not. It simply proposes that, if farming has any broader significance for the urban, non-farming population, it lies in such a transition.

4 Scholars have called for petty-bourgeois household production as the economic basis for their democratic theory. Roberto Mangabeira Unger (1987, 343) argued against deterministic assumptions about the continued dominance of large-scale corporations: 'working masses throughout the world stubbornly maintain the petty-bourgeois dream against almost universal advice insist[ing] that history has condemned this dream to frustration.' Christopher Lasch (1991) points out that owning and operating a small business is not just a personal goal, but a long-standing cultural ideal in Western history. A petty-bourgeois standpoint – namely, an acceptance of limits to economic growth and premium on family relationships – is the only solution to a perceived environmental and moral crisis. Cornel West claims Martin Luther King as a spokesman for a 'petty-bourgeois service ethic' that might still work for American blacks (cited in hooks 1990, 210). Finally, John Keane (1988) anticipates the end of a full-employment economy as a twofold opportunity to expand household-based economies and to enhance political participation in a revitalized civil society.

5 Rural sociologists have tended to adopt the model of the transition from feudalism to capitalism, but without explicitly situating their concerns about farm women's declining status in this perspective. For example, Linda Graff (1982) employed a sort of technological determinism to argue that the industrialization of agriculture marginalizes women from production. Alice Barthez (1982,184) argues that French legislation has transformed peasant families into capitalist families through ownership and credit policies favouring the family patriarch, thereby legally subordinating peasant women and (adult) children.

6 This argument lurks between the lines of past research and has yet to be empirically documented. At least three sources explicitly propose that farm women might pose a more interesting challenge to patriarchy than those women who face class and gender domination that are separated into public and private spheres. Sarah Elbert (1981, 389) speculates that an urban industrial model of feminism is individualist, corresponding to individual claims for individual wages, whereas a farm model of feminism is more collectivist, corresponding to a single farm receipt to be shared consensually among household members. French scholars have articulated this theme at more length. Feminism, Rose-Marie LaGrave (1982) advises, should recognize and integrate the creativity of farm wom-

en's struggles. Alice Barthez (1982, 184) concludes that the relations of domination based on age and sex in farm households explain the origin of all social hierarchies.

7 For later contributions to the debate between Lipset and Macpherson, see Conway 1981 and 1984; Finkel 1989; Richards and Pratt 1981; and Whitaker 1976 [1920]. For the United States see Goodwyn 1978.

8 For an attempt to remedy retroactively this lack of empirical information by reanalysing election data, see Bell 1990; and Finkel 1989, 202–13.

9 For example, David Laycock (1990, 122–3) quotes and measures Irene Parlby, a leading Canadian suffragist, against male theorists of agrarian democratic theory: 'Her [maternalist] comments can be seen as a folksy and popular articulation ... This is not the stuff of compelling political philosophy.' Laycock assesses Parlby simply as an agrarian theorist; he makes no allowances for her other foot in the women's movement and thus subsumes her under the gender-neutral category 'farmer.' William Irvine, who was Parlby's contemporary and colleague, avoided this error by a division of labour that attributed moral and aesthetic responsibilities to farm women and economic affairs to husbands (1976 [1920], 118–34).

10 For instance, Lipset's discussion of the CCF in power centres in politicians' confrontations with civil servants sympathetic to previous Liberal governments; it takes public policy disputes to reflect, in a fairly straightforward manner, party competition (Lipset 1971 [1950], chs. 11 and 12).

11 Apart from Yolande Cohen's research on the Cercles de fermières under the Union Nationale in Quebec (Cohen and Marchand 1989), there is no Canadian equivalent to Suzanne Berger's study (1972) of how French governments used the long arm of the Paris-based bureaucracy to manipulate isolated Breton peasants for their larger partisan agenda.

12 Agrarian populism, in David Laycock's opinion (1990, 82), was a mass democratic movement that offers insights far beyond its farming origins: '[The United Farmers of Alberta notion of citizenship] presaged the theory of participatory democracy that has been promoted by various radical academics and political activists since the mid-1960s.' Lawrence Goodwyn (1978, vii–xxiii) claims that agrarian protest is the only successful example of mass democratic insurgency in the United States.

13 External relations of commodity exchange with creditors and wholesalers are not, of course, unconnected from internal relations of marriage and family life. Marjorie Griffin Cohen, for example, showed that receipts from women's dairy and butter commodities subsidized men's less-profitable grain commodities and thereby contributed to the accumulation of capital in nineteenth-century agriculture. It was difficult for

spouses to recognize, Cohen explains, that the 'ordinary business of getting along in a marriage' corresponded, in fact, to the problems of coordinating two competing types of commodity production – dairy and grain –
on one farm (1988, 116).

CHAPTER 1   A History of Farm Women's Movements in
English Canada

1 Capital accumulation was critical to this process; see Graham 1988,
112–16, for a discussion of rural credit practices.
2 MacDonald 1986; Federated Women's Institutes of Ontario 1972, 3–11;
and Walker, Collins, and McIntyre Hood 1948.
3 WI members have commissioned an enormous oil portrait of Hoodless
for the MacDonald Institute at the Ontario Agricultural College and purchased her birthplace as a museum. See Crowley 1986A for just how irrelevant Hoodless was to the Women's Institutes.
4 Circular sent to prospective institutes in 1900: Federated Women's Institutes of Ontario 1972, 19. History of Ontario WI taken from ibid, 17–22.
5 Cohen argues that farm women's skills acquired 'exchange value' outside
the home, but does not specify to what extent handicrafts were sold for a
profit. Differences between the Cercles and Institutes in this regard may
be overdrawn; WI members continue to sell handicrafts at agricultural
fairs, which is Cohen's only example of 'exchange value' (Cohen 1989a,
130).
6 Speech, 13 June 1928, R-182, Violet McNaughton papers, Saskatchewan
Archives Board. McNaughton was convener of the research committee for
a survey done under the auspices of the United Farmers of Canada and
the Homemakers' Clubs for Extension Workers in Agricultural Engineer-
ing (22 May 1928), R-67, SAB. See also Report of Morning Meeting of the
Research Committee and Summarized Report of the Conference between
Women's Organizations and the Government of Saskatchewan on the subject of Home Economics, 8 November 1927. McNaughton papers, R-354
and R-341, SAB.
7 The line of descent from agrarian protest parties to the new farm women's
networks seems to be strictly conceptual, but it is possible that certain individuals, families, or friendships provide a more concrete line of descent
from one era to another.
8 See Bacchi 1979 and 1983, 123–32; and Rasmussen, Savage, and Wheeler
1976, 122–3.

9 Georgina Taylor (in preparation) suspects that, whereas McNaughton 'sought common ground' as a general principle, Parlby tended to fuel rivalries.

10 Cullip to Bradley and Bolton, 7 July 1927. Philip G. and Mabel M. Bradley papers, R-816, Saskatchewan Archives Board.

11 David Smith notes that political parties and their fragile governments were isolated from society in the newly created Prairie provinces: 'From the distance of more than half a century, it is difficult to appreciate the authority once possessed by the organized farmers. Certainly there are no comparable entities on the prairies today who wield their former influence ... Liberals and Conservatives were never so entrenched on the prairies that they could afford to forget the original non-partisan base of territorial politics or ignore the periodic threat of groups who challenged the utility, as well as ethics, of partisan politics' (1981, 37–9).

12 For similar WI activities in British Columbia, see Zacharias 1980, 67.

13 In Canada, the term 'maternal feminism' describes the maternal orientation of first-wave organizations and individuals who relied on women's presumed capacity for nurturance and moral instruction, based on all women's common experience as mothers or their biological capacity for motherhood (Kealey 1979, 7–8). In the United States, the term 'social feminism' describes women who were caught up in a series of social reforms such as temperance, abolition of prostitution, and labour legislation and who eventually coalesced into the reform or progressive movement at the turn of the century (Black 1989; Lemons 1973). The terms 'maternal' and 'social' are complementary; the first stresses maternal motivations and rhetoric for this orientation to public participation, whereas the latter is the organized and programmatic arm. The term 'relational feminism' describes the first-wave preference for a 'companionate, non-hierarchical, male-female couple' as the basic unit of society (Offen 1988).

A distinct complex of rhetoric, beliefs, practices, and programs has been identified and variously labelled as 'social,' 'maternal,' or 'relational' feminism. This complex has been subject to serious criticism, not in relation to the various modifiers, but rather in relation to whether it qualifies as feminist in view of evidently conservative commitments to gender difference, domesticity, and conventional family arrangements. A case can be made for claiming that such a complex of ideas and activities is indeed feminist because (according to its adherents) it facilitates women's entry into public political activity, and thus women's ultimate empowerment. Regardless of its qualifications to be 'feminist,' such a complex exists; it is salient to women's organized political activity, and thus deserves our attention (Offen 1989).

14 Continuities with well-established women's organizations were especially important in Canada at the time of feminism's second wave of collective political action in the 1960s. The second wave began with the women's liberation movement whose relatively young activists emerged from the New Left, anti-war, sexual liberation, and students' movements. Female activists became disillusioned with male-dominated protest movements and proceeded to develop their own version of liberation for women in an autonomous women's movement. The younger, much more radical women inevitably collided with the older women, who already maintained national organizations with similar agendas. In Canada, the two generations were able to converge in a national umbrella organization (NAC – National Action Committee on the Status of Women), in part, because criticism of American imperialism and the American war machine was compatible with the promotion of Canadian nationalism and an independent foreign policy on the part of the more established organizations. For personal testimonials from the Canadian radical left, see Adamson, Briskin, and McPhail 1988, 25–94; for an overview, see Prentice et al. 1988, 352–64.

15 'The OFA has done nothing but seek sources of more money to support its "bloated bureaucracy"': John Dowling, Ontario Coordinator, National Farmers' Union, cited in *Rural Voice*, September 1990, 2.

16 The author tried to learn more about FWIC's involvement in NAC by corresponding and speaking with two women who had been on the FWIC executive during the early 1970s. Both women recollected little about NAC other than to doubt that the FWIC had ever been involved with such a radical-feminist organization. Apparently, the FWIC's involvement in NAC was not an important event in the life of the organization. Kay Macpherson, who chaired NAC from 1977 to 1979, remembers that the FWIC and the National Council of Women both left NAC for the same reason (personal conversation, June 1993). Neither established organization had an ideological dispute with the fledgling NAC, but neither did they have an incentive to contribute to another national umbrella network when each organization already maintained a national structure.

17 Married women's property rights are a long-standing issue for organized farm women. Campaigns to guarantee wives equal rights to farm property date back to the United Farm Women of Alberta in the 1920s (Finkel 1989, 96). Such proposals are not a radical aberration on the part of the

FWIC; they are typical of the gap between the national body and the local Institutes, which are much more conservative.

18 This agency is now the Advisory Council on the Status of Women.

19 An FWIO president had also been a delegate on the same tour (Margaret Munro, 'Women talking to women on Oxfam tour,' *Home and Country* 56/1 [1989], 7).

20 One respondent, for example, said that UCW was much more exciting than the WI, recalling her participation in an anti-poverty march and conference in London, Ontario, where she met people (activists and social services workers) whom she would never otherwise meet.

21 Concerned Farm Women had its origins in the collapse in red meat prices that coincided with extraordinarily high interest rates in the early 1980s – a juncture that put many farms in the Grey–Bruce peninsula into bankruptcy. The crisis prompted armed stand-offs in which neighbouring farmers physically prevented bailiffs and bank officials, accompanied by local police, from repossessing indebted farms (Wilford 1984).

22 The family farm is the NFU's unit of membership. Instead of a separate women's auxiliary, it has a parallel, 'affirmative action' executive which consists of a women's president and vice-president, a women's advisory committee, and women's district directors. The purpose of a parallel executive is to facilitate women's participation throughout the NFU and to represent women's concerns to the executive (Wiebe 1987, 8–13).

23 'Quebec and Ontario state officials are committed to consultation with farm organizations ... [to] easy and constant informal personal contact. OMAF is extremely loath to act without first building a consensus in the farm community. To deal with conflict ... industry-wide committees find a consensus among competing interests and advise state officials' (Skogstad 1990, 73).

24 In response to the FWAP, the FWIO revived an apparently defunct agricultural committee to suggest projects that might qualify for funding. The WI has also been involved with Health and Welfare Canada on rural child-care facilities and with Consumer and Corporate Affairs.

25 The OFWN received conference funding from the Ontario Women's Directorate on the basis of almost 20,000 members in 1988. Its actual membership in 1989, after the first provincial conference, was 154 individuals and 19 organizations, but all WI members in Ontario were included on the basis of the FWIO's subscription to its newsletter. It was later agreed that a single subscription equalled a single associate membership ('Profile,' *Home & Country* 56/3 [1990], 5).

26 OFWN sponsors an annual provincial conference and sends representatives to the national CFWN conference.
27 Proposal for the Saskatchewan Women's Agricultural Network (SWAN), February 1985.
28 Taylor, in preparation.
29 Glenis Joyce, 'Report on Women in Local Decision-Making workshop,' presented to Canada–Saskatchewan Economic Regional Development Agreement, June 1988; and correspondence with Glenis Joyce, Extension Officer, University of Saskatchewan, March 1989.
30 Ongoing Tweedsmuir history collections were begun in 1936 at the encouragement of Lady Tweedsmuir, wife of Canada's governor general, to preserve local histories (Federated Women's Institutes of Ontario 1972, 60–2).
31 Maria Van Bommel, one of the original organizers of the WSA and OFWN, cited by Carol Stewart-Kirkby in 'Women in profile: Maria Van Bommel,' *Home & Country* 54/3 (1988), 22.
32 Claire Belluz, 'Women's equality on farm committees and boards,' *OFWN Newsletter* 2/4 (1990), 9.
33 Pat Salter, Reeve of Peel Township, cited by Janine Roelens-Grant in 'Salter encourages women to get involved in local politics,' *Home & Country* 57/2 (1991), 7.
34 'Women in profile: Brigid Pyke [former president of OFA],' *Home & Country* 53/4 (1987), 4.
35 General farm organizations lobby government to defend family farming against large-scale, capitalist corporate farms. This is all the more reason for farm women's organizations to make common cause with farm employees whose low wages ensure that corporate farming is profitable.
36 In their briefs to the Royal Commission on the Status of Women in 1967, the FWIC and the Edgewood (BC) and the Olds (Alberta) Women's Institutes recommended that women receive financial compensation and legal recognition for their unpaid work in agriculture. For example, farm wives had no legal 'dower rights' to farm property under the Homestead Act, which was still in force in 1967 (Royal Commission on the Status of Women 1970, 40–4).

CHAPTER 2   A Survey of Farm Women

1 The survey population was remarkably indigenous; 68 per cent of the sample had grown up in the same or adjacent township. The same proportion (68 per cent) was operating the 'home farm' of the husband's

family; only three couples had purchased or inherited property from the wife's family.

2 European immigrants outnumber immigrants from the United States and the United Kingdom in rural townships. Canada Census 1986, vols. 94-111, 94-112.

3 The WI divides Ontario counties into quadrants, which are called 'districts.' Branches originally corresponded to the same small areas served by local schools going up to grade eight. Just as rural schools have consolidated, so have WI branches generally consolidated to correspond to township boundaries.

4 There were estimated to be 70,000–150,000 non-family farm workers in Ontario in 1987, most of whom were guest workers or recent immigrants. In the absence of census data, this figure is an estimate from a labour organizer (Lee 1987, 100).

5 Janine Roelans-Grant, 'Russet says the WI keeps a community together,' *Home and Country* 58/4 (1992) 6. British research likewise identified the WI as an element of traditional farming communities that disappears with encroaching urbanization: 'A [Norfolk] farmer who denied any loss of community said: "We still have the WI in the village" and a Suffolk farmer noted the loss of community: "the cricket, WI, and that sort of thing, but it has all gone by the board nowadays"' (Newby et al. 1978, 202, 204).

6 OFWN Newsletter editor Corry Martens, 18 April 1991.

7 For example, professional occupations (teaching and nursing) formed the largest employment category, outnumbering even service and clerical occupations combined, in the Concerned Farm Women study. Professionals were surely overrepresented (Cebotarev, Blacklock, and McIsaac 1986, 18).

8 This study uses quotations from the works of short-story writer and novelist Alice Munro, who writes about the people who live in the area where the interviews were conducted, to add a cultural dimension to the analysis of southwestern Ontario. On the use of Alice Munro as a social historian, see Waver 1988.

9 For the impact of evangelical Protestantism on the society and physical landscape of nineteenth-century rural Ontario, see Graham 1988, 274–80.

10 The Concerned Farm Women survey found that women liked 'country living, independence, rural values, and production' best about farming (Ireland 1983, 61). British farmers claim to value husbandry and autonomy most about farming as an occupation (Newby et al. 1978, 153).

11 Whereas petty-bourgeois enterprises employ fewer than five people, small-business enterprises are usually defined as employing fewer than

thirty people. For a comparison of farming and small business, see Wilson and Finkle 1990.

12 Statistics Canada Health Reports, Supplement no. 14, 2/1 (1990), 14.

13 Seeing that employees hired, an employed husband, and or an extended-family enterprise do not directly pertain to women, farm prosperity seems to say more about husbands and in-laws than about women themselves. In this study, farms cultivate more acreage (r = .64) and hire more paid employees (r = .64) as capital value increases.

14 People holding formal paid positions in farm corporations were included. SES variables were not employed in final calculations for two reasons: first, various SES calculations were plotted against farm's capital value, acreage, and assorted demographics with no significant results; and second, because few women were employed either full-time or part-time, SES as a variable immediately slashed the sample to less than half its original size.

CHAPTER 3   Women's Work

1 See Boserup 1970, 16–31; Cloud 1988, 291; Garkovich and Bokemeier 1988, 222; Haney 1983; Lee 1987, 101; Rosenfeld 1985, 30, 72; and Smith 1987, 168–76.

2 For initial research, see Barthez 1982; Blumberg 1981; Boserup 1970; and Graff 1982. Rachel Rosenfeld's literature review of American rural sociology (1985, 3–35) may be supplemented with Fran Shaver's review of Canadian research (1989) and Barbara Cooper's review of research in both countries (1989).

3 Loadings near 0 indicate no association between the task and the factor, whereas loadings near +/–1 indicate strong association.

4 Reliability tests show the statistical coherence of these two combinations: husband's housework alpha = .66; husband's child-care alpha = .74.

5 The table entries are Pearson's r correlations, which measure the strength of the linear relationship between two variables. Values near +1 indicate a strong positive linear association; values near –1 indicate a strong negative association; and values near 0 indicate weak linear association (Norusis/SPSS Inc. 1988, 105).

6 In table 3.3, significance of prediction is indicated by asterisks, which represent ranges of probability (p) that the reported estimates arose by chance alone. One, two, and three asterisks represent progressively stronger relationships. Each numerical entry is an unstandardized regression coefficient whose sign indicates the direction (positive or negative) of the

relationship. A dash indicates that the corresponding characteristic was not included in the regression model because it did not help significantly to predict the measure of work involvement (Norusis/SPSS Inc. 1988, 168).

CHAPTER 4 Political Behaviour

1 Liberal modernization theory describes the fundamental transformation that began in Western Europe with the Renaissance and the Reformation, and eventually spread around the world. Whereas the traditional world was characterized by animal and human labour power, the bare physical subsistence of most people, spirituality, strict hierarchies ascribed at birth, and a static technological and social inertia that conserved past practices over many generations, the modern world is characterized by machine power running on natural resources (primarily fossil fuels), excess production leading to a rise in living standards for most people, secularism, fluid hierarchies achieved by individual effort, and rapid technological and social change that progresses to an ever-better world. Because the shift from a rural, agricultural society to an urban, industrial society is perhaps the single largest difference between traditional and modern landscapes, farming and farmers are immediately relevant. Classic texts on political participation that applied modernization theory include: Almond and Verba 1963; Deutsch 1961; and Lipset 1959.

2 Religiosity is always discussed because it is easier to use positive measures of church attendance and belief in God than to use the negative, secular absence of religion.

3 Bourque and Grossholtz 1974; Goot and Reid 1975; and McCormack 1975. Maurice Duverger's study of European women (1955) is an exception for the earlier period.

4 In this study, hours of housework reported measure a woman's focus on homemaking because, no matter that she may grumble, increased housework leaves less time for organizational or political work.

5 Inglehart (1979) identified two clusters of value priorities that correspond to Maslow's hierarchy of needs: materialist and post-materialist. Once people have satisfied their physiological or materialist needs for sustenance and safety, they progress to self-actualization or post-materialist needs. The distribution of materialist and post-materialist values in a nation's population will influence to what extent government policy favours either materialist priorities of a stable economy, law and order, and

national defence or post-materialist priorities of participation (in government and workplace), aesthetics in urban design and ecology, and self-fulfilment. Although the twin concepts of materialism and post-materialism were designed to transcend conventional distinctions between modern and traditional or left-wing and right-wing, post-materialism, the psychological basis of new social movements does so more successfully than materialism. Although trade-unionists may also qualify as materialists who favour intensive industrialization and security, materialism generally stands in for traditional, conservative right-wing priorities (Inglehart 1990).

6 Given this picture of non-political and traditionally 'privatized' home-makers, it comes as some surprise to find that older Canadian women tended to favour a party of the left – namely, the New Democratic Party (NDP). Sylvia Bashevkin (1985b, 48–9) suggests that this might be a historical artefact of the CCF/NDP's affiliation with suffrage: 'Western Canadian women in the enfranchisement cohort [born pre-1900] had the highest level of NDP partisanship of any female cohort sampled.' The CCF/NDP was also affiliated historically with the social gospel, which explains why religious women with limited education were slightly more likely to vote NDP than were comparable men and even more likely to vote NDP than were better-educated and secular men and women. Historical associations with both suffrage and social gospel are interesting because the enfranchisement cohort's partisan affiliation dates back to a rural and agricultural population. In other words, even though they were not farm wives in 1967 and 1979, their partisan loyalty only makes sense in the historic context of dominant political movements – agrarian populism, enfranchisement, and the social gospel – of the time when many were farm girls. Bashevkin's isolated finding is the only evidence available to make a transition from 'wife' to 'farm wife' on the subject of women's politicization.

7 This use of the term 'politicization' is similar to political sophistication, but excludes political knowledge and adds political participation (Neuman 1986, 191–5).

8 Ontario farm women's answers were compared to the following surveys: 1970–87 Euro-Barometer; 1981–2 World Values Survey; 1972–84 United States Election Studies (AES); 1988 and 1984 Canadian Election Studies (CES); 1987 Canadian Charter of Rights Study; 1981 Social Change in Canada Study; and 1975, 1980, and 1985 Project Canada surveys. In order to summarize the complex series of Euro-Barometer surveys of the twelve member-nations of the European Economic Community over two decades

and the 1981-2 World Values Survey (N = 1,245 Canadians), this discussion presents results from Inglehart 1990, 136-9, and Commission of the European Communities 1984 and 1987. Results from the Project Canada surveys are presented in Bibby 1987.

Comparisons of Ontario farm wives to the population of Canadian women have been drawn directly from original data sets. The 1988 and 1984 Election Studies were weighted to be representative in terms of urban–rural composition, but not all members of the rural population were farmers. Few respondents reported 'farmer' as an occupation, which implies that just as few respondents were farm wives. Calculations leading to analysis of left/right beliefs from the 1984 Canadian Election Study explicitly deleted farmers (Lambert et al. 1987, 546). If not deleted elsewhere, farmers are not isolated as a specific occupational stratum in published calculations from Election Studies. Even accounting for rural weighting, I assume results from election studies to represent opinions of predominantly urban populations, against which farm women's responses will be compared. For further details, see Northrup and Orum 1989 and Lambert et al. 1985.

9 Farm men apparently discuss politics more frequently than their wives; 70 per cent of wives interviewed credited their husbands with discussing politics often, and occasionally with his friends and neighbours. This gender gap is comparable to that between all Canadian men and women (Inglehart 1990, 348).

Since 1945, in Canada, neither urbanization nor industrialization has been associated with sex differences in 'psychological involvement' in politics or political salience. The gap between the political salience of farm men and women was no larger than the salience gap between urban men and women (Christy 1986, 16).

10 In a slightly different version, the Canadian Election Studies asked respondents how much attention they paid to politics generally.

11 When respondents were confused as to exactly who in the family held a party membership, the point was not pressed.

12 The table entries are Pearson's r correlations, which measure the strength of the linear relationship between two variables. Values near +1 indicate a strong positive linear association; values near –1 indicate a strong negative association; and values near 0 indicate weak linear association (Norusis/SPSS Inc. 1988, 105).

13 Reliability coefficient for political salience is .85. This procedure is similar to that used by Verba, Nie, and Kim 1978, 312-39.

14 In table 4.7, significance of prediction is indicated by asterisks, which

represent ranges of probability (p) that the reported estimates arose by chance alone. One, two, and three asterisks represent progressively stronger relationships. Each numerical entry is an unstandardized regression coefficient whose sign indicates the direction (positive or negative) of the relationship. A dash indicates that the corresponding characteristic was not included in the regression model because it did not help significantly to predict the measure of political involvement (Norusis/SPSS Inc. 1988, 168).

15 In the United States, respondents are asked to locate themselves on 'liberal/conservative' scale and to conceptualize 'liberal/conservative.' The 1988 Canadian Election Study was especially rigorous because it asked left/right location only of those women (12 per cent) who first admitted to using such labels to describe politics.

16 Insights from both farm women's 'centre principle' and the post-modern principle of 'difference' arise from the margins of relative powerlessness, but affinities should not be pushed much farther. Farm women seek unity and compromise in the centre, whereas post-modern theoreticians reject any imaginary centre where differences can be accommodated (Nicholson 1990).

17 Calculations were done to see if the proposed 'centre principle' is associated with political involvement, efficacy, and partisanship. But, remember that farm wives using 'left/right' in this sense meant it as a general principle of behaviour, usually in reference to domestic affairs. It would be surprising for such a diffuse preference for amiable cooperation to show statistical proof of association with political behaviour. Quantitative measures might be so weak precisely because such a preference is so widespread among respondents. Even respondents who correctly defined left/right in the usual sense also expressed their dislike for polar extremes.

18 'In democratic countries knowledge of how to combine is the mother of all other forms of knowledge ... If men are to remain civilized or to become civilized, the art of association must develop and improve at the same speed as equality of conditions spreads' (Tocqueville 1969[1848], 517).

19 The Women's Institutes have no direct equivalent in the United States; the Extension Service of the Department of Agriculture sponsors Homemaker Clubs, which do not form an autonomous organization.

20 For ACWW activities in Turkey, see Kiray 1984.

21 The category of professional organizations coded commodity groups and the Ontario Federation of Agriculture together with professional organi-

zations and trade unions derived from paid employment. Fair boards were coded as community organizations because most women affiliated with the Homemaking Agricultural Association.

22 The term 'existential' locates this tradition in the work of Hannah Arendt (1958). It also includes John Stuart Mill's and Jean-Jacques Rousseau's recommendations for political participation as a developmental and educational process (Porter 1989).

23 In table 4.13, significance of prediction is indicated by asterisks, which represent ranges of probability (p) that the reported estimates arose by chance alone. One, two, and three asterisks represent progressively stronger relationships. Each numerical entry is an unstandardized regression coefficient whose sign indicates the direct (positive or negative) of the relationship. A dash indicates that the corresponding characteristic was not included in the regression model because it did not help significantly to predict the measure of political involvement (Norusis/SPSS Inc. 1988, 168).

CHAPTER 5   Conservatism

1 Sources are *Election Returns, 1986 by-elections, 1987 general election,* published by the Government of Ontario; and *Thirty-fourth general election: Report of the Chief Electoral Office 1988,* published by the Chief Electoral Officer of Canada.

2 For the critical role of rural ridings in the rise of the New Democrats in the 1990 NDP sweep of Ontario, see John Phillips, 'The farmers did it! How Ontario's fields went pink,' *The Idler* 30 (1990), 6–9.

3 'FWIO have "Caught wave into the future,"' and Lori Jamieson, 'Morden says: "Put emphasis on fun and fellowship,"' *Home & Country* 57/1 (1991), 6 and 7.

4 'Speech,' Hilde Morden, FWIO 'Conference '90, Fragile Environment – Strong Caretakers – Women and Their Environment,' 6 March 1990.

5 'The appointment of the FWIO president to the Advisory Committee on Environmental Responsibility, chaired by the Minister [of Agriculture], is indicative of the respect and influence the organization has attained' (Geraldine Campbell, 'Minister Applauds FWIO Commitment to Improving Rural Life,' *Home & Country* 57/2 [1991], 11).

6 See Inglehart 1990, 169–76 and 377–80, for the connection between support for the environmental movement and privileged socio-economic characteristics.

7 While anything (whether hay, labour, or sex) becomes a commodity when

it is bought and sold for a price in the market-place, it becomes decom-modified when it is directly consumed by the producer or shared freely with other people. The definition of a commodity thus lies in the distinc-tion between hay that is grown for a farmer's own cattle to eat during the winter and excess hay that is sold to neighbouring farmers; between a meal prepared at home for guests and a meal prepared by a restaurant for paying customers; and between romantic love and prostitution.

8 Scepticism is surely warranted whenever claims are made that farmers are environmentalists. Howard Newby and colleagues argued that, despite skirmishes with conservationists over footpaths and hedgerows in rural England, farmers have selfish, instrumental reasons to be apparently al-truistic stewards of the land. Conservation of the rural environment pro-hibits industrial development of rural England, and thereby reduces wage levels of non-family agricultural workers to the benefit of capitalist farmers (Newby et al. 1978, 221–75). In contrast to England, rural Ontario is not dominated by capitalist squires, and Ontario farmers apparently welcome industrial and manufacturing enterprises as potential employers for themselves, judging from the occupations of fifteen respondents' hus-bands. The husbands' limited professional skills (eighteen in total had at-tended university) made the remunerative rewards of unionized, industrial employment apparent. Labour-intensive horticultural enterprises in On-tario's manufacturing heartland cannot compete with industrial wages, so agricultural guest-workers from Caribbean countries must be brought in for harvesting. None the less, even though uncultivated woodlands and scenic pastures are not quite the national heritage in Canada that they are in England, there is room for scepticism regarding farmers' environmen-talist credentials. So long as government reduces agricultural subsidies to farmers, and the terms of international trade in agriculture become ever more competitive, farmers will continue to maximize agricultural profits by intensive, petroleum-driven cultivation, and they will continue to seek industrial employment to subsidize their decreasing earnings from agri-culture. This situation puts into question farmers' ascribed anti-capitalist and environmentalist credentials.

This systemic conflict at the level of production, however, has barely begun to emerge as a political conflict in Canada. Judging from aca-demic environmentalist texts and newspapers, Canadian environmental-ists have yet to examine agriculture critically. Review of *Alternatives* from 1971 to 1989 revealed that, while the journal favoured organic farming technology, preserving prime agricultural land from urbanization, and animal rights, it did not criticize farmers.

Journalist Michael Valpy wrote a series of columns for the Toronto *Globe and Mail* in 1989 and 1990 on land-use planning in Grey County. His typically acerbic criticism was reserved for the Ontario environment ministry and developers while farmers were let off easily – until Grey County elected a pro-development farmer to Queen's Park in 1990 ('City-state, Toronto *Globe and Mail* 29 and 30 Aug.; 5 and 6 Sep.; 13 Dec. 1989, and 26 Oct. 1990).

9 This is not an eco-feminist argument because the unique insight of eco-feminism is missing – namely, the insight that connects the domination/domestication of women to the domination/domestication of nature and animals (*Hypatia special issue on ecological feminism* 6/1 [1991]).

10 Reg Bibby (1987), who thinks that Canadians could do with more religious devotion, has vainly sought evidence that religious commitment has some impact on people's opinions and personal happiness. Instead he found that religion is a marginal, fragmented consumer good which rarely has more impact than (his chosen analogy) one's choice of supermarkets. The only exceptions are conservative, Pentecostal denominations, whose memberships are declining.

11 Is Canada a Protestant or Roman Catholic country? Comparing Church attendance in Canada with that in other countries is complicated by a gap between lower Protestant and higher Roman Catholic attendance figures, especially outside Quebec (Bibby 1987, 17, 20).

12 Although the above results suggest that women have sexual relations only with men, this is not true, even in rural Ontario. Lesbians are farmers too (Eleanor Brown, 'Lives are changing in small towns,' *Xtra!* 252, 24 Jun. 1994, 18; and 'Rural lesbian roundtable,' in *The lesbian health guide*, ed. by Regan McClure and Anne Vespry [Toronto: Queer Press 1994], 52–9).

13 Examples are taken respectively from Environics polls conducted for Canadian Abortion Rights Action League, 1989, and 1987 Canadian Charter of Rights Study, York University. Both questions presume familiarity with specific legislative proposals.

14 'Do you agree or disagree with the federal government's plan to put abortion into the Criminal Code?': Environics Poll conducted for Canadian Abortion Rights Action League, 1989. 'Do you agree or disagree that the abortion decision should rest with a woman and her physician?': Gallup National Omnibus Poll, conducted for Canadian Abortion Rights Action League, 1988.

15 See Hong 1983 and 1984; Maret and Maret 1982; Stephan and McMullin 1982; and Weis et al. 1986.

16 The table entries are Pearson's r correlations, which measure the strength

of the linear relationship between two variables. Values near +1 indicate a strong positive linear association; values near -1 indicate a strong negative association; and values near 0 indicate weak linear association (Norusis/SPSS Inc. 1988, 105).

17 In table 5.6, significance of prediction is indicated by asterisks, which represent ranges of probability (p) that the reported estimates arose by chance alone. One, two, and three asterisks represent progressively stronger relationships. Each numerical entry is an unstandardized regression coefficient whose sign indicates the direction (positive or negative) of the relationship. A dash indicates that the corresponding characteristic was not included in the regression model becuase it did not help significantly to predict the measure of conservatism (Norusis/SPSS Inc. 1988, 168).

18 Abolition of the sexual double standard and upholding chastity for men and women alike were dominant themes of first-wave feminism. Except for sexual liberationists among anarchists and socialists, most notably Emma Goldman, first-wave feminists preferred to rely on chastity rather than contraception to limit family size (Dubois and Gordon 1983).

19 At the 1990 National Board Meeting, the Federated Women's Institutes of Canada (FWIC) passed a resolution that abortion *not* be reinstated in the Criminal Code. After considerable debate, this resolution was seen not to advocate either pro-life or pro-choice positions, but to affirm the WI's abstention from, in their view, a personal and private decision between a woman *and her husband* (Peggy Knapp, FWIO president, 15 May 1991). This resolution was sent to Prime Minister Mulroney prior to the defeat of legislation that proposed to recriminalize abortion.

20 Perhaps not coincidentally she was the only person to say that marital infidelity was 'normal' for men (although she didn't approve) but that women just weren't able to get away with it in suspicious rural neighbourhoods.

CHAPTER 6   Feminism

1 Ethel Chapman, Superintendent, Ontario Ministry of Agriculture, addressing the WI on its fiftieth anniversary in 1969, cited in Federated Women's Institutes of Ontario 1972, 65.

2 Patty Starr was a prominent, unelected member of the Ontario Liberal party who was eventually convicted of transferring funds from Toronto real-estate developers to Liberal party élites. Her name came up often in response to this question.

3 The 1984 and 1988 Canadian Election Studies used a 'feeling thermometer' to ask respondents to express like and dislike along a five-point interval scale from 0 to 100. This interval scale was combined here into ordinal
categories as follows: <25 = very bad opinion; 25–54 = rather poor opinion; 55–75 = quite a good opinion; >75 = very high opinion.

4 The original question focused on activists: 'What do you think of women
who claim that there should be fewer differences between roles of men and
women in society? Are they right or wrong?' When this question proved
too difficult to communicate orally, it was simplified to stress differences:
'That there should be fewer differences between men and women. What
do you think of people who say that? Are they right or wrong that there
should be fewer differences?' Previous use of this question in Euro-
Barometer surveys has indicated that it may also imply removing differences of prestige between the two different roles by giving equal value or
credit to women's traditional role (Brandt and Black 1990, 30).

   This question of gender-role differences is relevant to another set of
questions. This other set asked women to identify jobs from a list of farm
tasks that were most suitable for men in general, and most suitable for
their husbands personally, and to repeat the procedure for women in general, and themselves personally. Whereas masculinity proved to be relatively straightforward in that men's most suitable tasks were almost identical with husbands' preferred tasks, femininity was more complex. Those
tasks that respondents identified as being most suitable for women in general (dairy and bookkeeping) were not their preferred tasks; instead, many
women thought field-work would be the best job for them personally.

5 Apart from public-opinion research, there is another way to identify what
feminism means as a mass belief system. If feminism operates through the
women's liberation movement, it makes sense to take policies and activities of specific organizations such as the WI as surrogates for larger belief
systems. Such an approach taps ordinary women's understanding of feminism, but, to use an analogy from Marxism, women's organizations can
no more claim to represent individual women than can Communist parties claim to represent individual workers.

6 Loadings near 0 indicate no association between the task and the factor,
whereas loadings near +/–1 indicate strong association. The factor solution accounts for 30 per cent of the variation in responses; its KMO = .64.

7 The table entries are Pearson's r correlations, which measure the strength
of the linear relationship between two variables. Values near +1 indicate a
strong positive linear association; values near –1 indicate a strong nega-

tive association; and values near 0 indicate weak linear association (Norusis/SPSS Inc. 1988, 105).

8 In table 6.9, significance of prediction is indicated by asterisks, which represent ranges of probability (p) that the reported estimates arose by chance alone. One, two, and three asterisks represent progressively stronger relationships. Each numerical entry is an unstandardized regression coefficient whose sign indicates the direction (positive or negative) of the relationship. A dash indicates that the corresponding characteristic was not included in the regression model because it did not help significantly to predict the measure of feminism (Norusis/SPSS Inc. 1988, 168).

9 Since the highly educated husbands of this study attended the same professional school, this finding may say more about attitudes acquired at that particular school than about highly educated men's support for feminism in general.

CHAPTER 7   Marriage, Family, and Happiness

1 Reported problems of rural living are interesting in so far as they relate to domesticity and femininity. Two wives were distressed by their inability to maintain urban standards of domesticity: living on a gravel road causes so much dust that they wash windows once a week. One of these women was so self-conscious about barn odours in the house (manure on clothes bringing odours in) that she was embarrassed to invite town people in and hence restricted her friendships to other Institute members.

2 The question that asked about satisfaction with agricultural work was less successful because several women responded that they were 'perfectly satisfied' with their very minimal agricultural responsibilities. Others interpreted satisfaction from agricultural work to mean satisfaction with rural life in general.

3 In table 7.2, significance of prediction is indicated by asterisks, which represent ranges of probability (p) that the reported estimates arose by chance alone. One, two, and three asterisks represent progressively stronger relationships. Each numerical entry is an unstandardized regression coefficient whose sign indicates the direction (positive or negative) of the relationship. A dash indicates that the corresponding characteristic was not included in the regression model because it did not help significantly to predict the measure of personal and family happiness (Norusis/SPSS Inc. 1988, 168).

4 Table 3.4 confirmed that a husband's housework reduces a wife's hours of housework, and thus is a good measure of gender-role reversal.

CHAPTER 8   Towards an Agrarian Feminism

1 Not growing up on a farm significantly predicts salience (table 4.7), an equality definition of feminism (table 6.9), and farm-family criticism (table 7.2).

2 These results described white, but not black, women in the U.S. election studies during the 1970s (Fulenwider 1980).

3 Our research design and questions expect women to have already made the analytic leaps between public and private spheres of activity that feminist theory took the better part of two decades to articulate. To flesh out the aphorism 'the personal is the political,' scholars went to considerable intellectual effort to explain how domestic labour is inscribed within the reproduction of the capitalist workforce (Fox 1980) or how compulsory heterosexuality is inscribed within the legal structure of the state (MacKinnon 1983).

4 Pat Salter, Reeve of Peel Township, cited by Janine Roelens-Grant, 'Salter encourages women to get involved in local politics,' *Home & Country* 57/2 (1991) 7, 9.

5 A female landscape architect with the Bolivian Wild Life Society received $2,500 to attend a 'Windbreaks and Agroforestry Symposium' held at Guelph, Ontario. Two thousand dollars was allocated for training workshops for the rural women of Nicaragua (FWIO, *Annual Report*, 1991).

6 Further research into these examples might resolve theoretical debates between individualists and communitarians. This example suggests that apparently traditional face-to-face communities accommodate social deviance better than their critics claim. Iris Young, for example, argues that face-to-face communities repress 'deviants' (whether as independent women, lesbians, or socialists), whereas anonymous life among strangers in a city is liberating (1990, 317–19). Whether victims of domestic violence and single mothers experience their anonymity among strangers as liberating or lonely is open to question.

7 Chapter 1 discussed rural women's community service, particularly in the WI movement, as a precursor and aid to newly emergent provincial governments prior to the expansion of the postwar welfare state.

8 The international linkages made among rural women's organizations through ACWW offer an escape from this commodity-versus-community dichotomy. ACWW focuses on community development in society rather than government policy, but its events enable women to make conceptual linkages unifying agriculture globally. And judging from the beaming

faces of participants – whether in Nicaragua or eastern Europe – these events combine intellectual understanding with sociability.

9 In this respect, commodity prices are like workers' wages. Nicky Hart (1989) explained British working-class women's historically overwhelming support of the Conservative party in terms of Conservative policy that favoured working-class women more than Labour policy did. The basic (and relevant) point is that the size of working-class pay packets (the object of Labour policy) did not translate into increased household wealth unless the division of power was addressed inside working-class families, specifically unless working-class men stopped drinking away their pay packets. Alcohol expenditures are estimated as 15 per cent of household income during the mid-1930s; expenditure on alcohol and tobacco rose 400 per cent between 1938 and 1951, when average wages rose by just 200 per cent.

10 John Morris, publisher and editor of the *Manitoba Co-operator*, cited in OFWN 3/4 (1991) 2. The same OFWN issue noted that selected participants in the (Farm Women's) Advanced Leadership Program denied having a feminist perspective on women's role in agricultural organizations.

11 Consider this comment from a published professional who is committed to a theoretical vision of radical socialist transformation: 'By 1982 ... I no longer had the energy to put into working with IWDC [International Women's Day Committee] ... neither organization [Ontario Working Women and IWDC] offered the same sense of accomplishment [as earlier]. I wanted to build something solid, something concrete, something I had some control over – so I joined the parent committee for my daughters' day-care' (Adamson, Briskin and McPhail 1988, 81).

References

Adamson, Nancy, Linda Briskin, and Margaret McPhail. 1988. *Feminist organizing for change.* Toronto: Oxford University Press.

Alcoff, Linda. 1989. 'Cultural feminism versus post-structuralism.' In *Feminist theory in practice and process,* ed. by Micheline Malson, Jean O'Barr, Sarah Westphal-Wihl, and Mary Wyer, 295–326. Chicago: University of Chicago Press.

Allen, Richard. 1971. *The social passion: Religion and social reform in Canada, 1914–1928.* Toronto: University of Toronto Press.

Almond, Gabriel, and Sidney Verba. 1963. *The civic culture: Political attitudes and democracy in five nations.* Princeton, NJ: Princeton University Press.

Andersen, Kristi. 1975. 'Working women and political participation, 1952–1972.' *American Journal of Political Science* 19/3, 439–53.

Andrew, Caroline. 1984. 'Women and the welfare state.' *Canadian Journal of Political Science* 17/4, 667–83.

– 1989. 'Voluntarism and women's lobbying.' In *Women and counter-power,* ed. by Yolande Cohen, 118–23. Montreal: Black Rose Books.

Arendt, Hannah. 1958. *The human condition.* Chicago: University of Chicago Press.

Bacchi, Carol Lee. 1979. 'Divided allegiances: The response of farm and labour women to suffrage.' In *A not unreasonable claim,* ed. by Linda Kealey, 89–107. Toronto: Women's Educational Press.

– 1983. *Liberation deferred? The ideas of the English-Canadian suffragists, 1877–1918.* Toronto: University of Toronto Press.

Banaszak, Lee Ann, and Eric Plutzer. 1991. 'The social bases of feminism in the European Community.' Paper presented to the Midwest Political Science Association, Chicago, IL.

Banuazizi, Ali. 1987. 'Socio-psychological approaches to political development.' In *Understanding political development,* ed. by Myron Weiner and Samuel Huntington, 281–318. Toronto: Little, Brown.

Barnes, Samuel, and Max Kaase. 1979. *Political action: Mass participation in five western democracies.* Beverly Hills: Sage.

Barthez, Alice. 1982. *Famille, travail et agriculture.* Paris: Economica.

Bashevkin, S.B. 1985a. 'Political participation, ambition and feminism: Women in Ontario party elites.' *American Review of Canadian Studies* 15 (Winter), 405–19.

– 1985b. *Toeing the lines: Women and party politics in English Canada.* Toronto: University of Toronto Press.

Bates, Robert. 1987. 'Agrarian politics.' In *Understanding political development,* ed. by Myron Weiner and Samuel Huntington, 160–95. Toronto: Little, Brown.

Bechofer, Frank, and Brian Elliott. 1981. 'Petty property: The survival of a moral economy.' In *The petite bourgeoisie: Comparative studies of the uneasy stratum,* ed. by Frank Bechhofer and Brian Elliott, 182–200. New York: St. Martin's Press.

Bell, Edward, 1990. 'Class voting in the first Alberta Social Credit election.' *Canadian Journal of Political Science* 23/3, 519–30.

Berger, Suzanne. 1972. *Peasants against politics: Rural organization in Brittany 1911–1967.* Cambridge, MA: Harvard University Press.

Bers, Trudy Haffron, and Susan Gluck Mezey. 1981. 'Support for feminist goals among leaders of women's community groups.' *Signs* 6/4, 737–48.

Bescher-Donnelly, Linda, and Leslie Whitener-Smith. 1981. 'Changing roles and status of rural women.' In *The family in rural society,* ed. by Raymond Coward and William Smith, 167–85. Boulder, CO: Westview Rural Studies Series.

Beyrouti, M., M. Dion, and S. Welsh. 1989. *Socio-economic characteristics of the farm population.* Ottawa: Statistics Canada, Census of Agriculture.

Bibby, Reginald. 1987. *Fragmented gods: The poverty and potential of religion in Canada.* Toronto: Irwin Publishing.

Black, Naomi. 1989. *Social feminism.* Ithaca, NY: Cornell University Press.

Blishen, Bernard, William Carroll, and Catherine Moore. 1987. 'The 1981 socioeconomic index for occupations in Canada.' *Canadian Review of Sociology and Anthropology* 24/4 465–85.

Blumberg, Rae Lesser. 1981. 'Rural women in development.' In *Women and world change: Equity issues in development,* ed. by Naomi Black and Anne Baker Cottrell, 32–56. Beverly Hills: Sage.

Bokhemeier, Janet L., and John L. Tait. 1980. 'Women as power actors: A comparative study of rural communities.' *Rural Sociology* 45/2, 238-55.

Boserup, Ester. 1970. *Woman's role in economic development*. New York: St Martin's Press.

Bourque, Susan, and Jean Grossholtz. 1974. 'Politics an unnatural practice: Political Science looks at female participation.' *Politics and Society* 4/2, 225-66.

Branden, Victoria. 1985. 'A tough row to hoe: Farm women in Ontario.' *Canadian Forum* 64 (May), 17-21.

Brandt, Gail Cuthbert, and Naomi Black. 1990. '"Il en faut en peu": Farm women and feminism in Quebec and France since 1945.' Paper presented to the Canadian Historical Association, Victoria, BC.

Bruners, Daina. 1985. 'The influence of the women's liberation movement on the lives of Canadian farm women.' *Resources for Feminist Research/Documentation sur la recherche feministe* 11, 18-19.

Bujra, Janet M. 1979. 'Introductory: Female solidarity and the sexual division of labour.' In *Women united, women divided*, ed. by J. Bujra and P. Caplan, 13-45. Bloomington: Indiana University Press.

Burnet, Jean. 1951. *Next-year country: A study of rural social organization in Alberta*. Toronto: University of Toronto Press.

Burris, Val. 1983. 'Who opposed the ERA? An analysis of the social bases of antifeminism.' *Social Science Quarterly* 64, 305-17.

Burt, Sandra. 1986. 'Different democracies? A preliminary examination of the political worlds of Canadian men and women.' *Women and Politics* 6/4, 57-79.

– 1992. 'The greening of Ontario agriculture: Farm groups and the environmental agenda.' Paper presented to the Canadian Political Science Association, Charlottetown, PEI.

Butala, Sharon. 1988. *Luna*. Saskatoon: Fifth House Publishers.

– 1991. 'Holy Terror.' *NeWest Review* 17/2, 20.

Buttel, Frederick. 1989. 'The US farm crisis and the restructuring of American agriculture: Domestic and international dimensions.' In *The international farm crisis*, ed. by David Goodman and Michael Redclift, 46-83. London: Macmillan.

Buttel, Frederick, and Howard Newby, eds. 1980. *Rural sociology of the advanced societies: Critical perspectives*. London: Croom Helm.

Cebotarev, E.A., and Kathleen Beattie. 1985. 'Women strengthening the farming community: The case of the "Concerned Farm Women" group in Ontario.' In *Farming and the rural community in Ontario: An introduction*, 255-68. Toronto: Foundation for Rural Living.

Cebotarev, E.A., W.M. Blacklock, and L. McIsaac. 1986. 'Farm women's work patterns.' *Atlantis* 11/2 (Spring), 1–22.

Chambers, Rosalind C. 1954. 'A study of three voluntary organizations.' In *Social mobility in Britain*, ed. by D.V. Glass, 383–405. London: Routledge and Kegan Paul.

Chapman, L.J., and D.F. Putnam. 1966. *The Physiology of Southern Ontario*, 2d ed. Toronto: University of Toronto Press, published for the Ontario Research Foundation.

Christy, Carol. 1986. 'Canadian trends in sex differences in political participation: 1945–1984.' Paper presented to the Southern Political Science Association, Atlanta, GA.

Cloud, Kathleen. 1988. 'Farm women and the structural transformation of agriculture: A cross-cultural perspective.' In *Women and farming, changing roles, changing structures*, ed. by Wava Haney and Jane Knowles, 281–302. Boulder, CO: Westview Rural Studies Series.

Cohen, Marjorie Griffin. 1988. *Women's work, markets, and economic development in nineteenth-century Ontario*. Toronto: University of Toronto Press.

Cohen, Yolande. 1982. 'Des paysannes aux fermières: l'association des Cercles de Fermières Canadiennes françaises.' *Penelope, Femme et Terre*, Rose-Marie Lagrave, ed. 7 (autumn), 87–93.

– 1986/7. 'Les métiers feminins: Une conquête? Histoire comparée des fermières et infirmières dans l'entre-deux-guerres.' *Resources for Feminist Research/Documentation sur la recherche feministe* 15/4 (December/January), 54–5.

– 1989a. 'L'Association des Cercles de fermières in Quebec: Sociability and social influence.' In *Women and counter-power*, ed. by Y. Cohen, 124–41. Montreal: Black Rose Books.

– 1989b. 'The role of associations in democracy.' In *Women and counter-pwer*, ed. by Y. Cohen, 220–30. Montreal: Black Rose Books.

Cohen, Yolande, and Suzanne Marchand. 1989. 'Les relations entre les Cercles de fermières et l'état a travers leur correspondance (1920–1968).' Unpublished paper.

Collins, Robert. 1958. 'The biggest country club in the world.' *Maclean's*, 5 July, 19, 47, 48.

Commission des communautés européennes (Bruno Roche). 1979. *Femme et hommes d'Europe en 1978: Attitudes comparées a l'egard de quelques problèmes de sociétés*. Brussels.

Commission of the European Communities. 1984. *Women and men of Europe in 1983*. Brussels.

- 1987. *Men and women of Europe in 1987.* Brussels: Supplement No. 26, Women of Europe series.
- (Janine Mossuz-Lavau). 1991. *Women and men of Europe today: Attitudes towards Europe and Politics.* Brussels: Supplement No. 35, Women of Europe series.

Conover, Pamela Johnston. 1988. 'Feminists and the gender gap.' *Journal of Politics.* 50/4 985–1010.

Conover, Pamela Johnston and Virginia Sapiro. 1992. 'Gender equality in the public mind.' Paper presented to the American Political Science Association, Chicago, IL.

Converse, Philip. 1964. 'The nature of belief systems in mass publics.' In *Ideology and Discontent,* ed. by D. Apter, 206–61. New York: Free Press.

Conway, John F. 1981. 'Agrarian petit-bourgeois responses to capitalist industrialisation: The case of Canada.' In *The petite bourgeoisie: Comparative studies of the uneasy stratum,* ed. by Frank Bechhofer and Brian Elliott, 1–37. New York: St Martin's Press.

- 1984. 'The nature of populism: A clarification.' *Studies in Political Economy* 13 (Spring), 137–44.

Cook, Elizabeth Adell. 1989. 'Measuring feminist consciousness.' *Women and Politics* 9/3, 71–87.

Cooper, Barbara. 1989. 'Farm women: Some contemporary themes.' *Labour/ Le Travail* 24, 167–80.

Cooper, Barry. 1984. *The end of history: An essay on modern Hegelianism.* Toronto: University of Toronto Press.

Cott, Nancy. 1977. *The bonds of womanhood: 'Women's sphere' in New England, 1780–1835.* New Haven, CT: Yale University Press.

- 1987. *Grounding of modern feminism.* New Haven, CT: Yale University Press.

Crowley, Terry. 1986a. 'Madonnas before Magdalenes: Adelaide Hoodless and the making of the Canadian Gibson Girl.' *Canadian Historical Review* 67/4, 520–47.

- 1986b. 'Origins of continuing education for women: The Ontario Women's Institutes.' *Canadian Woman Studies* 7/3, 78–81.

Davidson, T. Arthur. 1972. *A new history of the County of Grey.* Published by the Grey County Historical Society. Owen Sound: Richardson, Bond and Wright.

de Lauretis, Teresa. 1986. 'Feminist studies/critical studies: Issues, terms, and context.' In *Feminist studies/critical studies,* ed. by T. de Lauretis, 1–19. Madison: University of Wisconsin Press.

Dennison, Carol J. 1984. 'They also served: The British Columbia Women's Institutes in two world wars.' In *Not just pin money: History of women's work in British Columbia*, ed. by Barbara Latham and Roberta Pazdro, 211–19. Victoria: Camosun College.

Deutsch, K.W. 1961. 'Social mobilization and political development.' *American Political Science Review* 55/3, 493–514.

Dion, Suzanne. 1983. *Les femmes dans l'agriculture au Québec*. Longueuil, PQ: Les Editions de la Terre de Chez Nous.

Dodson, Debra L. 1989. 'A Comparison of the impact of women and men's attitudes on their legislative behaviour: Is what they say what they do?' Paper presented to the American Political Science Association, Atlanta, GA.

Dogan, Mattei, and Jacques Narbonne. 1955. *Les françaises face à la politique: Comportement politique et condition sociale*. Paris: Armand Colin.

Drache, Daniel, and Meric Gertler, eds. 1991. *The new era of global competition: State power and market power*. Montreal and Kingston: McGill-Queen's University Press.

Dubois, Ellen Carol, and Linda Gordon. 1983. 'Seeking ecstasy on the battlefield: Danger and pleasure in nineteenth century feminist sexual thought.' *Feminist studies* 9/1 (Spring), 7–25.

Dumont-Johnson, Micheline. 1981. 'La parole des femmes: les revues feminines, 1938–1968.' In *Idéologies au Canada française, 1940–1976*, ed. by Fernand Dumont, Jean Hamelin, and Jean-Paul Montminy, 5–45. Quebec: Presse de l'Université Laval.

Dunn, John. 1990a. *Economic limits to modern politics*. Cambridge: Cambridge University Press.

– 1990b. 'Politics without greed or envy.' *Times Higher Education Supplement*, 2 March, 13.

Duverger, Maurice. 1955. *The political role of women*. Paris: UNESCO.

Eagles, D. Munro, James Bickerton, Alain Gagnon, and Patrick Smith. 1991. *The almanac of Canadian politics*. Peterborough, ON: Broadview Press.

Edwards, Rosalind. 1990. 'Connecting method and epistemology: A white woman interviewing black women.' *Women's Studies International Forum* 13/5, 477–90.

Elbert, Sarah. 1981. 'Challenge of research on farm women.' *Rural Sociologist* 1/6 387–90.

Federated Women's Institutes of Canada. 1990. *Rural child care survey project, 1988–1991*. Ottawa: Health and Welfare Canada.

Federated Women's Institutes of Ontario. *Ontario's Women's Institute story*. Toronto: Federated Women's Institutes of Ontario.

Fink, Virginia. 1988. 'The impact of changing technologies on the roles of farm and ranch wives in Southeastern Ohio.' In *Women and farming, changing roles, changing structures*, ed. by Wava Haney and Jane Knowles, 229-44. Boulder, CO: Westview Rural Studies Series.

Finkel, Alvin. 1989. *The Social Credit phenomenon in Alberta*. Toronto: University of Toronto Press.

Fox, Bonnie, ed. 1980. *Hidden in the household: Women's domestic labour under capitalism*. Toronto: Women's Press.

Freshwater, David. 1989. 'Canadian agricultural finance in the 1980s and 1990s.' *Canadian Journal of Agricultural Economics* 37, 1-27.

Friedmann, Harriet. 1980. 'Household production and the national economy: Concepts for the analysis of agrarian formations.' *Journal of Peasant Studies* 7, 158-84.

– 1986. 'Family enterprises in agriculture: Structural limits and political possibilities.' In *Agriculture: People and politics*, ed. by Graham Cox, Philip Lowe, and Michael Winter, 41-60. London: Allen & Unwin.

Fulenwider, Claire Knoche. 1980. *Feminism in American politics: A study of ideological influence*. New York: Praeger.

Garkovich, Lorraine, and Janet Bokemeier. 1988. 'Agricultural mechanization and American farm women's economic roles.' In *Women and farming, changing roles, changing structures*, ed. by Wava Haney and Jane Knowles, 211-28. Boulder, CO: Westview Rural Studies Series.

Ghorayshi, Parvin. 1987. 'Canadian agriculture: Capitalist or petit bourgeois?' *Canadian Review of Sociology and Anthropology* 24/3, 358-73.

– 1989. 'The indispensable nature of wives' work for the family farm enterprise.' *Canadian Review of Sociology and Anthropology* 26/4, 571-95.

Giangrande, Carole. 1985. *Down to earth: The crisis in Canadian farming*. Toronto: Anansi Press.

Githens, Marianne, and Jewel Prestage. 1977. 'Introduction.' In *A portrait of marginality: The political behaviour of American women*, ed. by M. Githens and J. Prestage, 3-10. New York: Longman.

Goodenough, Simon. 1977. *Jam and Jerusalem*. London: William Collins and Son.

Goodman, David, and Michael Redclift. 1986. 'Capitalism, petty commodity production and the farm enterprise.' In *Agriculture: People and politics*, ed. by Graham Cox, Philip Lowe, and Michael Winter, 20-40. London: Allen & Unwin.

Goodwyn, Lawrence. 1978. *The populist moment: A short history of the agrarian revolt in America*. New York: Oxford University Press.

Goot, Murray, and Elizabeth Reid. 1975. *Women and voting studies: Mindless matrons or sexist scientism?* Contemporary Political Sociology Series, vol. 1, by Richard Rose. Beverly Hills: Sage.

Graff, Linda. 1982. 'Industrialization of agriculture: Implications for the position of women.' *Resources for feminist research/Documentation sur la recherche feministe* 2/1, 10–11.

Graham, W.H. 1988. *Greenbank: Country matters in 19th century Ontario.* Peterborough, ON: Broadview Press.

Greer, Germaine. 1989. *Daddy, we hardly knew you.* London: Hamish Hamilton.

Gurin, Patricia. 1985. 'Women's gender consciousness.' *Public Opinion Quarterly* 49, 143–63.

Hamilton, Roberta A. 1978. *The liberation of women: A study of patriarchy and capitalism.* London: George Allen & Unwin.

Hamilton, Roberta A., and Michele Barrett, eds. 1987. *The politics of diversity: Feminism, Marxism and nationalism.* Montreal: Book Centre.

Haney, Wava Gillespie. 1983. 'Farm family and the role of women.' In *Technology and social change in rural areas,* ed. by Gene F. Summers, 179–93. Boulder, CO: Westview.

Hansen, Phillip, and Alicja Muszynski. 1990. 'Crisis in rural life and crisis in thinking: Directions for critical research.' *Canadian Review of Sociology and Anthropology* 27/1, 1–22.

Harding, Sandra. 1986. *The science question in feminism.* Ithaca, NY: Cornell University Press.

Hart, Nicky. 1989. 'Gender and the rise and fall of class politics.' *New Left Review* 175, 19–47.

Hause, Steven C., with Anne R. Kenney. 1984. *Women's suffrage and social politics in the French Third Republic.* Princeton, NJ: Princeton University Press.

Havens, Eugene A., with Gregory Hooks, Patrick H. Mooney, and Max J. Pfeffer. 1986. *Studies in the Transformation of U.S. Agriculture.* Boulder, CO: Westview.

Hayford, Alison. 1982. 'Different routes to different places.' *Resources for Feminist Research/Documentation sur la recherche feministe* 11/1, 17–19.

Hedley, Max J. 1976. 'Independent commodity production and the dynamics of tradition.' *Canadian Review of Sociology and Anthropology* 13/4, 413–21.

Hekman, Susan. 1990. *Gender and knowledge.* Boston: Northeastern University Press.

Holland, David, and Joe Carvalho. 1985. 'The changing mode of production in American agriculture: Emerging conflicts in agriculture's role in the reproduction of advanced capitalism.' *Review of Radical Political Economics* 17/4, 1-27.

Hong, Sung-mook. 1983. 'Gender, religion, and sexual permissiveness: Some recent Australian data.' *Journal of Psychology* 115, 17-22.

- 1984.'Permissiveness, more or less: Sexual attitudes in the general public.' *Australian Journal of sex, marriage, and family* 5/2, 89-96.

hooks, bell. 1990. *Yearning*. Toronto: Between the Lines Press.

Howell, Martha C. 1986. *Women, production, and patriarchy in late medieval cities*. Chicago: University of Chicago Press.

Hundertmark, Susan. 1985. 'Rural feminism.' *Healthsharing* (Winter), 14-17.

Huntington, Samuel. 1968. *Political order in changing societies*. New Haven, CT: Yale University Press.

Inglehart, Ronald. 1977. *The silent revolution: Changing values and political styles among western publics*. Princeton, NJ: Princeton University Press.

- 1979. 'Value priorities and socioeconomic change.' In *Political action: Mass participation in five western democracies*, ed. by Samuel Barnes and Max Kaase, 305-42. Beverly Hills: Sage.

- 1990. *Cultural shift in advanced industrial society*. Princeton, NJ: Princeton University Press.

Ingold, Tim. 1984. 'The estimation of work in a northern Finnish farming community.' In *Family and work in rural societies, perspectives on non-wage labour*, ed. by Norman Long, 116-34. London: Tavistock.

Institute for Social Research. 1982. *Social Change in Canada/Quality of Life, Technical Documentation*. Toronto: York University, Institute for Social Research.

Ireland, Gisele. 1983. *The farmer takes a wife: A study by Concerned Farm Women*. Chesley: Concerned Farm Women.

Irvine, William. 1976[1920]. *Farmers in politics*, ed. by Reginald Whitaker. Toronto: McClelland & Stewart.

Jackson, Wes, Wendell Berry, and Bruce Colman, eds. 1984. *Meeting the expectations of the land: Essays in sustainable agriculture and stewardship*. San Francisco: North Point.

Jensen, Joan. 1980. 'Cloth, butter and boarders: Women's household production for the market.' *Review of Radical Political Economics* 12/2, 14-24.

Johnston, Richard, Andre Blais, Henry Brady, and Jean Crete. 1992. *Letting the people decide: Dynamics of a Canadian election*. Montreal and Kingston: McGill-Queen's University Press.

Katzenstein, Mary Fainsod. 1987. 'Comparing the feminist movements of the United States and Western Europe: An overview.' In *The women's movements of the United States and Western Europe*, ed. by Mary Katzenstein and Carol McClurg Mueller, 3-20. Philadelphia: Temple University Press.

Kay, Barry, Ronald Lambert, Steven Brown, and James Curtis. 1988. 'Feminist consciousness and the Canadian electorate: A review of National Election Studies 1965-1984.' *Women and Politics* 8/2, 1-21.

Kealey, Linda. 1979. 'Introduction.' In *A not unreasonable claim*, ed. by Linda Kealey, 1-14. Toronto: Women's Educational Press.

Keane, John. 1988. *Democracy and civil society*. London: Verso.

Kechnie, Margaret. 1985. 'The United Farm Women of Ontario: Developing a political consciousness.' *Ontario History* 77 (December), 266-78.

Kiray, Mubeccel. 1984. 'Development in rural Turkey: Leadership or patronage.' In *Local politics and development in the Middle East*, ed. by Louis J. Cantori and Iliya Harik, 212-48. Boulder, CO: Westview.

Kirkpatrick, Jeane. 1974. *Political woman*. New York: Basic Books.

Klein, Ethel. 1984. *Gender politics: From consciousness to mass politics*. Cambridge, MA: Harvard University Press.

Klingemann, Hans. D. 1979. 'Measuring ideological conceptualizations.' In *Political action: Mass participation in five Western democracies*, ed. by Samuel Barnes and Max Kaase, 215-540. Beverly Hills: Sage.

Kohl, Seena. 1976. *Working together: Women and family in southwestern Saskatchewan*. Toronto: Holt, Rinehart and Winston.

Koski, Susan E. 1983. *The employment practices of farm women*. Saskatoon: National Farmers Union.

LaGrave, Rose-Marie. 1982. 'Introduction,' *Penelope, Femme et Terre*, Rose-Marie LaGrave, ed. 7 (autumn), 5-9.

Lambert, Ronald, James Curtis, Steven Brown, and Barry Kay. 1985. *The 1984 Election Study Codebook*. Waterloo, ON.

- 1986a. 'In search of left/right beliefs in the Canadian electorate.' *Canadian Journal of Political Science* 14/3, 541-63.

- 1986b. 'Effects of identification with governing parties on feelings of political efficacy and trust.' *Canadian Journal of Political Science* 14/4, 705-27.

- 1987. 'Social class, left/right political orientations, and subjective class voting in provincial and federal elections.' *Canadian Review of Sociology and Anthropology* 24/4, 526-49.

Langford, Nanci, and Norah Keating. 1987. 'Social isolation and Alberta farm women.' In *Women: Isolation and bonding. The ecology of gender*, ed. by Kathleen Storrie for CRIAW, 47-58. New York: Methuen.

Langford, Tom. 1991. 'Left/right orientation and political attitudes: A reappraisal and class comparison.' *Canadian Journal of Political Science* 24/3, 475–498.

Laponce, Jean A. 1970. 'Note on the use of the left-right dimension.' *Comparative Political Studies* 2/4, 481–502.

– 1981. *Left and right: The topography of political perceptions.* Toronto: University of Toronto Press.

Lasch, Christopher. 1991. *The true and only heaven: Progress and its critics.* New York: W.W. Norton.

Lash, Scott, and John Urry. 1987. *The end of organized capitalism.* Madison: University of Wisconsin Press.

Laycock, David. 1990. *Populism and democratic thought in the Canadian prairies, 1910 to 1945.* Toronto: University of Toronto Press.

Lee, Julie. 1987. 'Women as non-family farmworkers.' In *Growing strong: Women in agriculture,* ed. by Diane Morissette, 91–122. Ottawa: Canadian Advisory Council on the Status of Women.

Lem, Winnie. 1988. 'Household production and reproduction in rural Languedoc: Social relations of petty commodity production in Murviel-les-Beziers.' *Journal of Peasant Studies* 15/4, 500–30.

Lemons, J. Stanley. 1973. *The woman citizen: Social feminism in the 1920's.* Chicago: University of Illinois Press.

Lerner, Daniel. 1958. *The passing of traditional society: Modernizing the Middle East.* Glenco, IL: Free Press.

Lipset, Seymour Martin. 1959. 'Some social requisites of democracy.' *American Political Science Review* 53, 69–105.

– 1971[1950]. *Agrarian socialism: The Cooperative Commonwealth Federation in Saskatchewan.* Los Angeles: University of California Press.

Lovenduski, Joni. 1986. *Women and European politics: Contemporary feminism and public policy.* Amherst: University of Massachusetts Press.

Luxton, Meg. 1980. *More than a labour of love: Three generations of women's work in the home.* Toronto: Women's Press.

McClung, Nellie. 1946. *The stream runs fast.* Toronto: Thomas Allen.

McCormack, Thelma. 1975. 'Toward a nonsexist view of social and political change.' In *Another voice,* ed. by Marcia Millman and Rosabeth Moss Kanter, 1–33. New York: Doubleday.

MacDermid, Robert. 1990. 'Regionalism in Ontario.' In *Canadian politics: An introduction,* ed. by Alain Gagnon and James Bickerton, 360–90. Peterborough, ON: Broadview Press.

MacDermid, Robert, and Michael Stevenson. 1990. 'Identification with new social movements: The structure of Canadian public opinion on environmental issues.' Paper presented to the Canadian Political Science Assocation, Victoria, BC.

MacDonald, Cheryl. 1986. *Adelaide Hoodless: Domestic crusader.* Toronto: Dundurn Press.

McGhee, Molly. 1984. *Women in rural life today: The changing scene.* Toronto: Ontario Ministry of Agriculture and Food.

MacKinnon, Catherine. 1983. 'Feminism, Marxism, and the state: Toward feminist jurisprudence.' *Signs* 8/4, 635–54.

McLaren, Angus, and Arlene Tiger McLaren. 1986. *The bedroom and the state.* Toronto: McClelland & Stewart.

Macpherson, C.B. 1953. *Democracy in Alberta: Social Credit and the party system.* Toronto: University of Toronto Press.

Macpherson, Ian. 1988. 'Introduction.' In *Building beyond the homestead: Rural history on the prairies,* ed. by David Jones and Ian MacPherson, 1–3. Calgary: University of Calgary Press.

Magnusson, Warren, and Robert Walker. 1988. 'De-centring the state.' *Studies in political economy* 26, 37–72.

Mann, Susan, and James Dickinson. 1978. 'Obstacles to the development of a capitalist agriculture.' *Journal of Peasant Studies* 5/4, 466–81.

Marchildon, R.G. 1988. 'Improving the quality of rural life in Saskatchewan: Some activities of the Women's Section of the Saskatchewan Grain Growers, 1913–1920.' In *Building beyond the homestead,* ed. by David Jones and Ian MacPherson, 89–109. Calgary: University of Calgary Press.

Maret, Stephen, and Lezlie Maret. 1982. 'Attitudes of fundamentalists towards nonmarital sex.' *Psychological Reports* 51/3, pt 1, 921–2.

Marx, Karl, and Frederich Engels. 1972 [1888]. 'The Communist Manifesto.' In *Marx-Engels Reader,* ed. by Robert Tucker, 473–500. New York: Norton.

Mayer, Lawrence, 1990. 'Elite responses to feminism and other post-materialist issues: The case of Britain.' Paper presented to the American Political Science Association, San Francisco, CA.

Meanwell, C., and S. Glover. 1985. *To have and to hold.* Chesley, ON: Concerned Farm Women.

Menzies, June. 1968. 'Votes for Saskatchewan's women.' In *Politics in Saskatchewan,* ed. by Norman Ward and Duff Spafford, 78–92. Toronto: University of Toronto Press.

Mies, Maria, Veronika Bennholdt-Thomsen, and Claudia von Werlhof. 1988. *Women: The last colony.* Atlantic Highlands, NJ: Zed Books.

Miller, Lorna Clancy, and Mary Neth. 1988. 'Farm women in the political arena.' In *Women and farming*, ed. by Wava Haney and Jane Knowles, 357–80. Boulder, CO: Westview.

Morgan, April and Clyde Wilcox. 1991. 'Anti-feminism in Western Europe, 1975–1987.' Paper presented to the American Political Science Association, Washington, DC.

Morton, W.L. 1950. *Progressive Party in Canada*. Toronto: University of Toronto Press.

Mossuz-Lavau, Janine, and Mariette Sineau. 1981. 'France.' In *The politics of the second electorate*, trans. by Anne Batiot, ed. by Joni Lovenduski and Jill Hills, 126–9. London: Routledge and Kegan Paul.

– 1983. *Enquête sur les femmes et la politique en France*. Paris: Presses Universitaires de France.

Munro, Alice. 1968. *Dance of the happy shades*. Toronto: McGraw-Hill Ryerson.

– 1971. *Lives of girls and women*. Toronto: McGraw-Hill Ryerson.

– 1982. *The moons of Jupiter*. Toronto: Macmillan.

– 1990. *Friend of my youth*. Toronto: McClelland & Stewart.

Murphy, Brian. 1991. *The distribution of federal/provincial taxes and transfers in rural Canada*. Ottawa: Analytical Studies Branch, Statistics Canada.

Nelson, Joan. 1987. 'Political participation.' In *Understanding political development*, ed. by Myron Weiner and Samuel Huntington, 103–59. Toronto: Little, Brown.

Neth, Mary. 1988. 'Building the base: Farm women, the rural community, and farm organizations in the Midwest, 1900–1940.' In *Women and farming, changing roles, changing structures*, ed. by Wava Haney and Jane Knowles, 339–55. Boulder, CO: Westview Rural Studies Series.

Neuman, W. Russell. 1986. *The paradox of mass politics: Knowledge and opinion in the American electorate*. Cambridge, MA: Harvard University Press.

Neville, Mary Anne. 1985. *A history of Glenelg Township*. Compiled by the Glenelg Township Historical Committee. Owen Sound, ON: Stan Brown Printers.

Newby, Howard. 1978. 'The rural sociology of advanced capitalist societies.' In *International perspectives in rural sociology*, ed. by H. Newby, 3–30. Chichester: Wiley and Sons.

Newby, Howard, David Rose, Peter Saunders, and Colin Bell. 1978. *Property, paternalism, and power: Class and control in rural England*. Madison: University of Wisconsin Press.

- 1981. 'Farming for survival: The small farmer in the contemporary rural class structure.' In *The petite bourgeoisie: Comparative studies of the uneasy stratum*, ed. by Frank Bechhofer and Brian Elliott, 38–70. New York: St Martin's Press.

Nicholson, Linda, ed. 1990. *Feminism/Postmodernism*. New York: Routledge, Chapman & Hall.

Northrup, David, and Anne Orum. 1989. *The 1988 Election Study technical documentation*. Toronto: York University, Institute for Social Research.

Norusis, Marija/SPSS Inc. 1988. *SPSS-X Introductory Statistics Guide* Chicago: SPSS Inc.

Offe, Claus. 1987. 'Challenging the boundaries of institutional politics: Social movements since the 1960's.' In *Changing boundaries of the political: Essays on the evolving balance between the state and society, public and private in Europe*, ed. by Charles S. Maier, 63–106. Cambridge: Cambridge University Press.

Offen, Karen. 1988. 'Defining feminism: A comparative historical approach.' *Signs* 14/1, 119–57.

- 1989. 'Reply to Cott.' *Signs* 15/1, 206–9.

Ontario Ministry of Agriculture and Food. 1988. *Assessment of the impacts of the Canada–US Free Trade Agreement on the Ontario agriculture and food industry*. Toronto.

- 1990. *Agriculture in the Uruguay Round of GATT negotiations: The final stages*. Guelph: University of Guelph, Department of Agricultural Economics and Business (May).

Phillips, Susan. 1991. 'Meaning and structure in social movements: Mapping the network of national Canadian women's organizations.' *Canadian Journal of Political Science* 24/4, 755–82.

Piore, Michael, and Charles Sabel. 1984. *The second industrial divide: Possibilities for prosperity*. New York: Basic Books.

Plutzer, Lee Ann, and Erick Banaszak. 1991. 'Support for feminist in nine western democracies: The impact of national and subnational contexts.' Paper presented to the American Political Science Association, Washington, DC.

Poel, Dale H. 1988. 'Affective orientation towards the women's movement in Canadian politics: Gender, Class, ethnicity, and issues.' Paper presented to the American Political Science Association, Washington, DC.

Porter, Jene, ed. 1989. *Classics in political philosophy*. Scarborough, ON: Prentice-Hall Canada.

Prentice, Alison, Paula Bourne, Gail Cuthbert Brandt, Beth Light, Wendy Mitchinson, and Naomi Black. 1988. *Canadian women: A history*. Toronto: Harcourt Brace Jovanovich.

Rankin, L. Pauline. 1987. 'Beyond the kitchen and the cornfield: The political activism of Ontario farm women.' Unpublished MA thesis, Carleton University, Ontario.

- 1989. 'The politicization of Ontario farm women.' In *Beyond the vote: Canadian women and politics*, ed. by Linda Kealey and Joan Sangster, 309–32. Toronto: University of Toronto Press.

Rasmussen, Linda, C. Savage, and A. Wheeler. 1976. *A harvest yet to reap: A history of prairie women*. Toronto: Women's Press.

Richards, John, and Larry Pratt. 1981. *Prairie capitalism: Power and influence in the new west*. Toronto: McClelland & Stewart.

Roberts, Wayne. 1979. 'Rocking the cradle for the world: The new woman and maternal feminism, Toronto, 1877–1914.' In *A not unreasonable claim*, ed. by Linda Kealey, 15–46. Toronto: Women's Educational Press.

Rosenblatt, Paul C., and Roxanne M. Anderson. 1981. 'Interaction in farm families: Tension and stress.' In *Family in rural society*, ed. by Raymond Coward and William M. Smith, Jr, 147–66. Boulder, CO: Westview Rural Studies Series.

Rosenfeld, Rachel Ann. 1985. *Farm women: Work, farm, and family in the United States*. Chapel Hill: University of North Carolina Press.

Royal Commission on the Status of Women. 1970. *Report*. Ottawa: Information Canada.

Rural Women's Organisations, Liaison Committee. 1930. *What the Country Women of the World are doing – Links of friendship*, vol. II. Keighley, UK: Rydal Press.

Sachs, Carolyn. 1983. *Invisible farmers: Women in agricultural production*. Totowa, NJ: Rowman & Alanheld.

Salamon, Sonya, and Ann Mackey Keim. 1979. 'Land ownership and women's power in a midwestern farming community.' *Journal of marriage and the family* 46, 167–78.

Sapiro, Virginia. 1983. *The political integration of women: Roles, socialization, and politics*. Chicago: University of Illinois Press.

Scott, James. 1966. *The settlement of Huron County*. Toronto: Ryerson Press.

Shaver, Frances. 1980a. 'Farm and non-farm women in rural Quebec: A preliminary analysis.' Paper presented to the Sociology and Anthropology Association, Montreal (June).

- 1980b. 'Methodological notes for the study of the productive role of women in Quebec agriculture, 1940–1980. Paper presented to the Sociology and Anthropology Association, Halifax (June).

- 1982. 'Social science research on farm women: The state of the art.' *Resources for Feminist Research/Documentation sur la recherche feministe* 2/1, 3–4.

- 1989. 'Women and the farm family in Canada: A state of the art review.' Paper presented to the Congres de l'ACFAS, Montreal (May).

Shaver, Frances, and Bill Reimer. 1982. 'Social science research on farm women: The state of the art,' *Resources for Feminist Research/Documentation sur la recherche feministe* 11, 3-4.

- 1987. 'Economy and household: The gender based division of labour on the farm, Montmagny County, 1951-1981.' Unpublished paper.

Shorter, Edward. 1982. *A history of women's bodies.* New York: Basic Books.

Silverman, Eliane Leslau. 1984. *Last best west: Women on the Alberta frontier, 1880-1930.* Montreal: Eden Press.

- 1988. 'Women's perceptions of marriage on the Alberta frontier.' In *Building beyond the homestead,* ed. by David Jones and Ian MacPherson, 49-66. Calgary: University of Calgary Press.

Skogstad, Grace. 1987. *The politics of agricultural policy-making in Canada.* Toronto: University of Toronto Press.

- 1990. 'The farm policy community and public policy in Ontario and Quebec.' In *Policy communities and public policy in Canada: A structural approach,* ed. by William Coleman and Grace Skogstad, 59-90. Mississauga, ON: Copp Clark Pittman.

Smith, David, 1975. *Prairie liberalism: The Liberal Party in Saskatchewan 1905-1971.* Toronto: University of Toronto Press.

- 1981. *The regional decline of a national party.* Toronto: University of Toronto Press.

Smith, Dorothy. 1987. *The everyday world as problematic: A feminist sociology.* Toronto: University of Toronto Press.

Smith, Pamela. 1987. 'What lies in and behind the statistics?: Trying to measure women's contribution to Canadian agriculture.' In *Growing strong: Women in agriculture,* ed. by Diane Morissette, 123-209. Ottawa: Canadian Advisory Council on the Status of Women.

Staudt, Kathleen. 1979a. 'Class and sex in the politics of women farmers.' *Journal of Politics* 41, 492-512.

- 1979b. *Women and participation in rural development: A framework for project design and policy-oriented research.* Ithaca, NY: Cornell Center for International Studies, Rural Development Committee.

Stephan, G. Edward, and Douglas McMullin. 1982. 'Tolerance of sexual nonconformity: City size as a situational and early learning determinant.' *American Sociological Review* 47/33, 411-15.

Steward, Linda. 1991. 'A woman of courage: A biography of Agnes Campbell Macphail.' Unpublished Ph.D. thesis, University of Toronto.

Stoper, Emily. 1977. 'Wife and politician: Role strain among women in public office.' In *A portrait of marginality*, ed. by Marianne Githens and Jewel Prestage, 320–37. New York: Longman.

Strong-Boag, Veronica. 1986. 'Pulling in double harness or hauling a double load: Women, work, and feminism on the Canadian prairie.' *Journal of Canadian Studies* 21/3 (Fall), 32–52.

Taylor, Georgina. In preparation. 'Violet McNaughton and agrarian feminism.' PhD thesis, History Department, Carleton University, Ottawa.

Taylor, Norma. 1976. 'All this for three and a half a day: The farm wife.' In *Women in the Canadian mosaic*, ed. by Gwen Matheson, 151–66. Toronto: Peter Martin Associates.

Tibert, J., D. Bates, B. Bruce, D. Northrup, and A. Oram. 1987. *Civil Liberties and the Canadian Charter of Rights Project, Technical Documentation*. Toronto: York University, Institute for Social Research.

Tocqueville, Alexis de. 1969[1848]. *Democracy in America*, trans. by George Lawrence, ed. by J.P. Mayer. New York: Doubleday.

Unger, Roberto Mangabeira. 1987. *False necessity: Anti-necessitarian social theory in the service of radical democracy*. Cambridge: Cambridge University Press.

Van Herk, Aritha. 1978. *Judith*. Toronto: McClelland & Stewart.

Verba, Sidney, Norman Nie, and Jae-on Kim. 1978. *Participation and political equality: A seven-nation comparison*. Cambridge: Cambridge University Press.

Vernon, Richard, and S.V. LaSelva. 1984. 'Justifying tolerance.' *Canadian Journal of Political Science* 17/1 (March), 3–23.

Wagner, MaryJo. 1988. 'Helping Papa and Mamma sing the people's songs: Children in the Populist Party.' In *Women and farming, changing roles, changing structures*, ed. by Wava Haney and Jane Knowles, 319–38. Boulder, CO: Westview Rural Studies Series.

Walker, Annie, Edith Collins, and M. McIntyre Hood. 1948. *Fifty years of achievement*. Toronto: Federated Women's Institutes of Ontario.

Walker, Gerald. 1987. 'The farmers' class.' Discussion paper, Department of Geography, York University, Toronto, On.

Walzer, Michael. 1988. 'Socializing the welfare state.' In *Democracy and the welfare state*, ed. by Amy Gutmann, 13–30. Princeton, NJ: Princeton University Press.

Watt, Sholto, ed. 1933. *What the Country Women of the World are doing – Festivals number*, vol. IV. Associated Country Women of the World. Keighley, UK: Rydal Press.

Waver, John. 1988. 'Society and culture in rural and small-town Ontario: Alice Munro's testimony on the last forty years.' In *Patterns of the past: Interpreting Ontario's history*, ed. by R. Hall, W. Westfall, and L. Sefton MacDowell, 381-403. Toronto: Dundurn Press.

Weis, David, Michael Slosnerick, Rodney Cate, and Donna Sollie. 1986. 'A survey instrument for assessing the cognitive association of sex, love, and marriage.' *Journal of Sex Research* 22/2, 206-20.

Whitaker, Reginald. 1976[1920]. 'Introduction.' In *Farmers in politics*. Toronto: McClelland & Stewart.

Wiebe, Nettie. 1987. *Weaving new ways, farm women organizing*. Saskatoon: National Farmers' Union.

Wilcox, Clyde. 1991. 'The causes and consequences of feminist consciousness among western European women.' *Comparative political studies* 23/4, 519-45.

Wilford, Allen. 1984. *Farm gate defense: The story of the Canadian Farmers Survival Association*. Toronto: New Canada Publications.

Willick, Liz. 1986. 'Working to organize rural women in Canada.' *Canadian Woman Studies* 7/1&2, 168-9.

Willits, Fern, Robert Bealer, and Donald Crider. 1973. 'Leveling of attitudes in mass society: Rurality and traditional morality in America.' *Rural Sociology* 38/1 (spring), 36-45.

Wilson, Barry, and Peter Finkle. 1990. 'Is agriculture different? Another round in the battle between theory and practice.' In *Agricultural trade: Domestic pressures and international tensions*, ed. by Grace Skogstad and Andrew Fenton Cooper, 13-26. Halifax: Institute for Research on Public Policy.

Wilson, Jane. 1986. 'The feminisation of farming.' *Herizons* 4 (March), 12.

Wilson, John. 1986. 'The political economy of contract farming.' *Review of Radical Political Economics* 18/4, 47-70.

'Womanpoll: Women's role and rights.' 1970. *Chatelaine*, 3 March.

Women's Institutes of Saskatchewan. 1988. *Legacy, a history of Saskatchewan Homemakers' Clubs and Women's Institutes, 1911-1988*. Regina: Focus.

Wood, Louis Aubrey. 1975[1924]. *A history of farmers' movements in Canada*. Toronto: University of Toronto Press.

Young, Iris Marion. 1990. 'The ideal of community and the politics of difference.' In *Feminism/Postmodernism*, ed. by Linda Nicholson, 300-23. New York: Routledge and Kegan Paul.

Zacharias, Alexandra. 1980. 'British Columbia Women's Institute in the early years: Time to remember.' In *In her own right*, ed. by Barbara Latham and Cathy Kess, 55-77. Victoria, BC: Camosun College.

Index